Pleas... ...
You ...

SPITFIRE'S FORGOTTEN DESIGNER

SPITFIRE'S FORGOTTEN DESIGNER

The Career of Supermarine's Joe Smith

Mike Roussel

*This book, dedicated to all who worked for Supermarine, tells
the story of the famous design team and their inspirational and
innovative chief designers, R.J. Mitchell and Joseph Smith.*

Front cover illustrations: MV268 Spitfire FR Mk XIV, built at Eastleigh.
(Alan Mansell); Joe Smith. (Barbara Harries). *Back cover*: Original artwork
© David Hatchard, 2012; photographed by Alan Mansell.

First published 2013

The History Press
The Mill, Brimscombe Port
Stroud, Gloucestershire, GL5 2QG
www.thehistorypress.co.uk

© Mike Roussel, 2013

The right of Mike Roussel to be identified as the Author
of this work has been asserted in accordance with the
Copyrights, Designs and Patents Act 1988.

British Library Cataloguing in Publication Data.
A catalogue record for this book is available from the British Library.

ISBN 978 0 7524 8759 5

Typesetting and origination by The History Press
Printed in Great Britain
Manufacturing managed by Jellyfish Solutions Ltd

CONTENTS

FOREWORD

By Captain Eric Brown CBE, DSC, AFC,
QCVSA, MA, Hon. FRAeS, Hon. FSETP, RN

Chief Naval Test Pilot, RAE Farnborough, 1944–49

This is a book that just had to be written about a man who made a huge contribution to British aviation in the Second World War but was so self-effacing that he got little recognition for his demanding work, crucial to our war effort.

Stepping into the shoes of an inspirational chief designer at Supermarine would have daunted most men, but Joe Smith took it in his stride and without fuss while keeping the Spitfire in the forefront of fighter excellence. At the same time, he took a deep interest in adapting the Supermarine masterpiece to the naval environment, and so inevitably he and I came into close contact.

Joe took to carrier life like a duck to water and loved to attend deck landing trials of his products, and many an evening we would chat over a horse's neck (brandy and ginger ale) in the wardroom. He was a good listener and an innovative designer, so he kept the Seafire up with the performance hunt while making it safer and more robust for carrier operations.

By the end of the Second World War, I could see that it had taken its toll on Joe just as a new lease of life was needed to cope with the advent of the jet age. The jet aircraft coming from his drawing board showed his star was on the wane, but I shall always associate his name with the thunderous Seafire 47, which I loved to fly. This book is a tribute to a fine aircraft designer and a great man, whom I shall always remember with respect and affection, for he gave his all to his country, to his company, to the Fleet Air Arm, and to the RAF – with scant reward.

Eric Brown

PREFACE

Supermarine Inspirational and Innovative Design Engineers

Whenever the Spitfire is mentioned, the name of its famous designer R.J. Mitchell comes to mind, but few have heard of the man who led the development of the Spitfire throughout the war to become the deadly fighter that the Luftwaffe pilots feared. That man was Joe Smith. Reginald Mitchell sadly died of terminal cancer in June 1937 and was not able to see his prototype design progress into becoming perhaps one of the most famous fighter aircraft of the Second World War. Working under Mitchell as chief draughtsman was Joseph (Joe) Smith who was very involved with the early design of the Spitfire. After Mitchell's death in 1937, Smith first became manager of the Design Department, and then later chief designer.

There is a British wartime propaganda feature film about the Spitfire called *The First of the Few* (1942), directed by Leslie Howard, who takes the part of Mitchell in the film. The film is about him working alone to design and build a fighter for the defence of Britain in a future war, and does not refer to any other members of his design team, especially Joe Smith, who worked alongside him on all the design work of the Spitfire right from the beginning.

My own interest in the Spitfire goes back to the war years. When living near Yeovil, Somerset, I remember the searchlights criss-crossing the sky at night, the bombing and the 'dogfights' high up in the sky. For some time I lived with my uncle in Westland Road, close to Westland Aircraft Works where he worked. I would spend many hours near the main gates, watching the aircraft taking off and landing, and remember vividly the sounds of the engines as they were tested. My uncle could see how interested I was and bought a model kit, and together we made and flew my first model aircraft.

The idea for a Supermarine book came after talking to Dave Whatley, chief archivist at Solent Sky Aviation Museum, Southampton, who had loaned me some photographs from their collection to use in one of my books. He asked me what I was going to write next, and when I explained that I had not yet made up my mind, said, 'Why don't you write about Joe Smith and his work on the Spitfire during the war years?' I knew that Mitchell had designed the Spitfire, but was unaware of Smith and his leadership in the development of the Spitfire during the war. Dave Whatley told me that for many who knew Joe Smith and had worked within his design team, it was a great concern that there was very little written about his work on the Spitfire, and that credit for his leadership and dedication was long overdue.

I decided to undertake some initial research which confirmed to me that this was an interesting project that I would like to take on. I was able to gain the help of an ex-Supermarine apprentice who introduced me to other apprentices and this led to contact with the sons and daughters of the senior members who had already passed away, and so the list grew. My next task was to undertake the taped interviews, but I heard that Smith had a surviving daughter, Barbara, and after quite some time we made contact and so the story unfolds. All the interviews were recorded with the interviewees' permission and later transcribed. As quite a few of the interviewees still lived in the local area, I was able to meet them in person. Others, however, were further away, including some in Australia and the USA. These interviews were carried out over the telephone, but were still recorded and transcribed.

Experiences fifty or more years ago are understandably not always recalled accurately in every detail, so dates of events may not always be correct. It was necessary for me to check the factual and historical accuracy, but I was very surprised how accurate many of the interviews were. Furthermore, I wanted to capture and record their experiences in their own words for authenticity, and many of these interviews were backed up by documentary evidence, such as reports, test pilots' log books, and photographs. Furthermore, I was fortunate to be introduced to a number of people who had worked on the shop floor. Their interviews were very illuminating with regard to what it was like working in the various sheds, their experiences of the Luftwaffe bombing of works, and dispersal after the factory was destroyed.

I am deeply indebted to Barrie Bryant, who lives in Australia, and Murry White, who lives in the USA, for the amount of time and help they have given me over the years for my research. Barrie Bryant loaned me correspondence that he had with ex-Supermariners living in Australia and the UK, and with the permission of their relatives, I have been able to add interesting accounts of their experiences of working for Supermarine during the 1920s and '30s. Murry White has been a fount of all knowledge with his experiences of working for Mitchell as his runner, and later as Smith's technical assistant, and was able to describe vividly his personal experiences at Supermarine.

However, it was not possible to write the book without looking at the development of Supermarine and how the chief designer, Mitchell, started to build his young and talented design team in the 1920s. It was important to also look at how the team grew from small beginnings and the development of the company through to the 1930s when the prototype Spitfire flew for the first time, on 5 March 1936. After Mitchell died in 1937, the design team was seen as a closely knit 'family', which did not change after Smith took over as chief designer, successfully leading the team into the jet age until his death in 1956.

Mitchell was a prolific designer and by his untimely death had designed twenty-four different types of aircraft. However, with the prototype Spitfire he delegated the developmental work to Smith and the design team while he set about designing his first bomber. Sadly, he was not able to complete the project before he passed away, and both bomber fuselages under construction were destroyed when the works was bombed in September 1940. It is quite possible that had Mitchell lived, he would have wanted to design another fighter to take over from the Spitfire, but Smith knew that with the threat of war with Germany looming, there was not the time available to design a new fighter and have it in production within three years. He decided that the best course of action was to concentrate on the prototype Spitfire design to meet any developments in Luftwaffe fighters and bombers.

By the end of the war, the Spitfire was a vastly different fighter from the prototype that Mitchell had known. Since his death, the aircraft had doubled its weight and engine power, had vastly increased its speed, and its armaments were a deadly combination of machine guns and cannons that the German pilots feared. In addition, the naval version of the Spitfire, the Seafire, was popular with naval pilots operating from aircraft carriers and naval shore bases. I am privileged to have met Capt. Eric 'Winkle' Brown who shares his memories and close association with Smith during the development of the Seafire, and also agreed to write the foreword to this book.

Smith was later involved in the designs of other Supermarine aircraft, including the Spiteful and Seafang, leading into the jet age with the Attacker. This led to the Swift, which was the first swept back winged fighter in RAF service and also held the world speed record. The last aircraft designed by Smith was the Scimitar, which was the first British aircraft to carry nuclear weapons.

Historian J.D. Scott writes about Smith in his book *Vickers: A History*: 'Although he had been a great admirer of Mitchell, Smith had never tried to imitate his visionary boldness, for his own talent lay in developing things which were already known to be good. If Mitchell was born to design the Spitfire, Joe Smith was born to defend and develop it.' One of Jeffrey Quill's last actions before he passed away in February 1996 was to ask Gerry Gingell to compile a

Supermarine Spitfire memorial book, to be called *The Spitfire Book*, recording the names of all the members of the Supermarine Design Department responsible for the design and development of the Spitfire between 1932 and 1945, 'otherwise all these names will fade away and be totally forgotten'.

Shortly after Smith's death, the design staff were notified that the lease on Hursley Park was to end, and by 1958 the famous Supermarine design team was scattered to various sites, including South Marston, Hurn and Weybridge. However, a number of the long-serving senior members of the team remained in a small office in Southampton until retirement.

This book aims to tell the story of Joe Smith's drive, boundless energy and dogged determination to develop the Spitfire to meet any threat thrown at Britain by the Luftwaffe, and of his post-war work on the jet aircraft until his death in 1956. His dedication and leadership of the design team are demonstrated through the eyes not only of those that worked closely with him, but also of post-war apprentices, who have shared some interesting and often humorous anecdotes.

I hope that my contribution in the form of this book will add to the memory of the design team as listed in *The Spitfire Book*, and also give credit, which is long overdue, to the leadership and dedication of Joe Smith.

Mike Roussel

ACKNOWLEDGEMENTS

I am indebted to all who gave me their support, advice and time while I researched this book, and my grateful thanks go to all who agreed to be interviewed, and also put me in contact with others who could share their experiences and involvement with Supermarine.

My sincere thanks to Capt. Eric 'Winkle' Brown for sharing his experiences while testing the Seafires on the aircraft carriers and writing the foreword to this book.

It has been a great privilege to meet and talk to the sons, daughters and grand-children of the senior management of the Design and Technical Departments who have now passed away. They include Barbara Harries, daughter of Joe Smith; Alan Clifton, son of Alan Clifton senior; Judy Monger, daughter of Ernest Mansbridge; David Faddy, son of Alf Faddy; Martin Davis, son of Eric John (Jack) Davis; Ann Crimble, daughter of Eric Donald (Bill) Fear; Jennie Sherborne, daughter of George Pickering; and Sarah Quill, daughter of Jeffrey Quill. My thanks also go to Rachel Faggetter, daughter of Ted Faggetter; Diana Landon, daughter of Denis Webb; Peter Marsh-Hunn, grandson of Alfred Ernest Marsh-Hunn; and Tim Labette, grandson of Charles Labette, for their permission to quote from material written by their fathers or grandfathers.

I am especially grateful to all who were interviewed and gave me permission to use some of their own material for my book. They include Lily Bartlett, Margaret Blake, Barrie Bryant, Bryan Carter, Mary Collier, Cliff Colmer, David Coombs, Norman Crimble, David Effney, Frank Fulford, Tony Kenyon, Christopher Legg, Joy Lofthouse, Jessie Mason, Gordon Monger, David Noyce, Garth Pearce, Leo Schefer, John Thomson, Fred Veal, Muriel Wanson and Murry White.

My special thanks go to Sqn Ldr A. Jones MBE, CRAeS (Ret'd), Director of Solent Sky Aviation Museum, and I am also deeply indebted to its Archive Department, led by Dave Whatley, for the encouragement and support for my research; to Alan Mansell, for his photographs of air shows and his ongoing support in the photographic archives; and to Dave Hatchard, for assisting in accessing relevant historical documents and for his original painting of Joe Smith. I would also like to thank all who have loaned me photographs and other illustrations from their collections, including Raymond Crupi and Ron Dupas. My thanks also go to Nick Forder, curator of the Air and Space gallery at the Museum of Science and Industry, Manchester, for his help with my research studies. Visits to other aviation museums, including the RAF Museum at Hendon, Tangmere Military Aviation Museum and Fantasy of Flight, Florida, have added further value to my research studies.

Barrie Bryant and Murry White have provided valuable professional advice, consistent support and encouragement for my project, and checked my work for accuracy. My sincere thanks also go to David Key for his invitation to look around Hursley Park, which brought back treasured memories for those who had worked there.

I would also like to thank all those whom I have met not in person but through our respective websites around the world, and my special thanks go to Flightglobal.com and Murdo Morrison (RBI UK) for their courtesy in allowing me to use material from the Flightglobal archives.

Finally, I am eternally grateful to my wife Kay for her constant encouragement, especially in the past months when her loving support and care have seen me through to the completion of this book.

PART I

REGINALD JOSEPH MITCHELL (1895–1937)

INSPIRATIONAL DESIGNER

FLYING LIKE BIRDS

Humans have always been fascinated by flight. Observing birds in flight was the stimulus for early attempts to build wing-like structures and imitate the flight of birds by jumping from towers and high places. Because most attempted to fly by beating their wings like birds, this often led to disastrous results. It was in the late fifteenth century in Italy when Leonardo da Vinci studied the flight of birds and drew the first designs for a flying machine. These flapping-wing machines are known as ornithopters, and, interestingly, designs and prototype machines are still being made and tested in flight today.

It was in the eighteenth century that the idea of lighter-than-air flight using hot air balloons, and eventually airships, was developed, and the first rigid airship to fly, on 2 July 1900 over Lake Constance, was the original *Zeppelin*, built with a metal frame structure. The development of airships continued; they were used for passenger flights as well as in both World Wars, and can still be seen flying today. However, in the early years there were some fatal accidents, with airships catching fire because of the use of hydrogen. The two most famous Zeppelins were the *Graf Zeppelin* (D-LZ127), which first flew on 18 September 1928, and then transatlantic to North America in October 1928, and the *Hindenburg* (D-LZ129), which in 1936 was observed on photographic missions over the Solent area as well as other parts of Great Britain.

There were experiments with heavier-than-air winged aircraft such as model gliders, and attempts at a an early hang-glider whereby German engineer Otto Lilienthal became the first man to launch himself into the air, fly for some distance and land safely. This became the inspiration for Wilbur and Orville Wright for their first powered, heavier-than-air and controlled flight at Kitty Hawk, North Carolina, USA, on 17 December 1903. The challenge and excitement in building and flying winged aircraft soon caught on, and it was in 1908 that Samuel Cody, an American who took up British citizenship, was credited with the first British powered flight. A year later, Louis Blériot made the first

Edwin Rowland Moon, just visible in the cockpit, ready for his first powered flight with *Moonbeam II* in 1910. *Solent Sky*

crossing of the English Channel in a heavier-than-air machine, winning the *Daily Mail* £1,000 prize.

In 1907, a motor racing circuit was opened at Brooklands, Weybridge, and by the following year the site had become one of the first aerodromes in Britain. The interest in aviation was such that the first air show was held from 19–27 March 1909 at Olympia in London. Furthermore, many people wanted to become aviators, and to meet that need the first aviation school was opened at Brooklands by Hilda Hewlett and Gustav Blondeau in 1910. Other flying schools were also beginning to attract potential aviators around the British Isles, but Brooklands seemed to be the centre for such establishments. These included the Sopwith Flying School in 1912, Vickers Flying School in 1913 and the Handley Page Flying School in 1914.

As a consequence, the interest in powered flight increased and resulted in some aviators making their own aircraft. Edwin Rowland Moon, who owned the family boatbuilding business of Moonbeam Engineering, based at the Wool House, Southampton, decided to build his own homemade aircraft named *Moonbeam I* and *Moonbeam II*. *Moonbeam I* was first tested near Calshot, but the flight consisted mainly of short hops. His first successful powered flight was from a level field at North Stoneham Farm with *Moonbeam II* in 1910. This is now the site of Southampton International Airport, and was the Eastleigh aerodrome that K5054 flew from on its first test flight on 5 March 1936.

It is this interest in the development of aviation that quite possibly stimulated Noel Pemberton Billing, the founder of Supermarine, to get involved in flying and the designing and building of aircraft, especially when local interest was centred on the exploits of Moon. In the First World War, Moon joined the RNAS and after the war became a flight commander in the newly formed RAF, but was sadly killed in a flying boat accident in April 1920.

The result of the early experiments and developments in flying, including gliders, hang-gliders, hot air balloons and airships, can still be seen today. There remains a great interest in learning to fly, and many flying schools and clubs are available to meet that need. The opportunities are very wide-ranging, and include training as pilots for the RAF and commercial airlines.

1

THE EARLY YEARS

Noel Pemberton Billing

Born in 1880, Noel Pemberton Billing was an adventurous young man whose exploits led him into some dangerous moments and, it seems, challenged him even more to undertake a wide range of activities including aviation and aircraft design. An inventor with a large variety of patents, a seller of steam yachts, an actor and a playwright, and with a turbulent life as a politician during the First World War, he was a very determined man and would not be held back in whatever he chose to do. In 1908, Wilbur Wright sailed from the USA, complete with aeroplane, to demonstrate to Europe what he and his brother Orville had achieved with powered flight. Billing had heard and read about the Wright brothers' experiments with powered flight in America, and his enthusiasm for aviation drove him to experiment with his own flying machine. Billing's first effort was to build a glider, which when launched from the roof of his home fell apart on hitting the ground. His main problem was lack of capital, but his enthusiasm led to a wealthy friend financing the construction of an experimental aeroplane. The problem was getting a suitable site for the work to begin, but not far from his home was a disused factory in the village of South Fambridge, Essex.

Not only did he work on his own experimental aircraft, he was also keen to invite other aircraft designers whom he had met at the March 1909 air show at Olympia to build their prototype machines at his newly acquired site. He also founded a monthly magazine, *Aerocraft*, for which he became writer and editor, mainly to inform others interested in aviation on the progress of the ongoing experimental work and also to promote his aerodrome.

On 25 July 1909, the same year that Billing was trying to get his experimental work off the ground at his aerodrome, Louis Blériot created further interest in aviation by being the first person to cross the English Channel, from Calais to near Dover Castle, in his Blériot XI monoplane. This caused Billing to have some hope that other aviators would be interested in building their own aircraft at his aerodrome, but a series of mishaps and problems with drainage on the site, which was reclaimed marshland, led aviators to look for more suitable sites, which was not good news for Billing.

Also in 1909, Pemberton Billing had built three prototype aircraft of his own. The first was an open-cockpit pusher monoplane. He claimed his first flight as successful, but it was no more than a few short hops off the ground before it crashed in pieces. His second attempt ended similarly, despite having a more powerful engine. Billing was injured and spent a month in hospital. His third aircraft, an improved version with another new engine, was never flown because it had to be sold to settle debts, and so Billing's Fambridge venture came to an end.

After attempting other ventures, he became involved in selling steam yachts from 1911 to 1913. This was at a time when a young Hubert Scott-Paine had joined him as his assistant and was living with Billing and his wife on board a three-masted schooner named *Utopia* berthed on the River Itchen, Southampton.

The Foundation of Pemberton-Billing Ltd

It was in April 1913 that the first Schneider Trophy competition took place at Monaco, and possibly spurred on by the publicity of this event, Billing made a £500 wager with another aviation pioneer, Frederick Handley Page, that he would gain his Royal Aero Club's Aviators Certificate within 24 hours. In fact he did even better, achieving the certificate at the Vickers School of Flying at Brooklands early in the morning of 17 September 1913, even before having breakfast.

The wager of £500 came in useful, allowing Billing to purchase a disused coal wharf alongside the Woolston ferry on the River Itchen in Southampton as a site for a factory to design and manufacture marine aircraft. The overall aim was to build 'boats' that flew over the sea rather than those that sail on it. Interestingly, the telegraphic address chosen was 'Supermarine', indicating a craft that was above the sea, rather than a 'submarine' which was below it, and so Supermarine was born.

The first Pemberton-Billing Ltd aircraft was the biplane P.B.1. It was a flying boat and was exhibited at the Olympia Air Show in March 1914, where it was inspected by King George V. It was at this exhibition that the Germans first became interested in the P.B.1 design. The aircraft had a hull built of spruce

Flying boat P.B.1 at the Olympia Air Show in 1914. *Solent Sky*

and was powered by a 50hp Gnome engine driving a three-blade tractor air-screw mounted in the gap between the wings of the biplane.

One of the earlier designs was for a flying boat advertised as the 'Supermarine Flying Lifeboat'. This was the P.B.7, designed with its hull constructed as a motorboat, including a cabin for the pilot and passengers, with the wings, engine and tail section at the rear, which could be detached if the aircraft ditched in the sea. The pilot and passengers would then be able either to use the motorboat to make for safety or wait until rescued. The Germans had placed orders for the P.B.7, but following delays to the construction, the First World War had started so the German orders were cancelled. In the end, the P.B.7 was never flown, although plans had been made for initial water trials.

Pemberton-Billing Ltd in the First World War

In June 1914, Pemberton-Billing was formed as a limited company with a share capital of £20,000 put up by Noel Pemberton Billing and Alfred de Broughton, who became the directors of the company. The First World War began on 28 July 1914 and Pemberton-Billing built its first land plane, a single-seat scout biplane, just over a week later. This was the P.B.9, which was powered by a 50hp Gnome engine at a speed of 78mph (152.52km/h) and climbed at 500ft

(152.4m) per minute. It became known as the 'seven-day bus' because it was reputed to have been designed and built in seven days. It had not been decided to build the P.B.9 scout until a Monday morning, when Carol Vasilesco, the draughtsman, started on the design. Construction of the aircraft commenced on the Tuesday and by the following Tuesday, 11 August 1914, the P.B.9 was built and ready to be flight-tested. Its first flight was made at Netley Common, near Southampton, in the presence of Hubert Scott-Paine; Victor Mahl, Sopwith's chief mechanic, who was loaned by Tommy Sopwith to make the first flight; Vasilesco, a Romanian immigrant draughtsman working for Supermarine; and test pilot Howard Pixton. The first test was for taxiing, but Mahl went too close to a fence and damaged a lower wing. A repair was completed in a few hours by workmen from the factory, and Mahl then took the P.B.9 into the air for a successful first flight. Vasilesco sadly died at the age of 19 of heart failure on Christmas Eve 1914. Later another young man was to replace him at Supermarine; his name was Reginald Joseph Mitchell.

The P.B.9 went to Brooklands where it was tested by John Alcock for just two flights. However, he was not happy to continue flying the aircraft and it was later transferred to serve as a trainer at Hendon until taken out of service. John Alcock later became famous when, along with Arthur Whitten Brown, he was the first to fly non-stop across the Atlantic in June 1919.

The work at Supermarine during the First World War concentrated on the repair and maintenance of aircraft from the battlefields of France, as well as building under licence Norman Thompson RNAS NT2B flying boats for the Admiralty. The company was also subcontracted to build the Short 38 trainer and experimental biplanes as well as the Short 184, a patrol seaplane and torpedo bomber carrying two crewmen.

Billing decided to volunteer for the Royal Naval Volunteer Reserve (RNVR) and from October 1914 was given the rank of sub-lieutenant. This was to be a temporary commission as he was chosen mainly for the planning and execution of the attack on the Zeppelin airship factory at Friedrichshafen on Lake Constance because of his organisational ability. During the time that Billing was away from the factory serving in the Royal Navy the works was managed by Scott-Paine. At the time, there was little work coming in, but Scott-Paine managed to get some work from Sopwith who had a shed nearby. The work increased when the factory started to build aircraft under licence and repair damaged aircraft, and trade really started to build up when the Royal Aircraft Factory at Farnborough began to use the Woolston works.

In 1915, the P.B.23E 'Push Proj' (Pusher Projectile) was designed and built at Supermarine. The pusher configuration has the propeller facing in a rearward direction, making it look like the aircraft is being 'pushed' through the air, as opposed to the tractor configuration whereby an aircraft with a propeller in the front is 'pulled' through the air. At first the Push Proj had straight wings, but these were later changed to swept back wings. This pusher single-seat scout biplane had a 100hp Gnome Monosoupape engine powering the aircraft at 98mph (157.71km/h) and was armed with a single .303 (7.7mm) Lewis machine gun. The forerunner of the P.B.25 single-seat scout which came into service for the Royal Naval Air Service (RNAS) for the rest of the war, it was difficult to fly, especially on take-off and landing, and its performance was not the most successful.

Billing was given leave from the RNAS in 1915 to concentrate on designing aircraft for the war effort, and especially aircraft to target the German Zeppelin threat. In the First World War, the early fighters had little experience of night fighting, but when the Zeppelins started their bombing missions at night it was down to the early form of night fighter to attack them. They started using

The P.B.9 was the first land plane built by Pemberton-Billing Ltd. *Solent Sky*

incendiary flares that could be dropped over the airships, but the flares would leave a clear trail when dropped and this could aid the observation of the direction of the attacks on the Zeppelins. However, two quadruplane prototypes, the P.B.29E and the Supermarine Nighthawk, were specifically designed to attack the German Zeppelins.

The P.B.29E of 1915 was a quadruple wing, twin-engine night fighter aircraft in which the fuselage was attached to the second wing, with a gunner's nacelle between the third and fourth wings. The aircraft had two 90hp Austro-Daimler engines powering two airscrews, but flew at a slow speed. It had two flight crew and a gunner with a single .303in (7.7mm) machine gun seated in the fuselage section attached to the second wing. The test programme lasted only for the winter of 1915/16, but the development continued with a new Zeppelin killer, the Nighthawk.

The Nighthawk (P.B.31E) flew in early 1917 and was powered by two 100hp Anzani 9-cylinder radial engines powering two airscrews at 75mph (120.7km/h), although in tests it did not reach this speed. However, the armaments were increased from the P.B.29E to include a 1½-pounder Davis gun mounted to fire forward, and two Lewis .303in (7.7mm) machine guns, and incendiary flares that could be dropped on Zeppelins. The aircraft was able to

Supermarine Nighthawk P.B.31E quadruplane. *Solent Sky*

remain in extended flight for up to 18 hours, but there were some added crew comforts for these long hours of flight as it was equipped with a heated and enclosed cockpit with a bunk for an off-duty crew member. There was also a trainable searchlight in the nose of the aircraft to aid the pilots in finding and destroying Zeppelins in the air at night. Two Nighthawks were constructed, but the prototype did not come up to expectations and was eventually scrapped.

Future Senior Managers

A number of young apprentices working in well-known British engineering companies were forging their future careers in aviation just before the start of the First World War. One name that was to feature in the senior management of Supermarine after the conflict was James Bird who was educated at Marlborough and had an engineering background. After serving an apprenticeship at the Elswick shipyard of Sir W.G. Armstrong, Whitworth & Co., he became a qualified naval architect and later bought and ran a small shipyard in Wivenhoe, Essex. Bird became interested in aviation and built himself an aeroplane in early 1914, obtaining his pilot's licence. At first he joined the RNVR, but when the First World War broke out he transferred to the RNAS.

Reginald Joseph Mitchell became deeply interested in the development of aviation while a student at Hanley High School. It was then that he started to design, build and fly his own model aircraft. So interested was he in his hobby, his school friends commented that 'he was mad about aeroplanes'. On leaving school in 1911, he joined join Kerr, Stuart & Co., a locomotive engineering firm in Stoke-on-Trent, as an apprentice. After starting in the engine workshop he was transferred to the drawing office where his interest and talent for design work began to be recognised. Mitchell's drive to succeed in this area led him to attend evening classes to increase his knowledge and skills in technical drawing, mechanics and higher mathematics. At the time he was an engineering apprentice, major events were beginning to bring the development of aircraft and aviation to the fore. Among these events were the Schneider Trophy races, which were to become a great influence on his future career in aviation.

While Mitchell was still an apprentice at Kerr, Stuart & Co., his future chief draughtsman and colleague Joseph Smith had left Birmingham Municipal Technical School in 1914 to start an apprenticeship at Herbert Austin's motor works at Longbridge. This was at the beginning of the First World War and Smith was just old enough to serve in RNVR. There is a story that, in 1917, he was involved in taking a naval motor launch through French rivers and canals all the way to the Mediterranean, finishing up in Malta at the end of the war. Eight motor launches had left Portsmouth for the Mediterranean before eventually arriving in Marseille, some with damaged propellers after striking underwater obstructions. Two of the motor launches went on to Gibraltar for repairs, four sailed to Italian ports and two sailed to Malta, Smith being a crew member of one of them.

After the war, Smith returned to complete his engineering apprenticeship. Austin's had by this time moved into aircraft production and Smith was transferred to the aircraft section where he became a junior draughtsman in their aeroplane drawing office. It was an interesting and exciting period to be part of the development of aviation. In 1919, the Austin Whippet, a single-seat biplane, was being designed by the company's chief aircraft designer, J.D. Kenworthy.

When Austin's withdrew from aircraft production, Smith was keen to continue in the field of aviation design so he left to join Mitchell at the Supermarine Aviation Works in Southampton in 1921. This was a case of being 'in the right place at the right time' because Mitchell was then looking to build a team of young engineers for his future design and technical team. He knew exactly what kind of man he was looking for, and Smith was one of the first to be appointed. Little was Smith to know at the time that he would eventually become the chief designer and leader of the design team at Supermarine.

Another young man who undertook his engineering apprenticeship about the same time as Mitchell and Smith was Alf Faddy. He grew up in Wallsend and gained a scholarship to the Royal Grammar School in Newcastle upon Tyne. However, when his father became unemployed and shortly afterwards passed away, he had to leave school and go to work to support his mother, younger brother and sister, becoming an apprentice at Parsons of Newcastle. The company were famed for their development of the steam turbine and for their introduction of the launch *Turbinia* that

Joseph Smith joined the RNVR in 1914, serving on the motor launches. *Barbara Harries*

reached a speed in excess of 34 knots when it was shown at Queen Victoria's Jubilee review in 1896. At that time, it was the practice for apprentices to be sacked on completing their apprenticeship. This was so that they moved to other engineering firms to gain a wider experience and develop their skills further, before perhaps moving back to the firm where they had undertaken their original apprenticeship. However, this was not the case with Alf Faddy as he was retained by Parsons, who offered him a job as a chargehand.

Alf Faddy, similarly to Smith, also served in France during the First World War after joining the RNAS. He was fortunate when returning from France to be stationed at RNAS Felixstowe where he was able to work alongside Lt-Cdr John Cyril Porte on the Felixstowe flying boats. Felixstowe was an experimental station for the designing and building of flying boats that had been set up at the start of the war under Porte's command.

John Cyril Porte

Lt-Cdr John Cyril Porte initially joined the Royal Navy submarine service, but after contracting tuberculosis was discharged from the Royal Navy in 1911. This did not deter him and he went on to learn to fly, taking part in air races. His interest in flying boats developed when he met American Glenn Curtiss, also an experienced air race competitor, in Brighton. Both men joined together with the aim of designing and building an aircraft that would fly the North Atlantic. This design work was carried out in the USA and the result was the 'America' flying boat. However, with the start of the First World War the plan was dropped. From his work with Curtiss, Porte first equipped the station at Felixstowe with American Curtiss flying boats, but when they were used on patrol in the North Sea it soon became apparent that their hulls were not suited to the rough sea conditions they encountered. There was an urgent need for Porte to redesign and replace the old hulls, but by that time the experimental designs and development of the Felixstowe flying boats gradually took over.

Some of the Felixstowe flying boat hulls were constructed at the May, Harden & May sheds on Shore Road, Hythe, Hampshire, which had been built by the Admiralty for flying boat construction in the First World War. May, Harden & May was a subsidiary of AIRCO (the Aircraft Manufacturing Co.) based in Hendon. The Felixstowe flying boats were used to fly on patrols from their base at RNAS Felixstowe, looking for the German fleet and U-boats. They were also used to spot and attack Zeppelins, which had become more prominent from their bombing missions on British towns and cities.

When the RAF was formed in 1918, the base was renamed the Seaplane Experimental Station, but was closed in June 1919, the same year that Porte died from tuberculosis. The site of the Seaplane Experimental Station was eventually taken over by the Marine Aircraft Experimental Establishment (MAEE) in 1924. This was where the RAF High Speed Flight was formed for the Schneider Trophy race in 1927. However, after the 1927 race, which was held in Venice, the government disbanded the High Speed Flight, partly because of cost but also because there were no serving officers taking part in the races. The High Speed Flight had been formed initially because other competing countries were using military pilots, which was felt to be a disadvantage to the British entries for the Schneider Trophy. The High Speed Flight was later re-formed and was then based at Calshot for the 1929 and 1931 Schneider Trophy races, both won by Britain, which then retained the Schneider Trophy. The MAEE Felixstowe was visited by Mitchell regularly in connection with his design and production of flying boats. He was often flown from Southampton to Felixstowe by George Pickering, who was later to become a test pilot for Supermarine.

2

Supermarine Aviation Works Ltd

Billing decided to become a Member of Parliament in 1916 and sold his shares in Pemberton-Billing Ltd to Hubert Scott-Paine, who promptly renamed the company Supermarine Aviation Works Ltd. Billing's decision to become an MP followed his many contributions and reviews in newspapers on aviation development in which he also set out his views on the part aviation could play in warfare.

Admiralty Air Department

The government had assumed control of the Supermarine works to construct Admiralty designs, and also for repairs. The twin-float Navyplane and A.D. (Air Department) Flying Boat, designed by the Admiralty, were constructed at the works.

Seaplanes differ from amphibians in that they can land only on water whereas amphibians can land both on water and a runway. Seaplanes can be either a flying boat or a floatplane. A flying boat has a single hull and floats on water, and the floatplane is an aircraft that has streamlined floats instead of wheels.

The Navyplane was a twin-float pusher seaplane designed by Harold Bolas for the Admiralty Air Department in 1916 to undertake the role of a reconnaissance aircraft. Flight tests from August 1916 revealed that the aircraft was underpowered and its original engine, a Smith radial, was replaced by a Bentley BR1 rotary engine powering a pusher propeller. Lt-Cdr John Seddon then conducted the trials with the new engine, but the performance was still not good and only the 9065 was built.

Also in 1916, the A.D. Flying Boat, powered by a 200hp Hispano-Suiza engine driving a single pusher propeller at 100mph (160.93km/h), was designed by Flt Lt Linton Hope for the Admiralty Air Department. It was a two-seat patrol

Pemberton-Billing Admiralty Navyplane. Built in 1916, it carried two crew, a pilot and observer, and was armed with one Lewis machine gun and carried a torpedo. Only the 9065 was built. *Solent Sky*

biplane flying boat with a biplane tail and twin rudders. Its role was to support Royal Navy warships at sea, so it had fold-back wings to enable easy stowage on a ship. The aircraft, although essentially a flying boat, had wheels that could be used to take off from land or a ship. Once airborne, the wheels could be jettisoned. It had a crew of two, a pilot and an observer who would be responsible for firing the single .303in (7.7mm) Lewis machine gun, and wireless for communication with the ground. Two prototypes were built, the test programme proving that the prototypes had handling problems, both on the water and in the air. However, the problems were successfully remedied and orders for production placed.

Reginald Joseph Mitchell CBE, AMICE, FRAeS

That same year, a young man who was eventually to become a world-famous aircraft designer was looking for his first job. That young man was R.J. Mitchell. Having just completed his apprenticeship, he had seen an advertisement for a job as an assistant to Hubert Scott-Paine at Supermarine Aviation Works. He decided to apply, was successful in obtaining the post, and was invited to join Supermarine. Thus began his journey to becoming a famous aircraft designer.

Mitchell got to work immediately and was available to assist Bolas in the design of the Navyplane, which made its maiden flight in August 1916. During his twenty-year career with Supermarine, Mitchell was to continue the company's tradition of manufacturing flying boats before culminating in the design of the prototype Spitfire fighter aircraft. He was also to work with the chief designer, F.J. Hargreaves, on the Supermarine Baby. As a new member of the design team, Mitchell was given the task of producing some of the drawings for the aircraft.

The Supermarine Baby (N1B) was a single-engine pusher biplane flying boat with a wooden hull designed by Hargreaves to Admiralty Air Department requirements in 1917. It was powered by a 200hp Hispano-Suiza engine at a speed of 116mph (186.68km/h). The pilot's cockpit was situated in the nose of the aircraft. Although its tests proved encouraging, the Royal Navy was looking for a land plane design that could take off from a ship, and only one prototype eventually flew before the project was abandoned in 1918. However, the design work on this aircraft was not lost as it became the forerunner of the Sea King fighter and the Sea Lion racing aircraft.

By 1918, Mitchell had been promoted to the post of assistant to Mr Leach, the works manager, and the same year Mitchell married Florence Dayson, headmistress of Dresden Infants' School, Stoke-on-Trent, whom he had been courting before his move to Southampton. They had one son, Gordon, who was born in 1920.

Mitchell made his mark early in his career at Supermarine and was destined to become chief designer in 1919, at the age of 24, when Hargreaves left. In 1920, he was appointed chief engineer, and was promoted to become technical director just seven years later.

N13 Section

Cdr James Bird's service records show that in about 1915 he was posted to Southampton to take charge of the N13 Section of AIRCO as Admiralty overseer of aircraft and boat builders on Southampton Water, including Supermarine. The N13 Section later included the subsidiary May, Harden & May which occupied the old Admiralty sheds in Hythe for building the Felixstowe flying boats. It was the yacht-building yards that became part of the N13 Section because they had the skilled workmen creating wooden craft and these skills were transferred to manufacturing the wooden hulls of the flying boats. When Bird's demobilisation came along in 1918, it was on the strong recommendation of the Director of Inland Ports and Waterways to the Admiralty that he should leave with the rank of squadron commander, on condition that he continued to serve N13 Section as before but as a civilian. As a keen supporter of the flying boat, Bird then joined Scott-Paine at Supermarine Aviation Works.

Another future member of the Supermarine management team was Alfred Ernest Marsh-Hunn. In 1911, he started an apprenticeship at a Whitworth shipyard and qualified as an associate member of the Institution of Civil Engineers in 1916. His grandson, Peter Marsh-Hunn, remembers his mother saying that her father originally came from Woolwich, and when aged about 17 his interest in aviation led him to invent a method for mending the fabric wings on aircraft. As he was too young to patent it himself, a businessman from London, Mr Grey, patented it for him on the understanding that the profits would be shared. These monies were paid to him until he retired.

Because of the First World War, Marsh-Hunn was recruited into a temporary Civil Service post as an aircraft inspector in N13 Section of AIRCO. At the end of the war, when the N13 Section temporary staff were being demobilised, Marsh-Hunn consulted with Bird on his future career and Bird persuaded him to take a business management course with a view to working under him in the future. In July 1919, after completing the course, Marsh-Hunn was appointed as business manager to Supermarine Aviation Works at the time when Supermarine were seeking commercial work to replace the Admiralty contracts.

When Bird purchased the company from Scott-Paine in 1923, Marsh-Hunn's position in the firm was strengthened, as it was when Vickers purchased Supermarine, due to the good relationship he had developed with Head Office. Along with Joe Smith he was later appointed a special director to report to the Vickers board on finance and contracts. When in the 1950s Supermarine were beginning their transfer to South Marston, Marsh-Hunn at the age of 60 decided to retire and concentrate on his private business interests.

Building the Supermarine Design Team

Mitchell had already been 'hooked' into aviation by the time he was appointed assistant to Scott-Paine in 1916 and was working with design staff, some of whom had started in 1913, probably with Pemberton-Billing Ltd, and then transferred to Supermarine Aviation Works Ltd. They included Frank Holroyd, who later became assistant chief designer to Mitchell; W.T. Elliott, who was to become the works manager; Arthur Shirvall, who joined as an apprentice in 1918, specialised in hull design and later became head of new projects; Cecil Gedge, who started in 1919; and George Kettlewell, who started in 1920, the latter two both eventually becoming senior draughtsman.

The management of the company was in the hands of Scott-Paine from 1916, with Bird joining in 1918, and his 'lifelong colleague' Charles G. Grey appointed as company secretary in 1919. Joe Smith joined as senior draughtsman in early 1921, and soon proved himself by his drive, energy and technical skills which led Mitchell to promote him to chief draughtsman in 1926. Harry Tremelling followed in 1922 as senior draughtsman, and also taught drawing skills part-time at evening classes. Jack Rice also started as an apprentice the same year and was later to become head of electrical systems.

Until the early 1920s, the Royal Aircraft Establishment (RAE) at Farnborough had responsibility for airworthiness. Firms were required to provide the RAE with copies of their drawings, plus evidence from calculations and tests already performed. Most detail design relied on the eye and experience of the draughts-man; Mitchell undertook the calculations necessary to determine principal airframe dimensions. His growing workload led to an advertisement for a technical assistant to help him with calculations, and he also wanted to attract a young team of keen, interested engineers to become part of the Supermarine design team.

Alan Clifton had graduated in 1922 with a BSc in aeronautical engineering, and his first job was at a patent agent's office for a very short time. In 1923, he saw an advertisement for a technical assistant and was very keen to get the job, so rode his motorbike to Supermarine at Woolston. In his lecture to the Southampton branch of the Royal Aeronautical Society in 1976, he talked about his appointment: 'Mitchell did all the calculations relating to performance and stress, and in 1923 he employed me as his technical assistant to carry out such work – a great stroke of luck for me.' This was a good move for Clifton, especially at a time when Mitchell was choosing and building up his future design team and the Schneider Trophy racing seaplanes were being developed. Clifton was often referred to by the team as 'Cliffy', his son, also named Alan, being referred to as 'Little Alan' or 'Young Alan'. Where there is a need in this book to distinguish between Clifton senior and junior the reference will be 'Cliffy' or 'Young Alan'.

From about 1923, university graduates were recruited to undertake calculations to do with structural strength and aerodynamics; then, in 1924, came the Air Ministry 'Approved Firms Scheme' which transferred certain airworthiness responsibilities from the RAE at Farnborough to airframe constructors. These graduates formed the nucleus of the technical office, as distinct from the drawing office. Later, all were classified as 'stressmen', a term borrowed from marine engineering. Gradually young recruits from school became junior technical assistants, who after attending night school for a number of years became recognised members of the technical office. Early tasks for a junior were the keeping of weight records, weighing parts, measuring the weight and centre of gravity position of the complete aircraft, and preparing loading instructions for test flights.

In 1924, Ernie Mansbridge BSc joined the Mitchell design team. His daughter, Judy Monger, refers to her father's studies at the East London College, London University, where he did two courses in one under the tutorship of Professor N.A.V. Piercy, who is credited as writing many of the books used by aeronautical students. Mansbridge undertook the aeronautical course and also the civil and mechanical engineering course, which gave him an extra day a week to study aerodynamics and aeroplane design. When Mansbridge finished at university, Professor Piercy wrote this reference on 12 September 1924 for him:

> He proved a very satisfactory and diligent student and is confidently recom-
> mended for a drawing office post in an aeronautical firm. He has first-hand
> acquaintance and experience of wind channel testing and is competent to
> carry out testing, performance and strength calculations. I have no doubt he
> will prove a very useful man.

Mansbridge received a letter dated 17 September offering him a job at £2 10s for the first year, signed by Mitchell, and one dated 22 September adding: '… note that you consider our offer satisfactory; please could you start as soon as possible?' He started on 25 September 1924, straight from university.

At the time of joining Supermarine in 1924 there was a design team of twenty-four, Mansbridge becoming the third member of the Supermarine technical office. By 1929, he was responsible directly to Mitchell for aerodynamics, performance, weights and flight-testing.

Eric Lovell-Cooper also joined Supermarine in 1924. He had started his training at the Norwich aircraft firm of Boulton & Paul in 1918, and having proved himself as a promising aircraft engineer was advised to try for a job at Supermarine 'as they had a very bright designer working there'. This designer was, of course, Mitchell. Others who joined in 1924 were Reginald Caunter; Oliver Simmonds, an aerodynamics specialist who also taught the subject part-time; Oscar Sommer, who specialised in airscrew design and structural testing; Wilfred Hennessy BSc; and Harold Holmes BSc, both of whom worked in the Stresses Department. Miss J. Leach joined in 1925 as a tracer and was an assistant to the chief tracer Miss Farley, later taking over the position.

The team was getting larger, with William Conley joining in 1926 and Harold C. Smith in 1928. The same year, Simmonds left Supermarine to set up his own aircraft factory at the Government Rolling Mills at Weston, which he named Simmonds Aircraft Ltd. His first prototype was the Spartan biplane, christened by the Mayoress of Southampton on 31 December 1928. The company gained further financial support from an investment company and changed its name to Spartan Aircraft Ltd in 1930, moving to the Isle of Wight. However, it went out of business in 1935 and was merged with Saunders-Roe.

The Supermarine Metallurgical Department

Arthur Black was recruited by Mitchell as a metallurgist to develop a metallurgical department in 1926. He later became head of research and systems testing. In 1928, he was joined by Harry ('Griff') Griffiths as his laboratory assistant. After his scoutmaster informed him that there was a vacancy in the Supermarine laboratories, Griffiths had been keen to find out more about the job, and the next morning he travelled over to the Supermarine works on the Woolston floating bridge where he met the chief metallurgist. In his book *Testing Times: Memoirs of a Spitfire Boffin*, Griffiths describes his impression of Black's office:

> His office was most interesting – half of it was taken up with bits and pieces of aircraft; panels, tanks and what looked like the beginnings of a pair of skis. By the desk was a discarded fuel tank which served as a wastepaper bin. On the bench behind was a laboratory balance, microscope and other bits of apparatus.

With an interest in chemistry, he was fortunate to see in the chemical laboratory next door a labelled bottle showing the formula for nitric acid, because that was one of the questions he was asked by Black. Griffiths got the job and was asked to start work the following Monday morning at nine o'clock, and as part of his apprenticeship was required to attend night school for five years.

In his book, Griffiths refers to works laboratories being regarded as a supplier of anything that was remotely connected with chemicals and also acting as a general test facility. He mentions checking the accuracy of all the instruments used, including pressure gauges, altimeters and air speed indicators. In the early days, improvisation was the key to the success of some of the test situations and Griffiths mentions Sommer, who was in structural testing, as being a past master in improvisation. When a problem arose whereby the team had to find the best arrangement for the landing wheels of the Walrus amphibian flying boat, Griffiths searched in his attic at home and found some Meccano parts which they improvised to make a trolley to test the best stability for the wheels.

At the time when drop tanks were being developed to extend the range of the Spitfire, the pilots reported that they had difficulty in releasing the tanks. To gain an idea of the problem, Black and Griffiths flew alongside a Spitfire in the Supermarine 'Dumbo' and filmed the dropping of the tank. The analysis of the film revealed the tank sliding back until it hit the tailwheel before dropping away. As they had no access to a wind tunnel, the team used cardboard boxes and an industrial blower to undertake a test, and a solution to the problem was identified: 'Finally two hooks were fitted just aft of the tank to limit the distance over which it could slide, and in our cardboard "wind tunnel" the hooks were drawing pins!'

Premium Apprenticeships and Trade Apprenticeships

It was possible in the 1920s and early 1930s for employers to offer two types of apprenticeships: premium apprenticeships and trade apprenticeships. With the premium apprenticeships the parents paid £100 per year during the length of the apprenticeship, which could be up to five years. Most premium apprentices had stayed on at school until the age of 16 before taking up their apprenticeships.

Murry White believes that by 1930 there was also another grade of apprentices who did not pay a premium, namely the design apprentices: 'I think Roger Dickson was one followed by George Nicholas, myself, Doug Scard and Barrie Bryant.' The design apprentices usually joined the technical office after working as office boys and runners for Clifton (Cliffy) and Mitchell, and would attend Southampton University either one or two days per week. However, Murry White wanted to gain practical experience in the factory working in the different departments, but by doing so it took him six years to complete his courses.

The trade apprentices left school at the age of 14 and then undertook part-time studies at a technical college. It was the trade apprenticeships which most draughtsmen took up; some moved around to other companies for a time but many returned to their original company as a section leader. H.C. (Harold) Smith was a trade apprentice who became a foreman and progressed to structural engineer and by 1945 was a section leader in the technical office in charge of stresses. It was the premium apprentices that had the opportunity to take up positions in the more senior management positions of the company.

Eric John Davis, better known over time as Jack Davis, was awarded an Entrance Scholarship to Taunton's School, Southampton, on 17 September 1920 and did quite well, gaining his School Certificate before leaving on 28 July 1925. Both his parents were qualified teachers and supported him at school until he left at the age of 17. His father, who was Head of Craft at Southampton Technical College, suggested that aviation was the coming thing, so Davis became a premium apprentice at Supermarine. He took part-time day and evening classes to study for his National Certificate in Mechanical Engineering at University College, Southampton, gaining the qualification on 20 July 1928. He entered the drawing office as an improver draughtsman in 1929, and was involved in the work on the Schneider Trophy racing aircraft.

When Davis left Supermarine on 20 May 1930 to gain wider experience, he was provided with a good reference from T.C. Westbrook, the assistant superintendent, confirming that he had successfully completed his apprenticeship on 10 May 1930, and adding: 'Throughout his employment with us he has given every satisfaction.' After working at Westland Aircraft, Yeovil, and then Boulton & Paul Aircraft at Norwich, he returned to Supermarine in 1933 as a draughtsman, where he was able to work on the development of the Spitfire, progressing to design draughtsman, section leader and finally design co-ordinator.

Denis Webb became a premium apprentice in 1926. While considering what career he could take up, Webb had been reading *Aeroplane* and *Flight* magazines and saw an advertisement placed by Supermarine Aviation. He was eventually invited for an interview with Charles Grey. Webb's father paid £400 for him to become a premium apprentice; he subsequently discovered that his father had knocked Grey down from £500!

Cdr Bird took over Supermarine Aviation Works Ltd from 1923, at which time the senior management included Mitchell as chief designer, Elliott as works manager, Marsh-Hunn as commercial manager and Grey as company secretary. The chief test pilot was Capt. Henri Biard, who had joined Supermarine in 1919 after service in the RNAS.

3

SUPERMARINE FLYING BOATS IN THE 1920S

Mitchell and Smith were destined to work together at Supermarine at a time when the works were designing and building flying boats, and there is no doubt that Smith made a very large contribution to the success of the Supermarine flying boat designs. Scott-Paine had a keen interest in developing high-speed racing aircraft, enabling Smith to work alongside Mitchell in the designs of the Schneider Trophy racers and later the steam-cooled F.7/30 that led to the prototype Spitfire fighter aircraft.

In early 1920, the Supermarine Scylla was designed by Mitchell for the Air Ministry as an experimental wooden twin-engine biplane amphibian military aircraft to replace the RAF Felixstowe F.5, a First World War flying boat designed by John Porte at the Seaplane Experimental Station, Felixstowe. In April 1920, the Air Ministry announced that it was to hold a competition for land planes and seaplanes. Supermarine entered the competition for the seaplanes with the Commercial Amphibian designed by Mitchell specifically for the competition. The new single-engine amphibian biplane, powered by a 350hp Rolls-Royce Eagle VIII engine with pusher configuration, was built with a wooden hull and could carry two passengers and the pilot. The competition was held in September 1920 at the Aeroplane and Armament Experimental Establishment (A&AEE) at Martlesham Heath, near Ipswich, and although the Supermarine entry came second to a Vickers Viking, it so impressed the Air Ministry that it doubled the second prize money to £8,000. This aircraft became the Supermarine Seal and was designed and built as an amphibian biplane reconnaissance flying boat. It was later converted to become the Supermarine Seagull. As well as having more powerful 450hp Napier Lion engines, the Seagull changed from a pusher to a tractor configuration and was of wooden construction with a retractable undercarriage. It was put into production in 1922 for the Air Ministry. This amphibian successfully operated from

Supermarine's Woolston works in the early 1920s, with the Pemberton-Billing boatyard on the left and the Supermarine flying boat factory on the right. *Solent Sky*

Supermarine Commercial Amphibian with 350hp Rolls-Royce Eagle VIII engine giving a maximum speed of 95mph. It carried a pilot and two passengers. *Solent Sky*

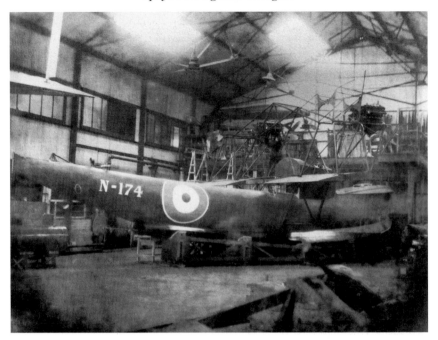

Scylla N174 was built and transported by road to Felixstowe for taxiing trials, but there is no evidence that it was flown. *Solent Sky*

aircraft carriers as a deck landing amphibian, but could also be used on land-based aerodromes. There were two marks of the Seal and four marks of the Seagull, with the exception of the Seagull V which later became the Walrus. The Seagull was first used by the Fleet Air Arm as a reconnaissance flying boat from 1923 to 1925, later being transferred to the Royal Australian Air Force (RAAF) to be used for aerial survey.

Supermarine's Australian Seagull

It was on 6 February 1926 that Lady Cook DBE, the wife of the High Commissioner for Australia, launched the first Supermarine Seagull three-seat amphibian flying boat destined for Australia. It was planned to use the Australian Seagulls at first to survey the Great Barrier Reef as well as for flight training and other tasks. The guests for the ceremony travelled by train from London to Southampton and were taken on a tour of the Supermarine works before the Seagull was brought out of the flight shed, down the slipway and into the River Itchen. Supermarine's test pilot Henri Biard then took off for a short flight along Southampton Water and landed back near the factory, where the Seagull was moored to a buoy.

Seagull N9605 was built as a Mk II in 1923 and converted to a Mk IV. It was later given the commercial registration G-AAIZ. *Solent Sky*

Supermarine Sparrow Land Plane

Mitchell designed his first land plane, the Sparrow I 'light plane', for the 1924 Lympne light aircraft trials. It was the first Supermarine land plane to be built since the Noel Pemberton Billing era and was powered by a Blackburne Thrush three-cylinder radial engine giving a maximum speed of 72mph (115.87km/h), flying at a ceiling of 11,000ft (3,352.8m). The first Sparrow was a biplane, known as a sesquiplane, with the lower wing smaller than the other. The pilot of the Sparrow I in the initial trials was Capt. Biard, but due to problems with its engine, the aircraft could not be completed within the time limits of the trials.

The Sparrow II was built as a parasol monoplane in 1926. The wing of a parasol monoplane is above the fuselage and is not directly connected to it, being supported by struts fixed to the fuselage. The Sparrow monoplane was powered by a Cherub III two-cylinder engine, built by the Bristol Aeroplane Co. Introduced in 1923, it was especially suitable for smaller aircraft. Biard was again the pilot, but the Sparrow II was not a powerful aircraft and could not maintain the 50mph (80.46km/h) speed required. It had to turn back and suffered a burst tyre on landing at Lympne.

The speed of the Sparrow was a source of fun in the Supermarine works, as highlighted in a story suggesting that Elliott, the works manager, could over-

The Sparrow I biplane, G-EBJP. It had two seats for dual control. *Solent Sky*

The Sparrow II parasol monoplane, G-EBJP (like the Sparrow I biplane), also had two seats for dual control. *Solent Sky*

take Biard flying the Sparrow while driving one of the Supermarine staff cars! While testing the aircraft, Mansbridge would be required to fly with the pilot to monitor and record test data. Judy Monger has this to say about the work her father did with the Supermarine test pilot Biard:

> The well-known pilot Henri Biard would fly an aircraft with my father developing schedules for flight test observation and analysis while sitting

behind the pilot. He would have an alarm clock to measure climb rates, and to adjust the weight he would be responsible for throwing bags of sand out of the aircraft. The Supermarine Sparrow, designed by RJM, was one aircraft that Henri Biard and my father flew for special tests. This aircraft, the first and only land monoplane that R.J. Mitchell designed at Supermarine before the development of the Spitfire designs, was used as a testbed for wing forms, and they flew the aircraft with five different wing shapes in a week at Worthy Down in 1927. The aircraft chosen for the tests was the experimental Sparrow II high wing parasol monoplane and it was designed specifically for testing different wing shapes. Henri Biard and my father undertook the performance trials that required 500ft (152.5m) steps up to 5,000ft (1,524m). However, one of the wing forms took 25 minutes to get to 5,000ft, but the best performance wing form was the SA12 and this was chosen for the Solent flying boat.

In 1921, the Air Ministry issued a contract to build a commercial flying boat which was to be the Supermarine Swan. It was designed and built in 1924 as an experimental amphibian biplane for reconnaissance, but had only just completed its trials when it was converted for commercial use. Supermarine had a royal visit from HRH the Prince of Wales on 27 June 1924. After he had opened Southampton's new floating dry dock, he travelled on the Woolston floating bridge to visit the Supermarine works where he saw the Swan.

Swan N175 wooden twin-engine amphibian. Henri Biard piloted the first flight on 25 March 1924. It was later converted to a ten-seat passenger flying boat and loaned to Imperial Airways. *Solent Sky*

HRH Edward, Prince of Wales (centre) standing in front of the Swan on 27 June 1924. On his left are Sqn Cdr Bird and R.J. Mitchell. *Solent Sky*

A test flight with Mitchell and other Supermarine staff and visitors as passengers in a Swan. Notice the wicker seats that were used because they were lightweight. *Solent Sky*

The Swan was used by Imperial Airways in 1926 as a ten-seat passenger flying boat for service between England and France until scrapped one year later. However, the twin-engine Swan was in fact a prototype for the armed military flying boat known as the Supermarine Southampton biplane, ordered by the Air Ministry in 1924, after seeing the Swan's successful tests and even before the Southampton's maiden flight on 10 March 1925. There were two marks of the Southampton: the Mk I was a wooden hull construction and the Mk II had a metal hull, and both were powered by two Napier Lion V engines.

The Supermarine Southampton entered RAF service in 1925 and the success of this flying boat helped to establish Supermarine at the forefront of marine aviation in the British aircraft industry. However, the Mitchell Supermarine designs included civilian passenger flying boats that also could be converted for military use, some of which were experimental. For example, the Sea Eagle (1923) was developed for civilian passenger use, although it took part in the Schneider Trophy races, but the Supermarine Scarab (1924) was a military version of the Sea Eagle.

Supermarine Southampton wooden-hulled Mk I N9896 being launched. It first flew on 10 March 1925 and was in service with the RAF 480 Coastal Command Flight at Calshot from July 1925. *Solent Sky*

Future Supermarine Test Pilot George Pickering

The exploits of the First World War pilots had created a desire in many young men to join up and learn to fly. George Pickering was one of those young men, and his daughter Jennie Sherborne talks about her father's early experiences:

> My father was born on 21 October 1906 and was educated at Berkhamsted School with Graham Greene, the novelist, whose father was the headmaster. I believe he left school at the age of 16 and joined the RAF. At first he went to No 2 Flying Training School, RAF Digby in Lincolnshire, gaining his pilot's licence at the age of 17 in an Avro 504K biplane, a two-seat training aircraft. Despite having two crashes before he was 19, he went on to fly over 30 different types of aircraft before the Spitfire tests.

Jennie goes on to talk about her father's service in Malta and how he became involved in the testing of Supermarine seaplanes and flying boats:

> During his service in Malta in 1927 he received the AFC (Air Force Cross) for a daring rescue in a flying boat. I think it was the Bishop of Malta who he rescued from the sea after he was on a return flight from Syracuse, Sicily, but had crashed in rough sea. The escort seaplane landed and performed a

Southampton Mk I S1037 was built in 1926 and is seen moored in Southampton Water. *Solent Sky*

difficult rescue and the Bishop was safely taken back to Malta. The sea was so rough that the pilot could not take off again, but he powered up the motors and took the Bishop back to Malta on what was perhaps a rather uncomfortable journey, riding the waves all the way back to the island.

Scarab M-NSAH was the military version of the Sea Eagle. Twelve Scarabs were built for the Spanish Air Service. The M in the serial number then represented Spain. *Solent Sky*

Supermarine Erecting Shop with the Southampton Mk IIs S1158 and S1159 being built in 1927 for the RAAF as AII-1 and AII-2 for the Coastal Reconnaissance Flight at Point Cook. *Solent Sky*

In 1931, Pickering came back to England and was stationed at the RAF Experimental Establishment at Felixstowe, still flying seaplanes and flying boats. It was there that he flew the maiden test flights on the Supermarine Stranraer, the Scapa and the Southampton flying boats.

Mitchell became very good friends with him and mentions his friendship with Pickering and his wife, Gladys, in his diary:

Southampton Mk IIs S1233 and S1234 flying in 1927. The Mk II carried four crew and was powered by two 500hp Napier Lion engines giving a maximum speed of 95mph. *Solent Sky*

I am spending a few days with my beloved George and Gladys Pickering. George is to be one of the first test pilots of my new design. He was a MAEE test pilot and in April 1931 was much impressed when he flew the Southampton IV from Felixstowe to Kalafrana in Malta.

The Kalafrana seaplane station (originally Calafrana until the name was changed in the 1930s), was opened in 1917 as an RNAS seaplane station. It was at first used for patrols off Malta by five American Curtiss flying boats that had been flown out from Felixstowe in July 1916. The station became an RAF seaplane station in 1918, and during the inter-war years was used by various types of seaplanes, eventually becoming a base for the Sunderland flying boats. During the Second World War, the Supermarine Walrus was often used to rescue pilots who had been shot down by enemy aircraft.

Calshot Spit

Calshot had developed into an important RAF base for seaplanes and flying boats, and also became well known for the later Schneider Trophy races. The Calshot naval air station was opened by the Royal Flying Corps (RFC) in 1913 for testing seaplanes. It was an ideal location for landing on water because of its sheltered position. The Sopwith hangar was the first to be built, in 1913, for aircraft repair and maintenance, followed later by the Schneider hangar. The first seaplane used was the Sopwith Bat, and during the First World War the air station was actively defending the English Channel and the Solent from the threat of submarine attack. Further buildings were added in 1917 for offices and workshops, including a third hangar, the Sunderland hangar.

The RFC and the RNAS combined in 1918 to form the RAF. Three flights were based at Calshot and by 1920 the station had become RAF Calshot, mainly training crews for flying boats and also for coastal reconnaissance. Part of RAF Calshot was also used for the training of motorboat crews for the rescue of airmen who crashed in the sea. In addition, the motorboats were used to tow targets for ships and aircraft to shoot at, also acting as tenders for the flying boats.

At first, prior to the end of the First World War, the Felixstowe flying boats had been stationed at Calshot, but in 1925 the Southampton flying boats replaced the Felixstowe F5s. On 9 January 1928, the first of two twin-engine amphibian aircraft, the Supermarine Seamew N212, took off on its maiden flight. The Seamew had a retractable undercarriage and a crew of three: the pilot sitting in the nose cockpit, and a forward and rear gunner. The programme ended after trials and a crash in September 1929.

Seamew N212 first flew on 9 January 1928. Only two were built. The picture shows Biard with Mitchell (just out of the picture) approaching the Seamew. *Solent Sky*

Supermarine Aviation Works Ltd Sports and Social Events

The proverb 'All work and no play makes Jack a dull boy' certainly did not apply to Supermarine, with their sports and social club and the drawing and technical office dinners. James Bird was a good leader who generated enthusiasm in his staff and encouraged the workforce to socialise and engage in sporting activities. Sports and social events programmes of the 1920s show that the senior management were all involved not only in the organisation of activities but also in taking part in events such as the rowing competitions where drawing office and technical office competed against the boat shop, metal shop, mill shop, mill joiners and assembly shop. They also had regular social events with entertainment provided by professional artists from London and the presentation of sports cups and prizes being among of the highlights of the evening.

Mitchell's and Smith's Sporting Interests

Mitchell did have other interests apart from his work on aircraft, as referred to by Smith:

If you were away on a business visit with him and the day's work was over, there was always the possibility of some prank developing. He was literally the life and soul of the party on such occasions as the annual drawing office dinner, when with no thought of dignity he became the ringleader in any sort of fun and games, usually aided and abetted by the firm's test pilots. He smoked a pipe, with the aid of a plentiful supply of matches, and was keen on sport. He played tennis, and later, golf, not in order to excel, but as a relaxation, and he was a good loser. He was also fond of the game of snooker and took up sailing as a hobby in later years.

He also learned to fly, and was a founder member of the Hampshire Aeroplane Club. Interestingly, Smith also smoked and was often referred to as 'sucking away on his pipe'. His daughter, Barbara, mentions that he enjoyed salmon fishing on the River Test and was a very good sportsman who played cricket and golf. As well as playing at Stoneham Golf Club in Southampton, he was on call to play fixtures several times at Wentworth with an RAF team.

Development of Commercial Passenger Services

From its formation, Supermarine had specialised in flying-boat manufacture, and Mitchell was to build on the company's tradition. At the end of the First World War the fighter-bomber aircraft that had been designed in wartime had made an impact on their possible use for commercial work, such as delivering mail and the possibility of passenger transportation. Scott-Paine decided to purchase from the Admiralty sixteen of the A.D. Flying Boats used in the war, and the company then went about redesigning and renaming it the Supermarine Channel I to become an early civil passenger aircraft, carrying two crew and three passengers. The Channel I had a 160hp Beardmore engine but this was later changed in the Channel II to a 240hp Armstrong Siddeley Puma engine.

Supermarine then started operating experimental pleasure flights with the Channel I flying boat in the summer of 1919, from the Royal Pier in Southampton to Bournemouth and the Isle of Wight. The flight experience was fairly primitive at first because the pilot and passengers were seated in open cockpits and having to brave all weather conditions. On 28 September 1919, the company introduced passenger flights from Woolston to Le Havre but these were discontinued after a short time and nothing much happened until 1923 when the British Marine Air Navigation Co. began the first British flying boat commercial passenger service from Southampton to Cherbourg, Le Havre and the Channel Islands.

Channel I flying boat N1529, G-EAED. From September 1919, it was used for the first international flying boat service from Woolston to Le Havre. *Solent Sky*

Sea Eagle G-EBFK was built for the British Marine Air Navigation service to the Channel Islands that started in 1923. *John Thomson*

Hubert Scott-Paine and the British Marine Air Navigation Co.

Scott-Paine formed the British Marine Air Navigation Co. as a joint venture between Supermarine and the Southern Railway, the owners of Southampton

Docks, just before leaving Supermarine for new ventures after selling his remaining shares to Bird in 1923. For its cross-Channel passenger service from Southampton, the newly formed British Marine Air Navigation Co. used the Supermarine Sea Eagle, designed by Mitchell and powered by a Rolls-Royce IX engine driving a pusher propeller at a cruising speed of 84mph (135.18km/h). It carried two crew and six passengers. However, it was a short-lived venture because, on 31 March 1924, Imperial Airways was formed as the government's choice for the future of British air services. The British Marine Air Navigation Co. was then taken over, along with a number of other airlines, by Imperial Airways, Scott-Paine becoming a director. Imperial Airways then began operating a passenger and cargo flying boat service from the Marine Airport, based on the River Itchen at Woolston, to St Peter Port in Guernsey. During the summer months this was a twice-weekly service, taking 1 hour and 40 minutes. It operated only once a week during the winter.

In 1936, the Imperial Airways flying boat service was to increase when its first flying boat, G-ADHL Canopus, started the Empire service from Southampton. Imperial Airways later opened its Hythe flying boat base on Southampton Water, in March 1937, for the servicing and maintenance of its Empire services aircraft, and by 1939 had merged with British Airways Ltd to form British Overseas Airways Corporation (BOAC). However, due to the start of the Second World War and the risk of Southampton being attacked and bombed, the operations were moved to Poole, Dorset, from 1940 until 1948 when BOAC returned to its new terminal on Berth 50 at Southampton Docks.

When BOAC ceased flying boat operations, Aquila Airways took over the aircraft and terminal at Berth 50 for its scheduled services to Madeira and other European destinations. Aquila Airways was formed by Barry Aikman in 1948 and at first was involved in the Berlin Airlift. However, as a result of the rising cost of fuel, maintenance of its aircraft and a series of air accidents, the airline ceased operations in 1958. This was at the time of the development of the commercial passenger jet aircraft that caused the demise of the transatlantic ocean liners sailing from Southampton.

British Power Boat Co.

Flying boats were not all that Scott-Paine became involved in. He was also interested in powerboat racing and by 30 September 1927 he had bought the Hythe shipyard with the intention of developing one of the most modern mass-production boatbuilding yards in the country. He renamed it the British Power Boat Co. and together with his chief designer, Fred Cooper, started producing fast racing boats. The company built *Miss England I* for Henry Segrave in 1928, whose aim was to regain the Harmsworth Trophy (the annual international award for powerboat racing), an award that had been retained for a number of years by the American Gar Wood. Segrave, racing *Miss England I*, successfully regained the trophy from Wood's *Miss America VII* in Miami in 1929, and today *Miss England I* can be seen in the Science Museum, London.

By 1930, the British Power Boat Co. was building seaplane tenders for the Air Ministry, and it was at this time that T.E. Shaw (Lawrence of Arabia) became involved for a number of years in the trials of these craft on behalf of the RAF. Aircraftman Shaw had gone to Calshot to assist the RAF support team for the 1929 Schneider Trophy race but was then seconded to the British Power Boat factory in the early 1930s, working closely with Scott-Paine.

When their first seaplane tender, the 37ft 6in (11.43m) RAF 200, was delivered in March 1931 it was Shaw who was involved in its successful trials. Further orders were to follow, including a Royal Navy order for a craft to recover torpedoes, which Shaw was also involved in. It took some time for those with whom he worked to realise who he really was and one of the airmen said: 'We had a gentleman in charge. We didn't know at the time, but we found out after he had been there a few days that he was one of the greatest men from the First World War, Lawrence of Arabia.'

In August 1931, disaster struck when the factory burned to the ground, but it was rapidly rebuilt as the most modern and efficient boatyard in Britain and was able to meet the delivery dates for the seaplane tenders destroyed in the fire. Shaw also worked on other launches and powerboats, and the high-speed motor torpedo boats became a powerful weapon against German shipping. By 1933, Scott-Paine could see the value in the use of fast motorboats as torpedo boats in wartime, and eventually he managed to persuade the Admiralty to order some motor torpedo boats (MTBs). The MTBs became well known as the 'Little Boats' in the Second World War. The British Power Boat Co. also went on to build tenders for the Imperial Airways flying boats where Scott-Paine had been a director.

Mary Collier remembers seeing Shaw regularly when he visited Scott-Paine and the powerboat factory:

> I worked at the British Power Boat Company and I was there before the war and before I was married. I was working in accounts and in the office typing. I remember Lawrence of Arabia who used to turn up on his motorbike to inspect the work. He used to spend a lot of his time cleaning his motorbike outside my office window. He was a very quiet man.

Sadly, Shaw was killed in a motorcycle accident in May 1935, near his home in Dorset, just after retiring from the RAF.

4

SCHNEIDER TROPHY RACES 1913–1931

Jacques Schneider was a French industrialist who, on 5 December 1912 at the Aéro-Club de France, offered a trophy for a seaplane race and proposed a course of at least 150 nautical miles. The race was to be run annually, and the first competition was held at Monaco on 16 April 1913. It was won by Maurice Prévost in a Deperdussin floatplane at an average speed of 45.71mph (73.56km/h). On 14 April 1914, the second year of the competition, Britain won the Schneider Trophy for the first time. Howard Pixton was the pilot, flying the Sopwith Tabloid biplane fitted with floats and powered by a 100hp Gnome Monosoupape engine at an average speed of 86.83mph (139.73km/h).

Sea King II, a single-seat biplane with wooden hull and retractable landing gear. First flown in 1921, it was rebuilt as the Sea Lion II, winner of the 1922 Schneider Trophy race. *Solent Sky*

Sea Lion I was entered in the 1919 Schneider Trophy race and was flown by Flt Lt Basil Hobbs. *Solent Sky*

The Schneider Trophy races then ceased due to the First World War until 1919, when it was held at Bournemouth. This was when Mitchell's Sea Lion I flying boat, a little pusher plane powered by a Napier Lion engine and capable of 149mph (239.79km/h), first took part. It had been developed from the Supermarine Baby. Only one pilot completed the course – the Italian Sgt Guido Janello – but he was disqualified as the judges ruled that he had not completed the set route because he had not been observed negotiating the Swanage turn. The pilot of the Sea Lion I was Flt Lt Basil Hobbs, but the aircraft was damaged after hitting an obstacle in the water due to the foggy conditions, which in the event forced the cancellation of the race. With these developments in mind and the need to keep up with the developments of other nations' aviation designs, Mitchell was encouraged to design and build an aircraft for the 1922 race.

During this time Supermarine continued with designs for various commercial and fighter flying boats that included the Scylla and Sea Urchin, and the Sea King, a single-seat fighter flying boat.

Both the 1920 and 1921 Schneider Trophy races were held at Venice, but Britain did not enter these. The Italians won both times, and had they won again then they would have kept the trophy. However, this was not to be, as the 1922 competition, held in Naples, was won by Sea Lion II, powered by a 450hp Napier Lion engine, designed by Mitchell and flown by Biard, who won the race at a world record speed of 145.7mph (234.48km/h). No funding had been forthcoming from the government and so Bird had financed the race as a private venture.

There was a bit of a misleading impression given to the Italians watching the Sea Lion fly its first lap, when its speed was not very impressive and Biard did not appear to have the floatplane completely under control. What they didn't know was that Biard had not opened up to full throttle on the trials, so the Italians felt confident that they would win for the third time and therefore keep the trophy. However, Biard opened up to full throttle and the speed of his laps was over 160mph (257.49km/h), which he maintained to overtake the Italians. He then slowed up, allowing them to reduce his lead and think they had a chance, only to open up again and win the race.

The Supermarine Sea Lion III was built for the 1923 race which took place at Calshot and was won by the American Curtiss CR-3 floatplane, piloted by David Rittenhouse at a speed of 177.27mph (285.28km/h), with the Supermarine entry flown by Biard managing only third place. The following year's race was postponed and the Sea Urchin designed for it was never built. It was not until October 1925 that the next race took place, at Baltimore, USA.

In preparation for the 1925 race, Mitchell started to design the first of a series of four streamlined float seaplanes, the S.4, S.5, S.6 and S.6B, with the designation 'S' standing for Schneider. The S.4 was of wooden construction with wooden floats and was powered by a Napier Lion engine. The British team had sailed for America with the intention of taking part in the Baltimore race, but were dogged by bad luck. First, on the crossing of the North Atlantic,

Sea Lion II won the 1922 competition held in Naples. *Solent Sky*

Biard and Mitchell in front of the S.4. Biard served as a RNAS pilot and joined Supermarine as a test pilot in 1919. *Solent Sky*

Biard slipped on the liner's deck and badly injured his hand; then on arrival in America he caught flu. Combined with this, the S.4's tail was damaged when the tent housing the aircraft blew down in a storm. However, the necessary repairs were undertaken and while Biard was flying at approximately 800ft (243.84m) the aircraft developed wing flutter. (At that time, little was known about this problem.) He did manage to land the aircraft on the water, the force of the landing making the undercarriage collapse, but fortunately he escaped safely from the aircraft.

The 1925 Schneider Trophy race was won again by the Americans in a Curtiss R3C-2, flown by James H. Doolittle at a speed of 232.57mph (374.28km/h). In 1926, there was no British entry in the race held at Norfolk, Virginia, USA, which was won by Italian Mario de Bernardi in a Macchi M.39 at an average speed of 246.5mph (396.7km/h), thus denying the Americans the opportunity of retaining the trophy.

The following year, the race was again held at Venice, but this time the Air Ministry sponsored the Mitchell-designed S.5s and there was a very strong British entry flown by pilots of the RAF High Speed Flight. The main difference between the S.4 and S.5 was that the S.5 had a lower wire-braced wing, and the fuselage and floats were of metal construction. The S.5 was fitted with a special 875hp Napier Lion engine that gave it a higher speed. Two S.5s were

Supermarine S.4 ready to be launched in the River Itchen. Biard was the pilot for the first flight on 24 August 1925. *Solent Sky*

in the race and both excelled, one coming in first (piloted by Flt Lt Sidney Webster) at an average speed of 281.66mph (453.28km/h) and setting a new world speed record. The other pilot, Flt Lt E. Worsley, came second at a speed of 273.07mph (381.52km/h). This was the last annual competition, it then moving to a biennial basis. Sadly, Flt Lt S. Kinkead, who was in command of the RAF High Speed Flight, was flying an S.5 in an attempt to break the world speed record when he crashed and was killed at Calshot on 12 March 1928. However, during November 1928 one of the two S.5s of the High Speed Flight at Felixstowe was piloted by Flt Lt D. D'Arcy Greig to set up a new British speed record of 319.57mph (514.29km/h).

The S.6, although similar to the S.5, was much larger and much heavier due to a 1,900hp Rolls-Royce 'R'-type engine of all-metal construction that had been specially developed for racing. Clifton (Cliffy) in his 1976 lecture commented on the 'problems' and 'solutions' to the construction of the S.6:

The 1929 S.6 was similar to the S.5 but all surfaces were in a light alloy stressed skin. The wings and part of the floats had double skins separated to provide a passageway for engine coolant The stressed skin could never be soldered, and a very slight leak or two was cured with 'Neverleak' which was bought at a local garage!

S.5 N219 being launched, with Calshot Castle in the background. *Solent Sky*

Two S.6 racer aircraft, serial numbers N247 and N248, were built at Woolston and delivered in August 1929 to the RAF High Speed Flight. This was to support a strong British entry, and in 1929 the Schneider Trophy race was held again at Calshot, with the Supermarine S.6 (N247), piloted by Flg Off. Henry Waghorn and powered by a Rolls-Royce engine, winning at an average speed of 328.63mph (528.87km/h). The second S.6 (N248) entry was piloted by Flg Off. Atcherley, but he was disqualified for missing a turning point, although he completed the course and set a world record over the 50km (31-mile) and 100km (62-mile) distances at speeds of 332.49mph (535.09km/h) and 331.75mph (533.89km/h) respectively. However, just days later, Sqn Ldr A.H. Orlebar AFC, flying N247 raised the world speed record to 336.3mph (541.22km/h) and then to 357.7mph (575.66km/h).

Having won the 1927 and 1929 Schneider Trophy races, Britain had to win only once more to retain the trophy, but the government's support for the team was withdrawn in 1931, causing a public outcry. However, a donation of £100,000 from Lady Houston gave Supermarine the opportunity to compete with the new S.6B. With only nine months to the contest, not much could be done to the S.6 with the exception of fitting a more powerful 2,350hp version of the Rolls-Royce R engine. Two S.6Bs were built and the original S.6s modified and redesignated S.6A. Along with the S.6Bs, they had new larger floats to carry extra fuel.

S.6 N248 just launched at Calshot. The pilot in the cockpit, sergeant on the beach, and the aircraftmen appear to be looking very closely at the floats. *Solent Sky*

S.6B in the hangar, with work being done on the floats. *Solent Sky*

None of the competitors from Europe were able to have their aircraft ready in time for the 1931 competition, but despite this, the RAF High Speed Flight arrived at Calshot with six Supermarine racers to use for practice flights. These racing aircraft were the S.5 (N220), which won the 1927 Venice competition, and the S.5 (N219) that came second, and the two S.6s (N247 and N248) from the 1929 event. The two new S.6Bs were given the serial numbers S1595 and S1596.

The aim was to race the S.6B (S1595) with the S.6A (N248) in reserve due to the aircraft's already proven racing capabilities should the S.6B not achieve the required speed or breakdown. The other S.6B (S1596) was to be the aircraft that would attempt the world air speed record. However, the S.6 (N247), which was the second reserve to the S.6 (N248) flown by Lt G.N. Brinton, crashed on take-off and was written off for the race. This left just the two new S.6Bs and the S.6A (N248) ready for the race, although in the end, N248 did not fly on the day.

The 1931 race was again won by Britain (pilot Flt Lt John Boothman) with a new world speed record of 379.08mph (610.07km/h). Britain also won the trophy outright as it was its third win in a row. Only two weeks later the world record was broken again, in the S.6B with a new Rolls-Royce engine at a speed of 407.5mph (655.80km/h) by Flt Lt G. Stainforth, who was the first man ever to fly over 400mph (655km/h).

S.6B and the British team at Calshot in 1931. From left to right, Flt Lt Hope, Lt Brinton, Flt Lt Long, Flt Lt Stainforth, Sqn Ldr Orlebar, Flt Lt Boothman, Flg Off. Snaith, Flt Lt Dry (Engineering Officer). *Solent Sky*

Ted Faggetter joined Supermarine in July 1931, just six weeks before the last Schneider Trophy race, and was able to see the event first-hand. He describes what at first was to be a disappointment but would be a memorable event the next day:

In order to get a good view of the last Schneider Trophy race at Calshot in September 1931, George Kettlewell, a Section Leader in the office organised a trip to Ryde on the Isle of Wight, involving a paddle steamer to Cowes and bus along to Ryde. The Italians were the only competitors and as they withdrew at the last moment the race was to just be a 'fly over'. Alas, it turned out to be a rather wet day with low clouds, but when we reached Ryde via Cowes the weather had deteriorated and the race was abandoned, though despite the weather we had an enjoyable day. It was a somewhat bedraggled party that returned to the mainland.

The next day, Sunday, it was a brilliant morning. Faggetter discovered that at 10.40 a.m. there was a steamer going direct to Ryde and cycled the 3 miles down to the pier in record time, arriving just as the gangplank was being hauled up at 11 a.m.:

When the steamer was well down Southampton Water we were stopped short of Calshot, the seaplane operating base, and anchored for some hours, not only for the 'fly over' but also for the subsequent attempt on the world speed record. This involved three flights down Southampton Water in each direction by a special Supermarine S.6B fitted with an up-rated Rolls-Royce engine. The steamer eventually went on to Ryde with an immediate return, somewhat late, but it was a memorable day. A few days later it was announced that the record had been raised to 407.5mph, the first exceeding 400mph. and some achievement!

'The Phantom of the Night'

The engine used for the 1931 Schneider Trophy race and the world air speed record was the Rolls-Royce 2,350hp 'R' (Racing) engine which had a very limited flying time between overhauls. This could be something in the order of 1 hour for the race and 30 minutes for speed record attempts. In consequence there was a need to transport engines rapidly between Derby and Calshot so that the Experimental Department could rebuild, test and reinstall them in the aircraft. To transport the engines a Phantom I car chassis was fitted with a cradle for the engine.

The Phantom I car chassis that transported the 'R' engines between Calshot and Derby. *Solent Sky*

It was well known that there were 'speed' records broken by the driver who transported the engines to and from Calshot, and at one stage the press got hold of the story and wrote it up as 'The Phantom of the Night'. Unfortunately this slowed progress down a little because, from then on, the police kept a close lookout for the speeding vehicle, and did at one time catch them after they had gone through Calshot village at 80mph (128.74km/h)!

The Schneider Trophy races became a great influence on the design of the future high-speed aircraft, such as the Spitfire fighter of the Second World War, particularly in the area of aerodynamics and engine design. This development of high-speed streamlined float seaplanes demonstrated that the Schneider competition had had a direct effect on the designs for a high-speed fighter aircraft. As a result of his contribution to the development of high-speed flight, Mitchell was awarded the CBE in 1932. Today, S.6A (N248) can be seen on display at Solent Sky Southampton, and S.6B (S1596) is in the Science Museum, London.

Four Southampton flying boats flew on the Far East tour to identify future bases. After flying to Australia and Hong Kong they returned to Singapore to set up the first permanent base. *John Thomson*

One of the tasks for the Far East Flight to practise was fuel delivery by canoe. *John Thomson*

The Far East Tour

It was in July 1926 that two Southampton flying boats flew from Plymouth to Egypt and Cyprus and back, but this was followed in October 1927 by four Southampton Mk II flying boats of the RAF Far East Flight under the command of Gp Capt. Cave-Browne-Cave departing Plymouth for an extended cruise to Athens, Egypt, India, Australia, Japan and Singapore, where the journey ended on 10 December 1928. The aim was to identify suitable flying boat bases for the RAF, and the experience gained by RAF personnel working in different conditions around the world was also invaluable. Maintenance and repair of aircraft was undertaken in challenging circumstances, such as changing an engine using portable derricks and refuelling when the fuel was transported to the aircraft in local craft.

During the 1920s, Supermarine had gained a worldwide reputation for their aircraft, and for their designer, Mitchell. This was demonstrated by the

Not a lot of room, but there are the mugs and teapot and the crew member with the frying pan. On his left is a bottle of sauce. *John Thomson*

With no workshop facilities available, an engine had to be replaced using a portable derrick.
John Thomson

outstanding performance of the Supermarine racing seaplanes in the Schneider Trophy races, combined with the reliability of the Southampton Mk II flying boats during the extended Far East Flight. The outcome was to benefit Supermarine Aviation Works Ltd in terms of export opportunities during the 1920s and '30s, and kept the company in work during a time when others went out of business due to the financial crises of the late 1930s.

5

SUPERMARINE AVIATION WORKS (VICKERS) LTD

Vickers Airships (Barrow)

Vickers was a well-known British engineering firm that started in the early nineteenth century, first as a steel foundry but then gradually expanding into other engineering sectors supplying equipment for shipbuilding, including military and naval hardware, and the manufacture of Vickers machine guns.

The interest in lighter-than-air airships found the company involved in developing the first rigid airship for the Admiralty in 1909 to compete with the development of the Zeppelin airships in Germany. The craft designated as HMA No 1 (His Majesty's Airship No 1), also known as the Mayfly, was built at Vickers, Barrow, for the Royal Navy, but the airship did not fare well and due to strong winds broke in half before making its first flight.

The team working on the design for the company's second rigid airship was under the direction of their chief draughtsman for airships, H.B. Pratt, but he left Vickers in 1912 to join J. Samuel White, a shipbuilding firm in Cowes on the Isle of Wight. It was there that Pratt met Barnes Wallis, who had at first been an apprentice at the Thames Engineering Works, working on marine engines. Barnes Wallis was not happy there because of the decline in shipbuilding work and in 1908 decided to transfer his engineering apprenticeship to J. Samuel White's shipyard at Cowes, finishing up in the drawing office where he became good friends with Pratt.

With the news that Germany was building more Zeppelins, the pressure was on to have British airships in the air and, in 1913, Vickers invited Pratt back to Barrow to continue his work on airships for them. He agreed to return, but also brought Barnes Wallis with him as his assistant to design, construct and test more airships.

By the 1920s, the British Government had become concerned about the technological lead that Germany was gaining in the development of airships and wanted to do something about it. But should the airships be built by the government or by private enterprise? The problem was solved by having two airships built: the R100 was designed and built by Vickers as the private enterprise, and the R101 was built by a government agency. The R100 and R101 were constructed as part of the Imperial Airship Scheme. The design and construction of the R100 was undertaken by Vickers at Howden in Yorkshire, and the R101, designed by V.C. Richmond, was built at the Royal Airship Works at Cardington in Bedfordshire.

In 1924, Nevil Shute Norway was appointed to the Airship Guarantee Co., a subsidiary of Vickers Ltd, to work on the construction of the R100 as chief calculator. Shute Norway was an aeronautical engineer but is perhaps better known as the novelist Nevil Shute. From 1919, he had studied engineering science at Balliol College, Oxford, and during vacations had worked in an unpaid capacity at Geoffrey de Havilland's Aircraft Manufacturing Co. at Hendon. After Oxford, Shute Norway worked as a performance calculator for de Havilland. By 1929, he had become deputy chief engineer under Barnes Wallis, with the R100's first flight taking place in December 1929. The airship had successful trials and early flights, including a transatlantic flight from England to Canada and back. However, the R101, which had left for a trip to India on 5 October 1930, crashed in France and caught fire with the loss of forty-eight of the fifty-four passengers and crew. Following this crash, all work on airships was discontinued in favour of heavier-than-air craft. Shute Norway could not see any future in airships so decided to set up his own aeroplane manufacturing company, Airspeed Ltd.

Barnes Wallis continued at Vickers and transferred to working on aircraft. He was responsible for designing the geodesic airframe construction method. This was a result of his experience of the geodesic wiring harnesses in the airship design, especially his work on the R100, and was used for the design of Vickers bombers, including the Wellesley and Wellington. At the start of the Second World War he was the assistant chief designer in Vickers' aviation section, and it was Barnes Wallis, of course, who became famous for his design of the bouncing bomb which was used to destroy the dams in the Ruhr.

In 1927, Vickers merged with Armstrong Whitworth and became Vickers-Armstrongs Ltd. The Aviation Department was renamed Vickers (Aviation) Ltd in 1928.

Supermarine Aviation Works Taken Over by Vickers

In the period that Vickers were looking to take over Supermarine, work was ongoing and other Mitchell designs were being built, including the Supermarine Nanok (Inuit for 'polar bear') prototype 1 (1927), a three-engine development of the Supermarine Southampton, with a crew of five. It was designed and built to order for the Royal Danish Navy as a torpedo-carrying flying boat and first flew on 21 June 1927. However, only one was built because test results did not meet the performance required by the Royal Danish Navy so the order was cancelled. The aircraft was then converted to a twelve-seat flying boat for the Hon. Arthur Guinness, the Irish owner of the Guinness brewing company, and was renamed the Supermarine Solent in 1928.

In the autumn of 1928, Sqn Cdr Bird sold Supermarine to Vickers (Aviation). The company was renamed Supermarine Aviation Works (Vickers) Ltd, but a condition of purchase was that Mitchell was to remain with the company and could not terminate his agreement before 5 December 1933. When Vickers took over Supermarine there were approximately 750 employees. This acquisition did not go down well with Mitchell due to the fact that Vickers sent their own man down from Weybridge to work alongside him. There has been some

Woolston works in the 1920s, with workshops modernised, at the time that Vickers-Armstrongs took over Supermarine Aviation Works. The Woolston ferry is on the far right. *Solent Sky*

The Nanok was a three-engine biplane built for the Royal Danish Navy. Armaments included two .303 machine guns and two torpedoes. *Solent Sky*

Rejected by the Royal Danish Navy, the Nanok was converted to G-AAAB and renamed Supermarine Solent, a twelve-seat aircraft for the Hon. Arthur Guinness. *Solent Sky*

speculation about the name of the Weybridge man, but this has been confirmed by Mitchell's son Gordon, who has said that Rex Pierson, the chief designer at Weybridge, released Barnes Wallis who then transferred to Supermarine to assist Mitchell in the design of the Guinness Air Yacht as well as in the general organisation. Mitchell was angry at what he saw as interference, and if Barnes Wallis walked into a room, he would immediately walk out.

Eric Lovell-Cooper remembers Barnes Wallis arriving just after Christmas and installing himself in Mitchell's office, even sitting in his chair! Eric was approached by Mitchell who told him, 'You might put a desk up in the loft for Wallis, but don't make him too comfortable!' The situation became so serious that Weybridge recalled Barnes Wallis, replacing him with Major Harold Payn AFC, an ex-RFC pilot from the First World War with an engineering background and some technical knowledge, as Mitchell's personal assistant. Although Weybridge were keen to keep Mitchell, it appeared that they wanted to make further changes and sent Trevor Westbrook as factory superintendent.

From the takeover in 1928, production of the Southampton flying boat continued, not only for the RAF but also for other countries such as Japan and Argentina which were also interested in the aircraft.

Trevor Westbrook

It was thought that Trevor Westbrook had been sent from Weybridge to be factory superintendent at the Woolston works for the purpose of organising the Supermarine work systems, which it was felt needed tightening up. This was not far from the truth, because at the time Supermarine's production system and stores were known to be very poorly organised. Mitchell was focused on his design work, and basic administration was very low in his priorities. When Vera Cross took over as his secretary, she found his desk full of unanswered letters and there was no organised filing system.

Westbrook was heavily involved in getting the factory organised for the future mass-production of the Spitfire and set about the task with vigour. There was an urgent need to sort out the organisation of the records system to make the factory more efficient, but at first Westbrook's methods did not meet with the approval of the Supermarine workforce. At the time of his arrival, production was mainly in timber, but he recognised that with the coming changes to all-metal aircraft, and possible future contracts for more modern metal aircraft, the stores would not be efficient enough to manage the demands, and he set about replacing some foremen. Not a popular move.

Reorganisation of the Stores Systems

In the course of improving the production system organisation Westbrook found his attention drawn to the work of the stores. Part of the problem was that the same system had been running for years. It had not been effectively updated for the new materials and parts required for the new aircraft, first for the 180 Walrus that had been ordered, and then for the Spitfire which was being redesigned and planned for production.

Denis Webb was appointed assistant to Westbrook and was not at all impressed with the systems in place for monitoring the parts needed for the production of the aircraft. He saw that the responsibility of the Progress Department was to 'chase up' a foreman when an assembly line ran short of a part. Westbrook had also spotted men waiting at the Finished Part Store for a set of parts, or even one part, with long delays due to the primitive type of storage bins and unsatisfactory systems that were in place. After observing the inefficient storage system, Westbrook set about sorting it out. However, after failing to get any action out of the chief storekeeper, he sacked him. Webb recalls, 'He then rang me and told me to do something about it!' This was a massive task that took Webb many hours of planning and making changes, funded by money that was earmarked by the Vickers board. Once the planning and changes had been completed, they finished up with an efficient stores record system which enabled them to warn foremen when stocks of any particular item were getting below a safe level.

Southampton Mk X N252 was a three-engine sesquiplane (wider-span upper wing) built with a stainless steel hull. Capt. 'Mutt' Summers undertook the trials on Southampton Water in March 1930. *John Thomson*

The Southampton Mk X

The Mk X was a three-engine version of the Southampton ordered by the Air Ministry in 1928, and was undergoing tests in March 1930. At first the engines were three Armstrong Siddeley Jaguar IVs; these were changed to the more powerful Bristol Jupiter engines but with disappointing results, so only the prototype was built.

The Supermarine Air Yacht

The Supermarine Air Yacht was a three-engine, all-metal luxury passenger-carrying flying boat designed and built in 1930 by the Supermarine Aviation Works for the Hon. Arthur Guinness for pleasure flights around the Mediterranean. It was powered by three engines, carried a crew of four and six passengers, and was to have replaced his Supermarine Solent, but was rejected by Guinness. The only one built, it was then sold to Mrs J.J. James who renamed it *Windward III*. The aircraft crashed on 25 January 1933 near Positano in the Gulf of Salerno with no casualties and was later scrapped.

Supermarine Air Yacht G-AASE was first flown in February 1930. Designed originally as an armed reconnaissance flying boat, it was later converted to a luxury yacht for the Hon. Arthur Guinness. *Solent Sky*

The wreckage of *Windward III* (ex-Air Yacht G-AASE) was taken to Giuseppe & Paolo Vigliar shipyard, Salerno, after it crashed in the Gulf of Salerno on 25 January 1933. *Solent Sky*

Alf Faddy's Journey to Supermarine

After leaving RNAS Felixstowe, Alf Faddy was employed by a firm with a contract to deliver the Vickers Vimy biplane, but the pilot had little confidence in the reliability of the engines and insisted that Faddy flew with him on every delivery flight. David Faddy remembers his father telling him about the occasion when they were forced to land on the front lawn of a vast mansion owned by a peer of the realm who had never seen an aircraft before. Both his father and the pilot were entertained 'royally' until the spare parts could be delivered and the aircraft could take off.

After the Vickers Vimy period, Faddy took a post at Parnall's, a small aircraft firm at Yate, near Bristol. Before the war Parnall & Sons had been a woodworking firm and with the increased demands for the production of wartime aircraft they were contracted to build aircraft, which at the time were constructed mainly of wood. The contracts issued included aircraft designed by other aircraft manufacturers. However, during the latter part of the First World War the Admiralty was interested in designing and building a two-seat reconnaissance aircraft that could operate from aircraft carriers. Harold Bolas, who was already an Admiralty Air Department designer and had experience in designing flying boats for the Air Department at Supermarine Aviation, was released to Parnall & Sons to work on designs for such an aircraft. The result was the Parnall Panther, which first flew in 1917.

While Faddy was at Parnall's he worked alongside Bolas on a number of designs for the RNAS that included the Plover (1923) and the Pipit and Peto (1929). The Peto was specifically designed in 1929 as a floatplane that could be launched from a submarine. However, one of the aircraft-carrying submarines, HMS *M2*, was wrecked in Lyme Bay in 1932 after leaving Portland for a naval exercise. It is thought that the hangar doors for the floatplane were opened too soon and flooded the submarine, with the loss of all the crew. At the time the submarine was carrying a Parnall Peto, but after this loss the Royal Navy stopped the practice of launching aircraft from submarines.

The valuable knowledge gained by Faddy over the years at RNAS Felixstowe, during the Vickers Vimy period and at Parnall's had prepared him so well that when he joined Supermarine in 1930, at the age of 38, he already had considerable experience in aeronautical design and was able to work on the Supermarine Type 179 Giant, a large six-engine monoplane civil flying boat powered by six Buzzard engines, built for seven crew and forty passengers and designed by Mitchell. The inspiration for this design was thought to have come from a visit to the Solent by the German Dornier Do X large flying boat in 1930.

After Faddy had settled down to his work in Supermarine he recommended a friend with whom he had worked at George Parnall & Co. in Bristol to Scott-Paine. This friend was Eric Donald Fear, who applied for a job at Supermarine and was recommended by Harold Bolas, the chief designer at Parnall's. Following this, Fear received a letter from H.J. Payn on 30 June 1931, signed on behalf of Mitchell, the director and chief designer, accepting his application for a position working in the drawing office. They offered him a position at a weekly commencing salary of £4 15s 0d. To all who worked in the Design Department, Fear was always known, for some reason, as Bill, and the fact that the initials E.D.F. on drawings stood for Eric Donald Fear came as some surprise to many who had talked about their career working at Supermarine.

Cancellation of the Type 179 Giant Project

Ted Faggetter was a new member of the design team when, due to economic problems, the Supermarine Type 179 Giant contract was cancelled in 1932. The job of laying off twenty drawing office staff was left to Joe Smith, as chief draughtsman. Faggetter remembered that it was one Friday in early 1932:

> The office boy emerged 20 times from Joe's office to tell draughtsmen that Joe wished to see them, but somehow I missed a call and survived to work

A model of the six-engine monoplane Type 179 Giant that was designed in 1929 and partly built before being cancelled. *Solent Sky*

on the Seagull Mk 5 amphibian, 26 of which had been ordered by Australia, 'off the drawing board'. I have often remarked that the Seagull Mk 5 took me through the 'Depression'. Eventually it was ordered by Britain and became famous as the 'Walrus', and was indeed a very interesting and versatile aircraft.

Lifelong Friends

From the start of his time working at Supermarine, Faggetter got to know Charles Blazdell and they became lifelong friends. Blazdell was responsible for the flying and engine control systems, and also the scarf ring for the aft firing gun of the Seagull Mk V. The control column was quite ingenious, the second pilot's wheel being detachable for storage at the side to allow access to the forward cockpit for mooring. After Faggetter left, Blazdell went on to be involved with the Spitfire and devised the ingenious landing gear locks, before he joined George Dowty, an old contact from Avro Hamble days. Faggetter's son, David, remembers his father talking about the design of the retracting undercarriage:

Dad mentioned several times Blazdell's initial design of the retracting under-carriage that cleaned up the aerodynamics so much. It was a simple twist and lock design, the first step toward the vast and intricate undercarriages of all the current aircraft. The air speed record had been taken by Supermarine's floatplane, but the drag of the floats was a barrier to really fast flight. There must have been a very high priority on a retracting design.

Working in the Drawing Office

When Faggetter joined in 1931, the design team consisted of about fifty draughtsman and ten technicians. He found that the old drawing office at Woolston was a happy, friendly place with quite a lot of good humour, although the general manager, Trevor Westbrook, did not appear very popular with everyone. Faggetter soon discovered that the office was on a mezzanine floor in the works and received the full effect of percussion riveting used in the assembly of flying boat hulls, thus providing a noise level which was not helpful to the draughtsmen trying to work out problems on a drawing board.

Another newcomer to the drawing office in 1932 was Charles Labette. He had attended Pear Tree Green Church School, Woolston, which was just 300 yards from the Supermarine works, and as he lived fairly close to the Supermarine Woolston works he would pass the old hangar doors of the dope shop several times a week. He remembers as a boy frequently pressing his face against the crack in the doors of the dope shop to see the girls doping the wings of the early Southamptons. At that time Supermarine aircraft were a part of life itself, and in those hard days provided an income for the family. Labette's father had worked for Supermarine since 1919, with Wilf Elliot as his boss, and at the time when Scott-Paine was the managing director. It was Labette's father who had taught Mitchell to drive a motor car. However, Charles Labette was destined to become a future member of Mitchell's design team:

> Joe Smith interviewed me in the office under the old Day and Night fighter mock up, by the side of the old Machine Shop. I started working in the old drawing office above the Machine Shop. However, the Machine Shop drive shafts were fastened to the floor beneath my bench, where the vibration and noise were often off-putting. On the stairs was the drawing office store with Mr Kerr in charge, and at the top of the stairs the technical office was on one side, and the tracer's office the other.

When Labette started at the drawing office he found the help and support he received working with others in the design team outstanding. He began work on the designs for the Seagull Mk V, Scapa and Stranraer where he was working for Reg Caunter, Bill Munro and Bill Case, and later with George Kettlewell on Walrus wings: 'I worked three benches from the front on the left-hand side facing Joe's office.'

The Joe Smith 1932 Sweepstake

Little has been written so far about Joe Smith, and it is interesting to hear some anecdotes from various staff who worked at Supermarine. Labette also remembers Smith's energy and the frequent times he was seen in the drawing office:

> In those days Joe was a pusher and would charge up and down the long aisle between the drawing benches once or twice every hour of the work day to ensure that everybody's head was down! If not, and one was away from one's desk talking to another drawing office staff member, Joe would come up quite often to enquire what was going on.

Smith was a an energetic person and this habit of his, passing up and down the office, was to a certain extent made necessary by the location of his office being at the opposite end of the main drawing office to the second drawing office and print room.

Christmas Eve 1932 was a short morning with everyone in a somewhat relaxed mood anticipating a snappy getaway at 12 noon to go shopping or catch trains:

> To provide some interest there was a bright suggestion for a sweepstake on the number of times Joe went up and down the office during the morning. It only counted if he passed the stairs half way along the office leading to the Stress office. All went well, with the score being chalked up on the wall just past the stairs for all to see, until Freddie Spur the R.T.O. came to see Joe and they settled in for a long end-of-the-year session. This caused terrible frustration especially among those who had backed higher numbers 25/30 and more. Then came a bright idea and a volunteer went to Freddie Spur's office and explained the problem to his secretary and she entering into the spirit of the day, rang Joe asking him to tell Freddie that he was wanted urgently on the phone, and it worked. However, any chance of high scores had gone and the final number was below 20 – but all good fun.

New Ventures in Australia

Faggetter did some work on the design of the Type 224 before leaving Supermarine in 1933 to work for a number of other aircraft firms. He went to Australia in 1938 to join the Commonwealth Aircraft Corporation as project manager, designing aircraft for the RAAF. He was later appointed to set up the

Australian Dunlop aviation industry manufacturing aircraft for the RAAF until he finally retired in 1971.

After his retirement, Faggetter heard that the RAAF were rebuilding a Seagull Mk V at Port Cook near Melbourne. On a subsequent visit with the Royal Aero Society he was able to see drawings that he had done for the original Seagull Mk V at Supermarine:

> I was amazed to see the parts of the Control Column laid out on a bench, and the Restorer was equally impressed when I told him I had drawn the parts more than 60 years before, as proved by the drawings.

Supermarine Flying Boats from 1932

The Supermarine Scapa of 1932 was also a development of the Supermarine Southampton and was powered by two Rolls-Royce Kestrel engines. It was of all-metal construction, and the open cockpits were replaced by an enclosed one, allowing the pilots to sit side by side. After service in the Mediterranean and British coastal waters it was retired in 1939. The production of the Scapa was then changed to the larger Stranraer, which was to be the last of the large biplanes.

The Scapa all-metal prototype S1648 was designed as a general reconnaissance flying boat and was test-flown by 'Mutt' Summers on 8 July 1932 before joining 202 Squadron in Malta. *Solent Sky*

Both the Stranraer (1932) and the Walrus (1933) were followed by a later version of the Supermarine Southampton as a military aircraft which saw action in the Second World War. The Stranraer had its first flight on 24 July 1934, entering service with the RAF in 1937, and at the start of the war was tasked with anti-submarine and convoy escort duties until being withdrawn from operational duties in 1941 to become a training aircraft until 1942. The Walrus was a development of the Seagull V, built for Australia, and was designed in 1933 as a catapult-launched amphibious biplane flying boat with a metal fuselage, an enclosed cockpit and a single-engine powering a pusher propeller. It was used by the RAF as a reconnaissance aircraft, and later in a SAR (Search and Rescue) role.

The Air Ministry issued specification 2/35 for a naval catapult-launched observation/spotting flying boat to be launched from cruisers. The name was then changed from Seagull to Walrus, with the first production Walrus having serial number K5772. A number of Walruses were used by the RNZAF and the RAAF. The Walrus was particularly successful during the war for reconnaissance, and attacking and destroying submarines.

The Stranraer prototype K3973. Air Ministry specification R.24/31 for a coastal reconnaissance flying boat was turned down, but Supermarine went ahead as a PV (private venture). It was test flown by 'Mutt' Summers. *Solent Sky*

The prototype Seagull V N2 became K4797 and was the prototype for the Walrus. *John Thomson*

The Walrus K8552 was a metal-hulled, single-engine amphibious biplane built in 1936 for reconnaissance and with a fully retractable undercarriage. It served with 715 (Catapult) Squadron on HMS *Suffolk* in 1937/38. *Solent Sky*

The Sheldrake N180 was intended as a development of the Seagull, but only one was built.
Solent Sky

Judy Monger talks about her father, Ernie Mansbridge, and his involvement in the flying boat test programme:

My father kept the records of the flying boat test flights that include the Scarab, Sheldrake, Scylla, Swan, Solent, Southampton, Scapa, Stranraer and the Seagull V. He was also involved in the Walrus, a World War Two air-sea rescue amphibian. I have some of them, and the names of all the people that joined the flying boat for the test flights. It is interesting to note how all the 'big chiefs' went for test flights in the aeroplanes, including Joe Smith, Trevor Westbrook, Alan Clifton, Shirvall, Black, Shenstone, Summers, Dixon and RJM himself on the Stranraer in 1934. The pilots were Summers and Pickering. Dad was on most of the test flights and was often joined by RJM.

Murry White Becomes a Design Apprentice

It was at the time that the first Spitfire designs were being produced in response to the F.7/30 specification that Murry White joined Supermarine as a design apprentice. Murry was born in November 1916 on the Isle of Wight in a small workman's cottage house on Maresfield Road, East Cowes. When they built the Princess flying boats the road was closed and the house pulled down, so Murry was actually born in the middle of Saunders-Roe's big hangar!

His father was a shipyard manager at J. Samuel White & Co. and when the family moved to Southampton in 1928 he attended Taunton's School. It was in September 1933, when he was in the lower sixth, that the headmaster asked if anybody would like to apply for an apprenticeship at Supermarine. Murry applied and was interviewed by Alan Clifton in the old hangar at Supermarine:

> I liked him very much right from the word go. He was a charming man and very kind and thoughtful. He made me feel very comfortable and I went back to my father and told him that I would really like to get that job. He told me to write Mr Clifton a letter expressing my wish to become a design apprentice in the technical office. I was accepted and joined the technical office with Alan Clifton and eighteen others, but was really the office boy for the first year. However, I hoped to go to Southampton University to get my National and Higher National Certificate.

A Brief Moment with R.J.

Mitchell was regularly in the drawing office, discussing matters about the draughtsmen's drawings on their drawing boards but had little contact with the young apprentices. However, when Murry joined Supermarine on 16 October 1933 as a design office apprentice in the technical office, his first year was as office boy and he had to run errands for Mitchell, one of which he remembers very clearly. The technical office at that time was a boarded-in section of a hangar roof, very primitive and very hot in summer and freezing in winter. The lunch hour was from noon to 1 p.m., but R.J. was in the habit of arriving at the technical office at about 11.30 a.m. where he would join Arthur Shirvall, the project engineer, and Clifton (Cliffy). However, when the noon bell rang they would continue their deliberations while those not involved went for lunch, but Murry would sit in the far corner of the office and eat his sandwiches:

> After a few moments Alan came over to me with a piece of tracing paper on which were some freehand lines of R.J.'s and asked me to obtain a copy of it from the print room. In my desire to be efficient and eager, I ran down a flight of stairs along another boarded-in section of the hangar forming the drawing office to the print room run by a really cantankerous old man by the name of Mr Bowdler who was also eating his lunch.

Mr Bowdler said that he was not going to interrupt his lunch for anybody, including R.J., but at the same time started the print machine. Murry soon had his print and ran all the way back to Shirvall's desk:

In my haste to spread the print out before R.J., I ripped it almost in half. I was awestruck and said I would get another, to which R.J. replied, 'No, White. Go and get the sticky tape and together we will join it up.' Now in those days the sticky tape was the type one had to lick. So I licked the tape while R.J., with a slight smile, held the two halves together. I went back to my corner expecting to be fired that afternoon. However, Alan Clifton, who some years later became a great friend, on receiving my lamentations, assured me that all was well!

Although Murry had other errands to run for R.J., that experience was perhaps his most memorable:

He was a kind and considerate man, even though he was very sick, and in fact, dying at that time. For all the errands I did for him he never failed to thank me. When R.J. died on 11 June 1937, I asked Alan for the afternoon off to attend the funeral. I had an old 250cc New Imperial motorcycle and on starting it the drive chain came off its sprocket. By the time I had taken the necessary bit apart to retrieve it, the funeral was over. I went home feeling very dejected.

My parents lived in the next street to R.J. in Highfield. Although they did not know R.J. they had a mutual friend who upon learning of my disaster offered to take me in her chauffeur-driven car to the cemetery to see the tributes to R.J. So I was able after all to say my final farewell to the man who had been my inspiration to join the aviation world and for which I am and always will be most grateful.

It is sad that Murry White was unable to make Mitchell's funeral at Highfield church, but Barrie Bryant did:

I was totally ignorant of RJM's fame. The verger was expecting a large attendance, but short of ushers on a weekday afternoon, asked me to help.

Help Given by Senior Members of the Design Team

As the design and technical team developed, it became almost like a family. Help, support and advice were never far away for the apprentices when they needed them. Murry remembers and appreciates the help he received from Harry Griffiths who was also an apprentice, but was three years into his apprenticeship and had been involved in the Schneider Trophy races, working on the Supermarine S.6 racer programme:

He was working for Arthur Black who was the chemist. 'Griff' took me under his wing and when lunch came along he would invite me to bring my sandwiches up to his laboratory. He became a lifelong friend and was about three years older than me, but has since died. Arthur Black had also been a great help to me. All these chaps were tremendous mentors in their particular field and Arthur Black was a good writer, amongst other things, and he helped me to compose reports on a pro forma for me, and how I should put reports together. That was a huge help to me.

Meeting Joe Smith for the First Time

Murry White remembers well the first meeting he had with Joe Smith. This was in his early apprenticeship where one of the jobs he had to do was make folders out of strawboard and file the *Flight* magazines by the month. To do this he had to go down to Mr Bowdler's room to cut the strawboard on the big guillotine:

> Mr Bowdler was always argumentative and he would talk to me. I was talking to him and suddenly I saw this chap coming into the office who said, 'Who are you?' I told him who I was and he asked what I was doing there. I told him I was cutting the strawboard and he said, 'No you're not, you are wasting my chap's time! Go on get out of here!' He chucked me out. I told Alan Clifton what had happened, and he laughed and said I could go back another day to finish the job. That was my first experience with old Joe, and he became more like a father to me and I became very attached to him.

Making Progress

The first year went well in the technical office; Murry was gaining more and more experience, making good progress and really enjoying his work. He worked with George Nicholas who taught him how to do weights estimation and C.G. (centre of gravity) on an aircraft, which he did for several years. In the early days of Murry's apprenticeship, Supermarine were building the twin-engine Scapa flying boat, the Seagull V (forerunner of the Walrus) and the prototype Stranraer, and it was on these aircraft that he gained his experience in the weights and balance department.

During his apprenticeship, Murry was keen to see the work of all the engineering departments and asked if he could visit the different shops. It was through his continual 'pestering' that they eventually agreed that he could go in the shops for a few months, although this lasted a whole year. He was able to work in the detail fitting shop, erecting shop and wing shop, and finished up in the tool room which he really enjoyed because of the precise engineering. His apprenticeship had involved all the various departments, including weights and balance, stressing, mechanical testing, the project office on new designs and finishing up in the Aerodynamics Department, which he thoroughly enjoyed.

6

DESIGN AND DEVELOPMENT OF THE SPITFIRE

The British Government became concerned in the early 1930s about the build-up of the German armed forces, especially the Luftwaffe. In response to this threat, the Air Ministry started to look for a new monoplane fighter to replace the Bristol Bulldog biplane that at the time was the main British fighter aircraft. The Bristol Bulldog had been designed by Frank Barnwell, chief designer of the Bristol Aeroplane Co., as a private venture to meet Air Ministry specification F.9/26 and first flew in May 1927. The Air Ministry had tested and evaluated both the Hawker Hawfinch and the Bristol Bulldog, culminating in the Bulldog being selected in 1928, after further modifications by its manufacturers.

Britain was aware of the threat from Germany and the design of the fighter aircraft it was developing, and it became essential that the RAF should have a fighter that could at least match the Luftwaffe aircraft. This resulted in the Air Ministry issuing specification F.7/30 that required a design for an aircraft armed with four machine guns and capable of functioning as a day or night fighter at a speed of 250mph (402.33km/h). Supermarine, already noted for their design and production of racing monoplanes for the Schneider Trophy competitions, were invited along with other aircraft manufacturers to submit designs.

The German aircraft already in production at the time included the Messerschmitt Bf 109 and Junkers Ju 87 Stuka dive bomber, which were used later in combat as part of the German Condor Legion during the Spanish Civil War of 1936–1939. It was in this war that the German pilots gained valuable combat experience while flying these aircraft and were to be well placed to use these skills to their advantage at the start of the Second World War.

The Supermarine 224

Supermarine designed the Type 224 K2890 prototype to meet specification F.7/30. It was an open-cockpit monoplane with inverted gull wings, also known as a cranked wing, with a fixed, spatted undercarriage. The armament consisted of four .303 machine guns; two were situated in the wheel spats and two in the cowling. The aircraft was powered by the 600hp evaporative-cooled Rolls-Royce Goshawk engine. Type 224 was first flown on 19 February 1934 by 'Mutt' Summers, but the Goshawk engine was not powerful enough and the aircraft could only reach a maximum speed of 228mph (366.93km/h) against the prototype Gloster Gladiator open-cockpit biplane, designed by H.P. Folland, chief designer of the Gloster Aircraft Co., which reached a speed of 242mph (389.46km/h). With a change to a more powerful engine and a fully enclosed cockpit, the Gloster SS.37 Gladiator then achieved 254mph (408.77km/h), 4mph (6.43km/h) above the F.7/30 specifications, and subsequently the Gloster Aircraft Co. was awarded the Air Ministry contract. The Gloster Gladiator was the first fully enclosed cockpit and last biplane introduced into RAF service.

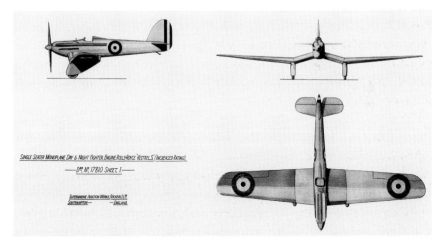

Supermarine tender drawing for the F.7/30 single-seat monoplane day and night fighter, powered by a Rolls-Royce Kestrel engine. *Solent Sky*

Type 224 K2890 was an inverted gull-wing monoplane fighter aircraft powered by the Rolls-Royce Goshawk engine. Type 224 first flew on 20 February 1934, piloted by 'Mutt' Summers. *Solent Sky*

The Gull Wing Design

The gull wing design was initially introduced by the Polish inventor Zygmunt Pulawski in 1928. The wing from the centre-section makes a sharp dihedral (upward) angle from the fuselage and the rest of the wing is flat. However, the inverted gull or cranked wing is where the centre-section makes an anhedral (downward) angle with the fuselage and the wing then rises at a dihedral angle to the tips of the wing.

The Heinkel He 70 was designed by Ernst Heinkel in the early 1930s with an inverted gull-wing shape, but also with retractable landing gear built into the lowest part of the wing. It first flew on 1 December 1932, and interestingly it was designed with a streamlined fuselage and elliptical wings. Another German aircraft with this design was the Junkers Ju 87 Stuka dive bomber, designed by Hermann Pohlmann, which first flew in September 1935. It had inverted gull wings and a fixed, spatted undercarriage, similar in wing design to the Supermarine Type 224. When the Ju 87 dived, it had a wailing siren that put fear into many who were witness to its attacks.

The 'Three Fs'

Alf Faddy had worked on the designs for the Ministry specification F.7/30 which eventually became the Type 224. Much of the detailed design work

Type 224 K2890 had one pair of guns either side of the cockpit and another pair in the 'trouser' fairings of the undercarriage. *Solent Sky*

appears to have been done by the 'three Fs' (Alf Faddy, Bill Fear and R.J. Fenner). Fenner had worked in the Supermarine Control Section, alongside Charles Blazdell on various contracts, but in the book *Spitfire: The History* by Morgan and Shacklady, he is quoted as saying:

> When Alf Faddy joined the design team in 1933 (I think) we formed the 'three Fs' with Bill Fear and did most of the work on the original Spitfire with the Goshawk steam cooled engine and the 'W' wing. This aircraft was built to the Ministry specification F.7/30 and it had gull wings with straight taper leading and trailing edges, the former helping the steam cooling.

(Alf Faddy did in fact join Supermarine in 1930, not 1933 as quoted by Fenner.)

Mitchell and his team were not satisfied with the design of the Type 224 and the flying capabilities of the aircraft during flight tests. Ernie Mansbridge observed at the time, 'We were too cautious. Choosing the thick section wing was a mistake when we could have used a modified thinner section as used on the S.5 floatplane.' Mitchell was thinking in a similar way and went on to use all the experience gained in the Schneider Trophy racing aircraft to redesign a new model. The prototype was to be equipped with the newly developed Rolls-Royce PV-12 engine and also included new construction techniques for the airframe.

Beverley Shenstone Joins Supermarine

Beverley Shenstone studied at the University of Toronto where he was awarded a Master's degree in aeronautical engineering in 1929. After leaving university he found that the opportunities for working in the field of aviation design and production were not as developed in Canada as in other countries, especially Germany. To gain experience in aircraft design and production he decided to go abroad and got a job working in the Junkers works in Dessau. It was there that he was able to work in the various shops and see the development of Junkers aircraft production, particularly the Ju W 33, a single-engine, all-metal transport aircraft. Shenstone also had an opportunity to meet Alexander Lippisch at the Wasserkuppe Gliding Centre in 1930, where he successfully gained his Glider Certificate. They became good friends, both having a deep interest in wing structure that led to Shenstone writing some papers on wing design.

Owing to a ban on powered flight brought about by the Treaty of Versailles, many Germans interested in aircraft design and flying were forced to turn to gliders. Gliding became a sport, and competitions were held from 1920 at Wasserkuppe. In 1925, Lippisch was appointed head of the technical branch of the RRG (German Gliding Organisation) and was later responsible for the delta wing design.

In 1931, Shenstone travelled to England with the aim of getting a job in a British aviation company, but was not very successful with most of the firms he visited. However, when he went to Supermarine Aviation Works (Vickers) Ltd he met Mitchell who was interested in his previous experience in wing design. It was at the time when Supermarine were engaged in designing the Type 179 Giant, a six-engine monoplane registered as G-ABLE. After showing him a drawing of the wing, Mitchell asked Shenstone's opinion of the design. His response to the question rather surprised Mitchell, and he asked Shenstone to leave an address in case he should need to contact him in the future. It was not long after that Shenstone received a letter from Mitchell, offering him a job as an aerodynamicist with Supermarine, which he accepted. He was involved for a short time on the Type 224, but mainly on the Type 300 prototype Spitfire, and in the introduction of the elliptical wing.

The Elliptical Wing Design

In *Spitfire: The History*, R.J. Fenner refers further to the F.7/30 development aircraft:

In conjunction with H. Holmes, Ernie Mansbridge, Alan Clifton and the 'three Fs' a number of different designs were produced – all as F.7/30 development aircraft. Drawing 30000, Sheet 11 was actually drawn by Alf Faddy who with me [R.J. Fenner] and Bill Fear [all three sitting in a row] did all the general arrangement drawings while the other two supplied the various schemes for the different parts of the aircraft, under direct supervision from R.J.M. of course, with various members of the Stress Office. We also had considerable advice from Beverley Shenstone on his return from the USA.

Shenstone, the chief aerodynamicist, and Trevor Westbrook, general manager, had visited the USA in 1935 as part of a fact-finding mission.

In 1935, Mitchell and his team concentrated on the Type 300 fighter built to the Air Ministry specification F.10/35. In discussion with his team, including Shenstone, Mitchell referred to the elliptical wing being used in the design for the Spitfire. Shenstone thought the elliptical wing was the best aerodynamically for the design because the induced drag caused in producing lift was less when a wing of this shape was used. The elliptical wing was thin at the tip but thicker at the root for the retractable undercarriage and to house eight machine guns, four on either wing. David Faddy refers to the credit given by Fenner to Alf Faddy, who was his section leader, for persuading Mitchell to adopt the elliptical wing proposed by Shenstone because it gave greater depth for the retracted landing gear and the outer ammunition boxes, all without the loss in performance.

The first design drawn by Faddy of the elliptical wing, Drawing 30000, Sheet 11, was not the final shape of the wing, but from it came the more recognisable elliptical wing of the final design. Within the 'three Fs' it was not the first time Faddy and Fear had worked together. Faddy had known Fear when they both worked at Parnall's in Bristol, Fear later joining him at Supermarine, and so the Mitchell design team developed.

As far as Mitchell was concerned, being a very practical man, the shape of the wing was unimportant. When the elliptical wing was suggested, he remarked to Shenstone, 'I don't give a damn whether it's elliptical or not, so long as it covers the guns!' Shenstone credits Joe Smith, who was in charge of structural design, for his work in overcoming problems in the development of the elliptical wing and also for his contribution to the success of the Spitfire.

After the design work was completed on the new Spitfire fighter, the team then worked on the B.12/36 specification four-engine bomber, and in 1938, Shenstone left Supermarine to work at the Air Ministry. Sammy Hughes, who had worked alongside Shenstone, assumed the role after he left the company.

The Heinkel He 70G

The elliptical wing had been used on other aircraft before the decision to use the same wing for the new Spitfire fighter, there being a suggestion that Supermarine had copied it from the German Heinkel He 70G transport aircraft. In fact, the Heinkel He 70G transport did have some influence on the Spitfire design.

Shenstone had seen the He 70 at the Paris Air Show and had observed the elliptical wing, but it was the smoothness of the skin that impressed him, so much so that he was not sure whether it was made of metal or wood. After contacting Ernst Heinkel, he found that it was a metal wing, but all the rivets were countersunk and filled before the final paint finish. This aerodynamic smoothness of the skin did have some influence of the design of the Spitfire. Mitchell and his design team also had the opportunity to see the He 70 when Rolls-Royce traded four Kestrel V engines with the German Ministry of Aviation *Reichsluftfahrtministerium* (RLM) for a Heinkel He 70G to test their own powerplants.

Detailed Design Work

Reference to the importance of detailed design work was highlighted in the 30th Mitchell Memorial Lecture to the Southampton branch of the Royal Aeronautical Society on 4 March 1986 by E.J. (Jack) Davis, who stated that:

> No detail design skill can rectify a poor basic layout, but a good project loses its edge if succeeding detail work is not of the highest standard. This stage was led by Alfred Faddy, who joined the firm circa 1930. He was a little older than the others and had played his part in the design of the six-engine flying boat. He was meticulous to the extreme and was not satisfied with anything less than the best. He used to say, 'draw with the pencil but design with the rubber'. Schemes prepared with his guidance were always revised once but usually more often. Thus the care and attention given to the basic design was matched by the effort in the drawing office. Other disciplines played their part. For example, Joe Smith, the Chief Draughtsman was always pressing for drawings to be issued to the works. Thus between the desire for perfection and the need to build the machine a fair compromise resulted.

David Faddy remembers that his father always carried very soft 4B or 6B pencils, and that he told him once that he did so because if there was an argument over a design drawing, the man with the softest pencil would usually win. Before he died in December 2006, Harry Griffiths told David that this was a habit of Mitchell's and David concludes that his father must have acquired the habit from Mitchell. This was also referred to by Joe Smith when he gave the first Mitchell Memorial lecture on 21 January 1954. When referring to R.J., he said:

> He was an inveterate 'drawer on drawings', particularly general arrangements. He would modify the lines of an aircraft with the softest pencil he could find, and then re-modify over the top with progressively thicker lines, until there was finally a new outline of lines about three-sixteenths of an inch thick. But the results were always worthwhile, and the centre of the line was usually accepted when things were re-drawn.

In the same lecture, Smith also comments on the amount of time Mitchell would spend in the drawing office:

> When in the throes of a new design, the arrangement of which had been decided, he would spend almost all his time in the drawing office on the various boards. Here he would argue out the details with the draughtsmen concerned, showing a complete grasp of the whole aircraft.

Making Landing Gear More Aerodynamic

From the early days of flight the importance of reducing drag was not fully understood, and it was not until the 1920s that the full significance was recognised of the effect reducing drag in flight would have on improving speed and fuel efficiency. Some of the main effects of drag came from aircraft with exposed engines, fixed landing gear and wing bracing. It was discovered that fixed landing gear contributed up to 40 per cent of drag, and by the 1930s aircraft engineers and designers had started to investigate ways of making landing gear more aerodynamic. They came to two possible solutions for reducing drag: enclosing the wheels in wheel 'pants' or 'spats', often referred to as trousered fairings; and landing gear that retracted into the wings or fuselage. Although retractable landing gear had already been used on some aircraft in the 1920s, most aircraft had fixed landing gear due to it being strong, yet cheap regarding cost of materials, requiring less maintenance and being fairly lightweight, which did not affect the overall weight of the design, one of the important factors the designers had to consider.

In the early 1930s, the American aircraft designer Jack Northrop looked at ways of streamlining aircraft when he designed his Alpha, Beta and Gamma series of fixed landing gear aircraft. It was in these designs that he introduced streamlined coverings that extended down from the fuselage with the wheels protruding from the bottom, which became known as 'trouser' gear. The Northrop Gamma designs in 1932, the Gamma 2A and Gamma 2B, had an enclosed cockpit on top of the fuselage, set back from the wings. The Gamma series was developed to the Gamma 2C, an attack aircraft armed with four wing-mounted machine guns and one gun in the rear cockpit. The Gamma 2C retained the same wings and trousered undercarriage of the 2A and 2B but with a new fuselage with a two-seat cockpit which was moved further forward, with the pilot slightly behind the wing.

Other aircraft of the Gamma series followed. The 2D, 2G, 2H and 2L were built mainly for civil customers, such as TWA, for mail carrying. One of the Northrop Gamma 2Gs, NC-13761, was used by the American aviatrix Jacqueline Cochran for aircraft races. Cochran was also influential in recruiting women ferry pilots for the British ATA (Air Transport Auxiliary) in the Second World War.

The Gamma 2E was built as a light bomber for the Chinese Government, its armaments consisting of four forward firing machine guns and a machine gun for the bomb aimer/gunner sitting in the rear seat in the cockpit. A single version of the Gamma 2E, designed in 1934 as a light attack aircraft, was built for demonstration purposes and registered as X13760. This aircraft was later purchased by the British Air Ministry in the summer of 1935 as part of its

Northrop Gamma 2E X13760 was bought by the Air Ministry and given the serial number K5053. *Raymond Crupi and Ron Dupas*

policy of evaluating aircraft from other countries. It first went to the RAE at Farnborough and then for flight tests at the A&AEE at Martlesham Heath. It was given the serial number K5403.

Comparing the 165mph (265.54km/h) maximum speed of the Gamma 2E with a bomb load, and 226mph (363.71km/h) without a bomb load, it was still 2mph (3.21km/h) less than the maximum speed of the Type 224. It could not have met the F.7/30 specification of 250mph (402.33km/h), but one of its advantages was that it had an enclosed cockpit which the Type 224 did not have, although both aircraft had a trousered undercarriage. By this time, Mitchell and his design team were well into the development of the Type 300 K5404, whose serial number followed on from the Northrop Gamma 2E K5403. As well as the Air Ministry purchasing a Gamma 2E, the Bristol Aeroplane Co. imported a Gamma 2L in 1937 without an engine to use for testing their Hercules engines. It had the registration number G-AFBT, but was broken up at Filton, Bristol, during the Second World War.

The Design and Construction of the Supermarine Type 300

This time Mitchell's design of a new land plane fighter was to have some influence from the Schneider aircraft designs. The design was focusing on an aircraft with a retractable undercarriage and an enclosed cockpit but retaining the Goshawk engine.

Mitchell was highly thought of by the chairman of Vickers Aviation, Sir Robert McLean, who gave great support to his work, and this was evident when Vickers gave the go-ahead on 6 November 1934 for the construction of a private venture prototype which was to be the Supermarine Type 300. However, it was just a month later that the Air Ministry reviewed the Type 300 while still in its design stage. The Air Ministry was favourably impressed and issued a contract on 1 December 1934, allocating £10,000 to Supermarine to develop a prototype to the specification F.37/34 for an eight-gun fighter with a Rolls-Royce PV-12 engine capable of 350mph (563.27km/h). The requirement for an eight-gun version was solved by building an elliptical wing which not only made an improvement on the aerodynamic qualities of the aircraft but importantly was also able to take the eight guns required by the Air Ministry, with four guns in each wing.

It was fortunate that at the same time as the prototype was being designed, Rolls-Royce produced their PV-12 engine which was later to be known as the Merlin. At last, Mitchell could use his Schneider experience, the Rolls-Royce Merlin engine enabling the aircraft to fly faster and in addition to carry more

Type 300 Spitfire I prototype K5054 with an enclosed cockpit, standing on the Eastleigh grass airfield with the hangar on the right. *Solent Sky*

ammunition and eight machine guns, double the original specifications. The two-bladed propellers were provided by de Havilland. The assembly of the hand-built prototype of the Supermarine Type 300 would take place at Eastleigh.

Eastleigh aerodrome had been a military aerodrome, used as a USNAF base in the First World War, and had two large wartime hangars. Between the wars the site was used mainly by the Cunard White Star Line as temporary accommodation for emigrants awaiting voyages overseas. The Southern Railway built a simple 'halt' for these travellers, but ordinary services did not stop there. In 1932, the aerodrome was purchased by Southampton County Borough and was renamed as Southampton Municipal Airport but was still referred to locally as Eastleigh aerodrome. Three years later, the Air Ministry, concerned with a possible war with Germany, gained permission from Southampton Corporation to have part of the site used by the RAF, and it was known briefly as RAF Eastleigh until 1936, when it became RAF Southampton. It was in 1936 that Supermarine started to use the site for testing the Type 300, but occupancy of the wartime hangars for final assembly of the fighters would not have been required before 1938 since the flight shed had space for only K5054 and two Walrus aircraft.

Mitchell met Faddy at his home in Southampton on a number of occasions to discuss early possible layouts for the Spitfire, drawing alternatives on the dining room wallpaper – much to the disgust of Faddy's wife! In April 1935, the wooden mock-up of the prototype was being prepared, but despite hopes that the Type

300 would fly by October of that year, it was the prototype Hurricane that flew first, on 6 November 1935. The Hurricane was also powered by a Rolls-Royce Merlin engine. Sydney Camm was the chief designer for Hawker Aircraft Ltd, and by 3 June 1936 the Air Ministry was suitably impressed and ordered 600 Hurricane fighter aircraft. In the event, the unpainted Supermarine Type 300 built to specification F.37/34 did not fly until 5 March 1936, having been built at Woolston and then taken to Eastleigh for assembly.

In the early days of Supermarine, the most well-known test pilot was Henri Biard, but Murry White remembers that in the early flying boat days there was a pilot who was quite famous in his day. His name was H.J. Payn, known generally as 'Agony' Payn, but he had never worked with him:

> In my time we were joined by George Pickering with whom I worked closely. He was a great personality and much later became a good friend of mine. He, incidentally, flew K5054 before Jeffrey Quill joined us from Weybridge.

Jeffrey Quill

Jeffrey Kindersley Quill OBE, AFC, FRAeS was born on 1 February 1913. His interest in aircraft and flying began during the First World War when at the age of 5 he saw an aeroplane land on the common near his house in Littlehampton, which he describes in his book *Spitfire: A Test Pilot's Story*. He had a ringside seat from his balcony for the take-off. Another incident occurred when he went with his elder brothers to see a plane that had crashed in a field at Rustington, and these two events were the start of his desire to be a pilot.

Quill was educated at Lancing College. On leaving school in 1931, he took a short service commission in the RAF as a pilot officer and trained at No 3 Flying School at Grantham, Lincolnshire, going solo in an Avro Tutor after only five hours of dual instruction. In the service flight of the school he flew Siddeley Siskins and passed out in August 1932 with an 'exceptional' rating. He was then posted to No 17 (Fighter) Squadron at Upavon where he was to fly Bristol Bulldogs, which had entered RAF service in 1929 and were the main RAF fighters in the early 1930s. (The Bristol Bulldog was the aircraft that Douglas Bader was flying when he crashed after performing an unauthorised aerobatic display that resulted in losing both his legs.)

In 1934, Quill was posted to the RAF Meteorological Flight at Duxford, which made two flights each day, climbing to between 18,000ft and 25,000ft to report, at 1000ft intervals, on the temperature, humidity and cloud formation. On landing, the results were signalled or telephoned to the Met Office in London. The pilots were flying obsolescent Armstrong Whitworth Siskin IIIA, formerly RAF front-line fighters, which had been replaced by the British Bulldog. The Siskin was an open-cockpit aircraft with rudimentary blind-flying instruments, and pilots had to wear electrically heated suits. This brought Quill invaluable all-weather experience, as well as many hazardous moments and forced landings in conditions that were sometimes considered 'unflyable'. For his achievement in this role he was awarded the Air Force Cross in 1936.

Late in 1935, Quill heard that 'Mutt' Summers, chief test pilot at Vickers, was looking for an assistant, and he flew to Brooklands where he was interviewed by Summers and Sir Robert McLean. He was offered the job and, relinquishing with some regret the opportunity of a permanent commission in the RAF, was released on 1 January 1936 to begin testing aircraft at Vickers, including the Vildebeest torpedo bomber, Valentia transport, and the prototype Venom fighter. The Venom was preferred to the Spitfire by Vickers senior management, but eventually it was proven that the Spitfire performed better and it was the aircraft that was eventually to go into production.

The dangers of test flying were experienced by Quill while testing a Wellesley bomber which went into a spin at 12,000ft (3,657.6m). Unable to regain control, he had to bail out at 3,000ft (914.4m). The following year a pilot was killed when the Wellesley was undergoing further tests at the RAE, spinning out of control during stalling tests. By this time Quill, who had 'an inner certainty that my destiny lay with the Spitfire', was about to move from Vickers at Brooklands to Supermarine in Southampton to concentrate on testing the Spitfire.

The First Flight of K5054

The prototype Spitfire K5054 was first flown in 1936 by Joseph 'Mutt' Summers, Quill flying him down to Eastleigh on 5 March in the firm's Miles Falcon Six for the first test flight. When Summers piloted the first flight of K5054 the undercarriage was not retracted, but after a number of initial checks during the 8-minute flight, Summers landed K5045 and said, 'I don't want anything touched.' As Quill points out in *Spitfire: A Test Pilot's Story*, this remark was destined to become widely misinterpreted:

> What [Summers] meant was that there were no snags which required correction or adjustment before he flew the aircraft again. Mutt's comment has crept into folklore as implying that the aeroplane was perfect in every respect from the moment of its first flight – an obviously absurd and impracticable notion.

For the initial flights of K5054 the aircraft was not painted, and the different shades of fuselage show that parts taken from other aircraft were used for the prototype. *Solent Sky*

A team from Rolls-Royce Motors painted K5054 in a pale blue gloss just in time for a visit by HM King George VI who is seen looking in the cockpit. *Solent Sky*

Quill says that Summers left the undercarriage down deliberately for the first flight, and recalls in his book:

> There was a light wind blowing across the aerodrome which meant that Mutt had to take the short run, and he taxied towards one of the large Chance lights (which in those days were situated round the perimeter), turned into the wind and opened up the throttle. The aeroplane was airborne after a very short ground roll and climbed away comfortably. Mutt did not retract the undercarriage on that first flight – deliberately, of course – but cruised around for some minutes, checked the lowering of the flaps and the slow flying and stalling characteristics, and then brought K5054 into land.

(Chance lights, similar to searchlights, were floodlights positioned on towers around the aerodrome and focused on the landing area.)

Quill made his first flight in the prototype K5054 on 26 March 1936, and thereafter cleared the aircraft, and all subsequent marks of Spitfires, for RAF service.

Test Flight Instructions

In the test flight instructions issued to Summers on 3 March 1936 for No 300/1 Fighter F.37/34 – Aircraft K5054 it stated that for the first flight certain conditions were to be noted, going on to list the instructions for the ailerons, rudder, elevator, chassis, exhaust system, airscrew and loading. In the chassis instructions it was clearly noted:

> The chassis is not to be operated during the first flight as it is considered necessary to check the chassis operation after taxying and landings have been carried out. All warning devices are to be completed and operating satisfactorily before the chassis is operated in the air.
>
> Pilots are to be given facilities for operating the chassis and familiarising themselves with the mechanism and its 'feel' on the ground before using it in flight.

Quite a few of the important people from the Supermarine design and technical team were present at Eastleigh aerodrome on the day, including Mitchell, Smith, Clifton (Cliffy), Shenstone, Faddy, Mansbridge, Davis and Payn together with Stewart Scott-Hall, the Air Ministry's resident technical officer. Also present were Supermarine test pilots Quill and Pickering, who would be flying the follow-up tests of the prototype. Ken Scales, the foreman in charge of the construction of the aircraft at Eastleigh, and other family members were also there on this historic occasion.

Judy Monger clearly remembers the first flight of K5054 and how lucky she was that she got to see it. The children were playing in their garden when their father, Ernie Mansbridge, came home at about 10.30 a.m. Judy can clearly remember hearing him saying to her mother, 'Would you like to see the first flight of a new aeroplane?' Her mother asked what she was going to do with the three children and because the neighbours were unable to look after them, her father decided to take them as well:

We all piled in the car and went off to Eastleigh. When we got to Eastleigh aerodrome we got down behind the seat so that the guard at the gate couldn't see us, and then my father drove over to park with the other cars.

It was a bit grey and I remember the aeroplane going up into the cloud, but not a wildly cloudy day as there was some sunshine, not a lot though. We got quite excited when the engine started up, and the sound of that engine still excites me. You hear it going over and you rush out to have a look. It wasn't the same engine because they had changed it. However, I preferred the sound of the Merlin engine to the Griffon. The Merlin was a very distinctive sound and you could pick it out from all the Junkers and the Heinkels coming over. You knew when it was a Spitfire.

Eventually we all wanted to go to the toilet and so we were taken into the hangar, under guard to go to the toilet.

Of course it takes time for the pilot to come and get in the aeroplane, but we stayed in the car. My youngest brother was in the front with mother because he was only aged one. Time passed and then this wonderful aeroplane started up and then it went off. It seemed to have been gone for quite a time, or so it seemed to us, but in that time R.J. Mitchell came and stuck his head through the front window, said hello to mother and asked how she was, and said hello to us in the back. The others in the group all stood around watching. There was Eric Cooper, Alf Faddy, Joe Smith, 'Agony' Payn, my father and Jeffrey Quill. Then the aeroplane came back again and the pilot in a white suit got out and we went: 'Gosh wasn't that wonderful!' At that moment I decided I wanted to learn to fly.

As well as the first 8-minute test flight of K5054 at 16.35 hours on 5 March 1936, Summers also did test flights on 6 March at 15.23 hours for 23 minutes, 10 March at 17.00 hours for 31 minutes, 14 March at 13.00 hours for 50 minutes and the fifth test flight on 24 March at 11.45 hours for 43 minutes.

The previously unpainted K5054 was then returned to the workshops to be painted in a high-gloss blue/grey and the aircraft was then handed over to Pickering and Quill for performance trials. Pickering flew K5054 for the first time on flight No 6 at 16.50 hours on 25 March and was in the air for 33 minutes. Quill then flew the next three test flights, Nos 7, 8 and 9, on 26 and 27 March.

Mitchell, Mansbridge and Faddy were all at Eastleigh that day to witness Quill's first flight. He describes how Ken Scales helped him with his parachute and the Sutton harness before he took off on his first flight at 17.45 hours, and was in the air for 18 minutes. Quill comments that the fixed-pitch propeller could only provide low revs during the take-off, the acceleration was sluggish and he had to use full right rudder to keep K5054 flying straight, but he was impressed with the rest of the test flight and thought, 'Here is a real lady.'

Mansbridge had a very busy schedule. Judy Monger remembers that her father was always there when the planes flew because he was in charge of the flight-testing. Quill would then have lunch with them as it was on his way home. After lunch, Mansbridge would take Quill back to his home at the River Barn in Old Bursledon.

Murry White Becomes Assistant to Ernie Mansbridge

Following the completion of his apprenticeship, Murry White had achieved his Higher National Certificate with distinction and Alan Clifton had asked him what job he would like to do next. Murry said that he would like to work with Mansbridge, and Clifton was happy for Murry to become a member of the Supermarine design team as an aerodynamicist and performance reduction engineer and assistant to Mansbridge.

At that time, they did very little flying but eventually, when getting near to the production stage, Mansbridge and Murry were undertaking a lot of full-time work on performance reduction, Mansbridge managing all the test flight work and loading work and teaching Murry how to do performance reduction. This involved calculating a conversion of the pilot's test flight figures into standard atmospheric conditions to give the true air speed. This figure is very different to the pilot's observed figures on his instruments. Murry remembers Quill's two flights on 27 March 1936, particularly the second test flight when Mansbridge gave him the task of working out the reduction figures.

On 27 March 1936, Quill went up again for two test flights and describes the outcome more fully in his book *Birth of a Legend: The Spitfire*. The first was at 15.25 hours, with a flight time of 35 minutes:

From the outset K5054 was a pleasure to fly and at first sight the performance seemed exciting. Nevertheless the first set of performance trials, which I carried out on 27 March, were disappointing, yielding a maximum true speed of little more than 335mph [539.13km/h] at less than 17,000ft [5,181m].

This proved disappointing compared to Mitchell's estimated speed of 350mph (563.27km/h). The problem was solved by replacing the fixed-pitch wooden propeller with a new propeller that Supermarine had been working on with modified tip sections. After the new propeller had been fitted, Quill took the aircraft up again at 18.00 hours, when his flight time was 36 minutes. He concentrated on a set of level speed tests and this time achieved 349½mph (562.46km/h), just short of Mitchell's estimated speed. After he landed he gave Mansbridge the test card to work out the true air speed. Mansbridge was very supportive of Murry White and passed the test card to him, asking him to calculate the true air speed:

> I did the reduction of the set of figures for the K5054 and thought I had got it wrong with the result of 349½mph [562.46km/h] True Air Speed. I thought I was 100mph [160km/h] out somewhere. I went to Ernie and told him that I had made a mistake, but couldn't see where. He looked through my figures very carefully and said that I hadn't made a mistake, and that my figures were exactly right, and was what they expected. I said I thought it would have been more like 250mph [402.33km/h], but he said that if it had been it wouldn't have been any good, 350mph [563.27km/h] was what they were aiming for.

The results of the test flight satisfied Mitchell and so it was planned to fly the aircraft to Martlesham Heath (near Ipswich) for RAF trials. Summers did further test flights in K5054 on 11, 13 and 14 May. The remainder of the twenty-three test flights were shared between Pickering and Quill.

K5054 is Delivered to Martlesham Heath for Official Trials

On 26 May 1936, K5054 was flown by Summers to the A&AEE at Martlesham Heath for official trials which were undertaken by Flt Lt Humphrey Edwardes-Jones, the first RAF pilot to fly the aircraft. His comment after the flight was that K5054 was a 'delight to fly'. Much more important was his positive answer to the Air Ministry question that the machine was suitable for an average RAF pilot, and possibly it was the comment that influenced the Air Ministry and Vickers to proceed with the development of the prototype. Judy Monger remembers that her father had had to look after the Spitfire when it went to Martlesham Heath, and that his task had been to write out the instructions regarding what they were doing with the aircraft.

Shortly afterwards, on 3 June 1936, the same day as the Air Ministry ordered the 600 Hurricane fighter aircraft from Hawker Aircraft Ltd, and before any test reports of the Spitfire had reached the Air Ministry, the RAF placed a production order for 310 Supermarine Spitfires. Once the order was placed, the standard drawings had to be completed and issued so that the tools could be made and the assembly jigs produced. Finally, all the sub-contract orders would need to be placed with the various firms, but it was possible that the first production aircraft would not be transferred to Eastleigh for assembly until about March 1938.

With substantial orders being placed for the Stranraer and Walrus from 1935, including the order for 310 Spitfires in June 1936, Supermarine had to increase their workforce considerably to meet the demand for aircraft that were deemed as being for urgent delivery. This was not easy as there were insufficient numbers of experienced aircraft workers, so others were recruited who had to 'learn on the job'. New recruits were needed not only for the workshops but also for the design offices, and so the small collegiate group of the design team began to enlarge.

Gaining Further Experience in Castle Bromwich

Murry White remembers assisting Mansbridge with the weight and centre of gravity, but in order to allow him to gain more experience Mansbridge gave Murry his first job away from home:

> I had to weigh the first production Spitfire aircraft at Castle Bromwich. Ernie Mansbridge was my immediate boss and sent me off early one morning. He told me that he wanted me to C.G. [centre of gravity] the first production aircraft and that I had to be there by 8 a.m. This was wartime of course, so I hurried up and got there, but it was not ready and I had to wait a whole week before I could do it. I got to know the people at Castle Bromwich very well, and returned to Southampton.
>
> I worked under him all the way through the war and did all the Performance Reduction and all other tests required on the Spitfire, like cooling and oil pressure tests, longitudinal, directional and lateral stability tests, take-off and landing distance measurement tests, propeller comparison tests,

particularly variable pitch and constant speed measurements, right through to the Spitfire Mk 21. I became very attached to the people with whom I worked, not only Ernie and Jeffrey, but all the other pilots we had, as well as the ground crews on our airfields.

The Final Decision on a Name for K5054

A day after the first flight of K5054 a Certificate of Design was issued, but at the time the aircraft was still referred to as the Type 300 as no name had been decided upon. Around 10 March 1936, Supermarine contacted the Air Ministry with the suggestion that the Type 300 should retain the same name as the Type 224, which was 'Spitfire'. The name 'Spitfire' had originated from Sir Robert McLean, using the letter 'S' which was linked to the company name 'Supermarine'. However, he particularly liked Spitfire because he compared it with his daughter, Annie, whom he considered 'a little Spitfire'.

Later on in the month, K5054 still had not been given a name, and Judy Monger remembers Sunday 31 March 1936 when George Pickering took K5054 up for two test flights. Test flight No 10 was at 15.30 hours and K5054 was in the air for 43 minutes, and later, at 17.25 hours, the aircraft was in the air for 30 minutes on flight No 11. As a small child, Judy was standing close to her dad and listening to the conversation between Smith, Faddy, Cooper and Mansbridge, in which possible names for K5054 were being discussed. The names included 'Shrew' and 'Shrike', but Smith suggested 'Scarab'. However, Mansbridge quickly reminded him that there had been a Supermarine flying boat with that name. Despite the suggestions put forward, Sir Robert McLean insisted on keeping the name 'Spitfire', which was finally confirmed by the Air Ministry on 10 June 1936. This was not altogether popular with Mitchell, who commented that it was, 'just the sort of bloody silly name they would give it!', especially as the Type 224 had not entirely met his expectation. (Annie McLean was known throughout her long life as 'Spitfire Annie'. She later married the actor Robert Newton and died at the age of 100.)

David Faddy vividly remembers the summer of 1936, especially when his father's car got buzzed by the Spitfire. His father had taken his mother, his brother Geoff and him to Eastleigh to see the Spitfire fly. Quill, who by this time had taken over as test pilot, had seen his father's car and flew very low over it. 'My brother and I were terrified and Geoff, who was only a little over a year old, tried to crawl under the front seat (there were no seat belts in those days).'

The Eastleigh hangar with teams of men and women working in the Spitfire production unit during the war years. *Solent Sky*

Trevor Westbrook is Recalled to Weybridge

Trevor Westbrook was very focused on getting the production difficulties sorted out when Vickers recalled him to take over their Weybridge factory because he was needed for the production of the Wellington Bombers. Westbrook's contribution was such that by the time he returned to Weybridge in December 1936, he had ensured that the Southampton works was the most up-to-date aircraft factory in England. Westbrook was replaced by H.B. Pratt, who had worked for many years at Vickers as chief draughtsman for airships. He had worked alongside Barnes Wallis, including on the R100 which was successfully flown. However, after the crash of the R101, which had not been built by Vickers, the airship project was cancelled. Pratt would not have been sent to Supermarine to replace Westbrook if he had not been highly thought of by Sir Robert McLean.

Cyril Russell remembers that after Pratt's arrival, the factory settled down with Pratt doing the administration work and Wilfred Elliot able to concentrate on his job as works manager, having been rather overshadowed previously by Westbrook. Quill also remembers that Pratt came from Vickers at Barrow in 1937 and had a completely different management style to Westbrook, but was the one who inherited the difficulties of Spitfire production and was the subject of the Air Ministry's wrath for the failure to meet delivery dates. Quill saw him as a calm, methodical and unexcitable man who set about recovering the situation and was able to get the production deliveries back on schedule by March 1939.

'Bent Tin Stuff'

Murry White remembers being called into the general manager's office where Pratt explained the new task that he wanted him to undertake. He told Murry how pleased he was with his work and said that the company wanted to send him, along with George Nicholas, to Barrow. He wanted them to understand what real engineering was all about instead of the 'bent tin stuff' in Supermarine:

> George and I went off to Barrow at the end of 1938 and spent four months there, but we couldn't do any real work. The Foreman and Chargehand of the shop told us to watch and see how they worked. The first shop I went in was the Pattern Shop where work models were made for making castings in brass, steel, or iron. Then to the Foundries to see how the patterns were used. This was followed by the Boilermaker's Shop, Diesel Engine Shop, the Turbine Erecting Shop, and finally the Field Gun Shop.
>
> I was in the field gun place where there was an old mechanic that must have been in the First World War, and the crisis of 1938 came along. He was absolutely furious with the government and Neville Chamberlain who had waved the paper when he got off the plane after seeing Hitler, and said 'Peace in our time'. He was obviously not in favour of appeasement.

Murry found that his time in Barrow in 1938 was arguably the happiest period of his apprenticeship.

Beaverbrook Investigators

Pratt was managing the works well between 1937 and 1940, but at that time Lord Beaverbrook had appointed small teams of investigators who would arrive without notice at an aircraft factory to produce a report on the production output and note especially if there were delays in production. However, when the Beaverbrook investigators arrived at the Supermarine factory without notice, Pratt refused them entry. The fact that wartime security clearance was important and Supermarine did not have advance notice, Pratt, as general manager, made a decision not to allow them access. This, of course, did not help him in future dealings with the investigators.

While under great pressure from his workload and the investigators, Pratt was injured when the Itchen factory was bombed and was off work for some time. During his absence Sqn Cdr Bird took over as temporary general manager. However, when Pratt eventually returned to his office at Hursley

Park he was becoming depressed and was effectively sacked after the negative reports submitted by the Beaverbrook investigators. It was all too much for him and he shot himself at home, following which Bird was appointed to his post. Murry White was saddened to learn later that Pratt had shot himself, not having known at the time that he had been fired and assuming that it was the strain of the work and being injured during the bombing of the Supermarine factories.

A Job in the Woolston Factory in the 1930s

After leaving Sholing Girls' School in 1933 at the age of 14, Jessie Mason worked for a time helping an elderly lady. One day, when cycling down to Woolston to get some shopping for the lady, she had second thoughts and cycled up to Harry Oven who was on the Supermarine main gate and asked if there were any jobs. He took down some particulars and then told her to turn up at 7.30 a.m. the following day. Jessie certainly had good cause to remember what happened on her first day. Her mother had prepared a sandwich for her to take to work, which she put in her coat pocket. When she arrived at the works a buzzer sounded and the rack where she had hung her coat was pulled up into the roof. Little was she to know at the time that her coat would remain in the roof until it was time to go home, so she had to go without her sandwich.

Jessie remembers seeing the first full-scale model of the Spitfire, which was built in wood. It was covered by tarpaulin screens which she believed was to hide it from the eyes of the German pilots who would deliver the mail to their base in the Supermarine office block. This was not the only time that she recalls seeing Germans around the factory:

> I remember seeing the Supermarine workmen with a sandbag on their bench and with a mallet they would bang away for ages to shape metal, but later some Germans came and fitted a machine which would do the job in seconds instead of using a mallet and sandbag.

Another memory that sticks out in Jessie's mind was when K5054 flew for the first time. Along with about six other women, she volunteered to go up to Eastleigh where their job was to polish the wings and fuselage of the prototype, which was standing on the grass outside the hangar:

> When we got there we saw the aircraft just had a metal finish and hadn't been painted. Our job was to clean and polish the wings and fuselage and by

the time we had finished it was really sparkling. We used some sort of polish which was similar to Brasso.

Jessie worked in the 'K' Shop time and checking office run by Mr Pomeroy, and her job was to meet the workmen and take their names and information about the job they were on. The rate fixer would check and time the jobs, and if the men finished earlier than the time set then they would get extra money. 'I remember the foreman was Mr Heaver, and also Les White who worked in the 'K' Shop Time & Checking Office. At that time the Walrus and Stranraer were being built.'

It was in 1936 that Frank Fulford joined Supermarine as a 'handy lad' and worked in 'K' Shop, along with Jessie. Frank was 16 when he started looking for a job, and had at first tried for a job in Woolston which meant that he had to pass the Supermarine works. After passing the gates a number of times and knowing it was an aircraft factory, he observed that the lights seemed to be on all the time, day and night. He decided that it seemed a good place to get a job so went to the main gates and told the doorman that he wanted to work in the factory. Frank was asked how old he was and told to wait while the doorman went and got one of the foremen:

> The foreman came down and I remember that it was Bill Heaver and he was the man in charge of the sheet metal shop. He asked what I was after and I told him that I was very interested in aircraft and wanted a job, and I thought

The new office block being built at the Woolston works in 1939. Although some men are at work, young boys are seen playing on the scaffolding nearby. *Barbara Harries*

Woolston works with its new office block and updated production workshops, all completed just before the war started in 1939. *Solent Sky*

it was a very nice factory. He asked what trade I was interested in and I told him I wanted to do sheet metal work. 'OK,' he said, 'you can start next week.'

In the meantime Frank had to get all his documentation together and arrived the next week in his new denim overalls. However, he realised that when he entered the 'K' Shop where the sheet metal work was done, everyone would know he was a new boy. He was put with a skilled man and the foreman told him that he was going to be a 'handy lad'. Frank really enjoyed the work, but found that he had to buy his own tools and had to stamp his name on them so that the other workmen would know that they belonged to him. He also had the same experience as Jessie Mason when he arrived at work in the morning to see a rack with hooks for the workmen to put their coats and personal belongings on:

These racks were then hoisted by pulleys up into the roof, so you couldn't get to your belongings until work finished at the end of your shift when the racks were then lowered down. The other thing was if you wanted to use the toilet you had to ask permission and you were only allowed 7 minutes, otherwise they would come looking for you.

The first aircraft he worked on was the Walrus which had a pusher engine and a machine gun at the front with an open cockpit and another cockpit aft. Frank worked on the main spar frame of the fuselage where the wing connects to the fuselage. The Walrus had a fitting in the upper wing centre-section for hooking and to lock the cable on and lift the aircraft on to a ship. Frank had some good times working in 'K' Shop and discovered when working with the skilled men that they only had a certain time to do the job. This was the piecework which had been assessed by the rate fixer, and they received a bonus if the job was completed in a faster time.

One interesting event occurred when Frank was taken to Eastleigh aerodrome by one of the fitters to take some measurements of the K5054 that had flown for the first time a few days before:

> The first Spitfire had flown just days before I got there and the skilled man I worked with took me to Eastleigh aerodrome which was then a grass runway. He told me that we had to go and get some dimension from K5054 which was standing outside the hangar. When we arrived we got the dimensions from the fairing between the wing and the fuselage. To me the plane didn't look anything out of the ordinary.

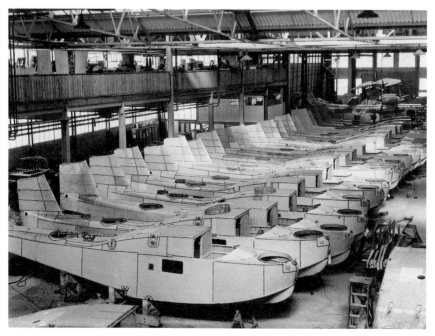

Walrus fuselages completed and waiting for the next stage of their production at the Itchen works. *Solent Sky*

While on reconnaissance in the South Atlantic, F9C Walrus L2261 from 711 Squadron, HMS *Sussex* was shot down by three Bf 109s on 31 October 1939. All three crew were killed. *John Thomson*

After this he worked on the engine nacelles for the Scapa and Stranraer, and found that they had to hammer the shape of the engine cowling which could take up the whole morning and even part of the afternoon to get it into shape. Afterwards the engine cowling was taken to the wheeling machine and Frank assisted the skilled workman in getting it curved. He also did some work on the flying boat floats, but thought that it was just like building a fuselage in miniature:

> Later on, there was the decision to put the Spitfire into production and I worked with another man producing parts of the aircraft. This was in 'K' Shop and I worked most of my time with Bill Heaver as foreman.

7

EARLY WARNINGS OF THE 1930S

In the 1930s it had become clear that Germany was beginning to build up its military hardware, especially with the development of the Luftwaffe bombers and fighter aircraft. Furthermore, in 1936, Adolf Hitler gave his support for Germany's involvement in helping the Nationalists in the Spanish Civil War, and this was undertaken by the formation of the Condor Legion under the command of General Hugo Sperrle. The Condor Legion was made up mainly of volunteers from the Luftwaffe, and some from the German Army, and they were involved in the conflict until the start of the Second World War in 1939.

The Condor Legion was equipped with aircraft that included a bomber group of Ju 52s, He 51 fighters, reconnaissance aircraft and floatplanes. However, more sinister was the request from Sperrle for higher-performance aircraft that included those that the RAF would come up against in the Second World War, such as the He 111, the Junkers Stuka bomber and the Messerschmitt fighters. For the volunteer pilots from the Luftwaffe this provided a good grounding in combat experience during their time with the Condor Legion, especially for Stuka pilots who gained plenty of practice in its use as a dive bomber in its 'terror bombing' missions.

Zeppelins in the Southampton Sky

In 1936, the German airship *Hindenburg* appeared in the sky over Southampton, causing great concern over the possibility that photographs were being taken of the port, aircraft factories and other possible bombing targets. Muriel Wanson and Lily Bartlett both saw the Zeppelin flying over the city. Lily remembers walking with her future husband in the park when a Zeppelin flew right over them and across the docks. David Noyce also saw a Zeppelin fly low over

Southampton while he was watching his father play cricket at West End. Tony Kenyon comments that security against foreign spies had always been a worry, as the fact that Southampton was a large passenger liner port meant that passengers from German liners were able to spread everywhere taking photographs. He also saw recalls seeing the Zeppelin very clearly:

> I can remember lying on the gravel and watching it come over. After it passed over us it went up the Itchen, but as we were on high ground we could see it flying low along the River Itchen, over the Supermarine works and then over the docks. Everybody was fuming because they thought they were taking photographs.

There was concern voiced in the Houses of Parliament in July 1936 about the *Hindenburg* flying low over British cities, but the official statement from the Under-Secretary of State for Air, Sir Philip Sassoon, was that both the British and German governments had come to an agreement that the airships *Graf Zeppelin* and *Hindenburg* would avoid flying over Britain, unless in cases of emergency, such as those caused by adverse weather conditions. However, further concern was raised over the German airships gaining information of British arsenals and dockyards by flying over them. This warning was made clearer when it was reported that the *Hindenburg* had flown very low over Southampton Water and over what was the prohibited area of Portsmouth. Further concern was raised by the question as to whether foreign aircraft were permitted to carry cameras. This brought the reply from Sir Philip Sassoon that foreign aircraft were not permitted to carry cameras unless special permission had been obtained. (*Hansard*, July 1936)

Sea Mail to Air Mail

Since the nineteenth century transatlantic mail had been delivered by steamship but following the introduction of aircraft, attention was paid to a possible airmail service. Developments in aviation led to attempts to cross the North Atlantic, and the possibility for speeding up the time it took to carry transatlantic mail.

The first transatlantic flight had been undertaken in May 1919, when Lt-Cdr Albert Read flew a Navy Curtiss NC-4 flying boat from New York to Plymouth, but the actual transatlantic crossing was to Lisbon in Portugal and then in stages to its final destination. However, it was not without engine problems and fortunately, being a flying boat, it could land and float on the sea for repairs to be undertaken. It was Alcock and Brown who made the first non-stop transatlantic flight just a few weeks later, in June 1919, flying in a Vickers Vimy bomber from Newfoundland to Ireland.

The first solo flight was undertaken in May 1927 by Charles Lindbergh flying the *Spirit of St Louis* from New York to Paris, followed one year later by Amelia Earhart as the first woman to fly transatlantic. Some reports state that she was the first woman to fly a solo non-stop transatlantic flight, but this is not exactly correct as she was the first woman to fly transatlantic as a passenger, because the aircraft was flown by pilots Wilmer Stutz and Louis Gordon. After landing at Burry Port in Wales, Amelia Earhart then flew on to Southampton where she was welcomed by the mayor, Mrs Foster Welch, on 20 June 1928.

Catapulting Seaplanes from Ocean Liners

At about the same time, an interest was shown in carrying a seaplane on board an ocean liner and then catapulting it from the ship with the aim of delivering the mail by air ahead of the arrival of the ship. This was first introduced on the French ocean Liner *Île de France* on which a catapult was installed in 1928 and the seaplane launched when the liner was a few hundred miles from her destination ports of New York and Le Havre. However, this proved to be too expensive to run and by 1930 the catapult was taken off the ship and the service discontinued.

On the other hand, NDL (Norddeutscher Lloyd) joined up with the German airline Lufthansa and installed catapults on their two new liners *Bremen* and *Europa*. A Heinkel He 12 was on board the *Bremen* for her maiden voyage in 1929, and was launched from the ship when approximately 250 miles from New York to deliver the mail a matter of hours later. On the return journey, the seaplane would be dispatched when in the English Channel to fly on to Bremerhaven. The aircraft were changed to the Ju 46 in 1932 on both the *Bremen* and *Europa*, but although New York remained as the westbound destination port for the seaplanes, the eastbound destination port was changed from Bremerhaven to Southampton. They would deliver any mail for Britain and then refuel to fly on to Bremerhaven.

German Air Mail Seaplanes Land on the River Itchen

Following the Zeppelin flights over Southampton, concern was growing about the German seaplanes that had been flying into Southampton with the mail for some time, landing on the River Itchen. These seaplanes were piloted by German

Lufthansa pilots that had been catapulted from the ocean liners *Bremen* and *Europa* off the coast of Ireland. What was even more worrying was that their Southampton office was at the base of the Supermarine office block where there were a couple of Germans working in the mail office. It does not take too much imagination to realise that with the Spitfires being built close by, they would have been able to see what was happening, and also that the Lufthansa pilots flying seaplanes in with the mail were gaining knowledge about the port of Southampton and the Supermarine works as well as other industries in the area. The same pilots were to become Luftwaffe pilots in the Second World War and would know exactly where to drop their bombs in future attacks on Southampton.

Supermarine Bomber Design

It was while the work on improvement and development of the prototype Spitfire was ongoing that Supermarine received a contract for a four-engine bomber to the Air Ministry specification B.12/36, which was to be the Supermarine 318 bomber. Mitchell, although seriously ill, put all his efforts into the bomber design, leaving his chief draughtsman Smith with the task of getting the Spitfire production up and running. Jeffrey Quill in *Birth of a Legend: The Spitfire*, records:

> Most of the design load in getting the Spitfire into production would have descended upon Joe Smith's shoulders anyway. In spite of the traumas experienced between 1936 and 1938 in producing the Spitfire – Smith's shoulders were broad enough to take the load.

However, despite the many delays, with dogged determination Smith went on to develop the Spitfire into a succession of variants to meet the wartime demands: fighters; fighter-bombers; photo reconnaissance; naval carrier operations and floatplanes. The B.12/36 bomber design, to be powered by four Rolls-Royce Merlin engines, was expected to be a highly efficient bomber, both in performance and in attack capability, and was under construction before the war in the Woolston works. Frank Fulford remembers working on the prototype:

> In the corner of the shop they were beginning to build the bomber that Mitchell had designed. That would have been a beauty! It was all metal sheeting of course. I did some work on the bomber and really enjoyed it. The fuselage was pretty well complete and it was a shame it was never flown.

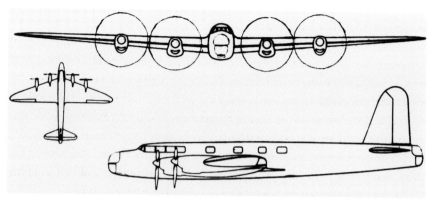

Design plan for Type 317 B.12/36 bomber. *Solent Sky*

The Type 317 B.12/36 bomber fuselage being built in the Woolston works. *Solent Sky*

The fate of the prototype bomber was finally decided when German bombs destroyed the Woolston factory in 1940. This was the end of what could have been a very successful front-line bomber, and the work was then concentrated on the production of the Spitfire.

Charles Labette had left Supermarine in 1936 to work for the Fairey Aviation Co. where he was responsible for work on the fuselage of the Sea Fox. In 1938, he returned to Supermarine to work for Eric Lovell-Cooper on the B.12/36 bomber. After a short time he was transferred to the technical office Project Department to work for Arthur Shirvall. He was involved in the upgrading and development of the Spitfire and its many marks for improved performance, both aerodynamically and militarily, his special job being the use of Spitfires/ Seafires for naval use for deck landing and taking off using RATOG (Rocket-Assisted Take-off Gear) and catapulting. In connection with this work he accompanied Roger Dickson to Scotland to work on the aircraft carrier HMS *Pretoria Castle* for a few weeks. The pressure on the workforce at the time often found them working from 7.30 a.m. to 9.30 p.m. seven days a week.

Reginald J. Mitchell Dies

Although Mitchell tried to continue with his work while he was terminally ill, he saw only his prototype Spitfire fly before he died on 11 June 1937. He was aged only 42, and his death was a great loss to the country and to the world of aircraft design. As one of the leading inspirational designers of the time, he had in his short working life as chief designer for Supermarine designed as many as twenty-four different types of aircraft, including flying boats, amphibians, the Schneider racing seaplanes, and the B.12/36 bomber, destroyed in the bombing of the Supermarine factory, and culminating in the famous Spitfire.

It has been said that Mitchell could at times be sharp in his dealings with his staff, and they quickly learned not to disturb him when he was in deep concentration over his drawing board. In the first Royal Aeronautical Society Mitchell Memorial Lecture given by Joe Smith on 21 January 1954, he reflected on his experiences and observations from the sixteen years he had worked with Mitchell. Smith said that R.J. was essentially a friendly person, and normally even-tempered, but 'occasionally let rip with us when he was dissatisfied with the work. The storms were of short duration and forgotten by him almost immediately – provided you put the job right!'

Mitchell was a gifted leader and was highly respected by his design team, who were very loyal and inspired to go that 'extra mile' in their work. Smith describes some of R.J.'s leadership qualities:

> He was known as R.J. to everyone from the lowest to the highest, and the fact that he accepted his nickname is one illustration of his friendliness and absence of false dignity.
>
> He never shirked full responsibility, and his technical integrity was unquestionable. He won the complete respect and confidence of his staff, in whom he created a continuous sense of achievement.
>
> As a person R.J. was a modest man who hated publicity and shunned public occasions. He was a shrewd assessor of other men and often showed great restraint in dealing with strangers with whose point of view he disagreed. When meeting people for the first time R.J. appeared rather shy, but once he knew them better he was more outgoing. Sir Henry Royce summed up R.J. as 'a man slow to decide, but quick to act'.

Joe Smith also refers to the human aspect that Mitchell's staff got to know, and that was his concern for the safety of the pilots who flew the aircraft he designed. Finally, Smith refers to the courage that Mitchell showed when he became terminally ill:

In the whole range of human emotions there is nothing as terrible as the realisation that an incurable disease makes one's death inevitable within a short space of time. To have the courage to face such a tragic fate unflinchingly must be the hope of every man, and adding a fervent prayer that may never happen to him.

It did happen to Mitchell, and I can personally vouch for the fact that he behaved in a way which is beyond praise. To talk to him during this period was to see a high form of courage, and the memory must always remain an inspiration.

Sadly, Smith also died of cancer at the age of 58, only two years after giving this excellent lecture.

PART II

JOSEPH SMITH
(1897–1956)

INNOVATIVE DESIGNER

INTRODUCTION

JOSEPH (JOE) SMITH

Much of the publicity about the design and development of the Spitfire has been solely attributed to R.J. Mitchell, but the design of any new aircraft will involve many others in the work. Supporting and working alongside Mitchell was his chief draughtsman Joe Smith, a modest man whose dedication and leadership of the Supermarine design team at a difficult but crucial time for Britain, with the growing threat of war, has largely been forgotten. While Mitchell was an inspirational figure who had designed a vast number of aircraft at Supermarine right up to the prototype Spitfire before he died, Smith could be described as an innovative designer who transformed Mitchell's original design through no fewer than twenty-four marks to a fighter aircraft that Mitchell could never have envisaged. It was a sad fact that Mitchell died in 1937 before he could see his Spitfire in action, but he would have been very proud of Smith for his consistent and focused work on the development of the aircraft.

Joe Smith CBE, AMIMechE, FRAeS

Joe Smith married Winifred Greaves, and had two children, David and his younger sister Barbara. David Smith followed in his father's footsteps, taking a five-year engineering apprenticeship followed by his National Service in the RAF. In 1954, he was working for BTH (British Thomson-Houston) in aircraft equipment technical sales in Coventry, and later as export manager for Lucas Aerospace, which took him on various business trips around the world. He was a very keen mountaineer, having climbed all the Scottish Munro peaks more than once and was responsible for getting the 83-mile (133.57km) Dales Way between Ilkley and Windermere accepted by the government as an official National Trail. He celebrated his 70th birthday trekking in the Himalayas. Sadly,

The Smith family in the early twentieth century. From left to right, back row: elder brother Sam; Joe Smith. Front row: Joe's father; youngest brother Bill; Joe's mother. Joe's daughter Barbara comments: 'That's Dad with hair!' *Barbara Harries*

David Smith passed away in August 2008, but his sister Barbara has been able to share her memories of their father:

> He was a wonderful father and a good family man, but unfortunately he died aged 58 in February 1956 when I was only 21. I gather that when my father passed away there was a letter from Yardley Secondary School saying they were amazed that they had such a distinguished old boy.

Joe Smith junior had two brothers, Sam who was the eldest and his younger brother Bill:

> My father came from Birmingham, brought up from grass roots of nothing; I think the family were butchers. He was not an educated man and didn't come from university, but his time in the RNVR during the First World War would have coloured his language at times. My father's brother Sam started work as a tea boy and ended up as company director. They made good.
>
> My father enjoyed being in the garden. He was no gardener, but would cut all the hedges and the lawn. They were immaculate, not a leaf out of place

and the lines were straight, as you can imagine from a draughtsman. We kept chickens because we had an acre of ground where we could do that sort of thing. We were quite self-sufficient because we grew all our own vegetables, and I remember mum had to get the broad beans in because it was dad's favourite vegetable. We then lived in Otterbourne, Hampshire.

Even during the war we managed seaside and country holidays, even if dad could only come for days of it, then shoot off and come back again. We had a wonderful time. He taught me to swim and appreciate the countryside, liked animals, and as far as I know was liked and respected by everybody.

We used to go down to see my brother who was at boarding school in Sherborne, and I think dad used to fit it in with his visits to Westland's Aircraft in Yeovil. He used to drop mum and me off for the weekend while he went off on business and then later came back to pick us up.

My mother was a wonderful mother, but she had a very hard life because my father didn't come home at night till 10 or 11 p.m., certainly during the war years. She also did an awful amount of war work with her knitting, balaclavas, socks and slippers I can remember her making.

Dad thought very highly of his test pilots and said they were all first class, but mum would have to comfort him when one of the planes crashed and the pilot was killed or injured.

I never heard my father say cross words at home and he and my mother were happy as anything. However, I know my father could swear like a trooper, but he didn't mean it at all. He could tell someone off, but the next minute, all was forgotten.

My dad was very shy, very modest and hated publicity. I remember him preparing for the first Mitchell Memorial Lecture because he was terribly nervous. He had never spoken publicly like that before.

Jeffrey Quill liked my dad immensely and always said that my dad did not get the recognition he deserved. I know that Mitchell designed the Spitfire and it was his idea, but he only saw the prototype fly. It needed an awful lot doing to it, and it was a completely different aircraft, especially by the end of the war. All the pilots and everyone still alive will say that my father did not get the appreciation he deserved.

I remember the Spitfire window at Bentley Priory and went to the unveiling of it. It was done by the Spitfire Society. In Hursley Church there is a plaque in the tower in remembrance of my father, donated by IBM to have the clock repaired, at about the end of the 1950s. There was also an embroidered altar cloth from the family.

Jeffrey Quill, in his book *Birth of a Legend: The Spitfire*, wrote:

> Joe was a man of great character and determination. He was tough, did not suffer fools gladly and was impatient of idleness or shoddy work. He inspired a genuine liking and respect amongst those who worked for him. He was a worthy, and perhaps in the dramatic changed circumstances of the time, the only possible successor to R.J.

8

FROM DESIGN MANAGER
TO CHIEF DESIGNER

After Reginald Mitchell's death on 11 June 1937 there were the inevitable changes in the organisation of the Design Department at Supermarine but there was a delay in appointing his final successor. Although this was eventually to be Joseph Smith, who as his chief draughtsman had worked alongside Mitchell for some considerable time and knew him well, the final appointment as chief designer did not come until much later. This was because at first Maj. Harold 'Agony' Payn AFC had been installed by Sir Robert McLean as the head of design after Mitchell's death. He had been sent down initially from Weybridge to help Mitchell after the Vickers takeover in 1928. However, he did not have Mitchell's training, experience or talents and, furthermore, in 1939 it was a particularly sensitive time in the country for security. It was discovered that Payn's wife had German connections so he could not get security clearance and was subsequently forced to leave Supermarine.

At first, Smith was to become the design manager. This has been confirmed by a letter of appointment received by Barrie Bryant dated 10 October 1939, inviting him to start work on 12 October 1939, and was signed by Smith as manager of the Design Department at the Supermarine works. The date of the letter indicates that more than two years after Mitchell's death, Smith's title was 'Manager, Design Department'. It was not until 1941 that he gained chief designer approval from the Ministry of Aircraft Production. During the interim period, Rex Pierson was the approved chief designer for both Vickers at Weybridge and Supermarine, and he signed certain legal documents during this period. When Smith did take over as the chief designer in 1941, Alan Clifton (Cliffy) became his principal assistant and Eric Lovell-Cooper became the chief draughtsman.

Smith was a man of great energy, determination, dedication and courage, and fully recognised that his main task from then on was to develop the Spitfire to its maximum potential in order to meet the might of the Luftwaffe in the skies over Britain, Europe and in other air battles around the world. Throughout the war years he was to be in the forefront, leading his design team and workforce to ensure that the Spitfire remained in the front rank of fighter performance. He was a down-to-earth practical engineer and knew the value of a good basic design, and had been directly involved in the development of the prototype Spitfire, much of which had been left to him while Mitchell concentrated on the B.12/36 bomber design. Furthermore, Smith was fully aware of the developing threat of war with Germany in the late 1930s, and subsequently of the need to meet the threat and might of the Luftwaffe fighters and bombers. He could not even contemplate the thought of a new design and was reputed to have said, 'It'll get us through the war.'

Memories of Young Supermarine Workers in 1937/38

Fred Veal was about 16 when he joined Supermarine in 1937 as a 'handy lad' in 'K' Shop where all the fuselages were built, and remembers seeing on the other side of the workshop the Walrus being built. At that time Supermarine had started building the Spitfire and Fred worked in the wheeling squad, shaping the skins of the aircraft: 'It's a skilled job which you cannot be taught, but gain the skills by practice over time.'

Lily Bartlett had a friend who worked for Supermarine who told her that they were looking for people to work at the factory. She was just 17 in 1937, and was fortunate to get a job at the works, starting on 1s (one shilling) an hour:

> I really felt lucky and at first I was working in the wood shop where we were fitting together the frames of the wooden planes. There were about a dozen of us girls. The frames then went in the dope shop where the fuselage and wings were covered in canvas and hand stitched. They would then put red dope on them and spray them silver. The planes were standing in rows. I only remember the Stranraer.

With the wooden planes, their job was to fit the frame together, but when they worked on the metal planes the job changed to bending the metal pipes filled with resin until the job was completed when the resin was taken out before the pipes were taken away. However, when engaged on the pipe work the girls were working on piecework with a set time of 20 minutes per job. If they completed the job earlier than the allotted time, then they got extra money:

I can remember that a man would come along and watch you working. The other girls used to tell me to go slow because if you went fast they would expect that every time. They said, 'Take your time on it'.

Muriel Wanson started work at Supermarine at the end of 1938, making ailerons for wings at Eastleigh aerodrome. Another job was cleaning sprockets that had been retrieved from crashed aeroplanes. She describes the sprockets as being at different stages of rust which they had to clean off, but some took longer than others because there was quite a bit of rust on them which needed to be filed away. The hangar they worked in was old and very cold, especially as they were standing on concrete the whole day. There were some interesting moments when the test flights took place, and Muriel remembers they would all rush out to watch 'Mutt' Summers taking off and flying around the aerodrome.

Production Difficulties for Supermarine

Putting the Spitfire into mass-production proved to be much harder than Supermarine had anticipated. Until they received the large order for 310 Spitfire fighter aircraft on 3 June 1936, the company had managed to keep regular production of basically hand-built flying boats and amphibians, especially through the early years and the difficulties of the Great Depression from 1929 until 1935, when the aircraft industry became busy with the Rearmament Programme.

To start production in response to a contract issued by the Air Ministry for 310 Spitfires was going to be difficult. At the time, the Woolston factory was working at full capacity building the Walrus and Stranraer flying boats to complete orders already placed, so it was not possible for the company to start production of the Spitfire immediately. One solution that they came up with was to use outside contractors to manufacture parts of the Spitfire for final assembly. This was not an ideal solution, but at least something was happening. However, the time taken to get all these production arrangements up and running was quite long and not to the Air Ministry's liking. It wanted deliveries of the Spitfire as soon as possible.

New Itchen Factory Built

A new factory was built in 1939 and was known as the Itchen works. The building of this new factory was undertaken on reclaimed land from the River

Itchen, and was similar to work on reclaiming land from the River Test for the New Docks in the late 1930s.

The Itchen works was established at first for the production of the Walrus and Sea Otter, but construction of Spitfire fuselages soon began there. However, the construction of the aircraft wings was sub-contracted to General Aircraft Ltd at Feltham in Middlesex and Pobjoy Airmotors Ltd of Rochester, Kent. Other sub-contracting firms were Folland Aircraft Ltd, Hamble (tailplane and rudder); General Electric Co., Preston (wing tips); Aero Engines Ltd, Kingswood, Bristol (ailerons and elevators); Singer Motors Ltd, Coventry (engine mountings); J. Samuel White, Cowes (fuselage frames); Westland Aircraft Ltd, Yeovil (wing ribs); G. Beaton & Son Ltd, Willesden, London (wing ribs); and Pressed Steel Co., Coventry (wing leading edge).

Vickers-Armstrongs were not altogether happy to see the process of sub-contracting the work, preferring all the work to be done in-house. To that end, they were not forthcoming with releasing the blueprints and other components in a hurry, which caused further delays in getting the Spitfire into production. By then the Air Ministry was dissatisfied with the time being taken in completing the order for the 310 Spitfire contract and said that after the order was completed, it would consider switching Supermarine from the production of the Spitfire fighter to building Bristol Beaufighters. This was a blow to Smith, and Lovell-Cooper advised him to call Sir Wilfred Freeman who was responsible to the Air Ministry as the AMDP (Air Member for Development and Production). Whatever Smith said to Sir Wilfred solved the problem, leaving Supermarine to continue building Spitfires.

The 'Shadow Factory' at Castle Bromwich

The government felt that the Supermarine works at Woolston would not be able to cope with the expected volume of demand for the new aircraft, and it also considered that Southampton was dangerously close to the French coast and could be easily attacked by the Luftwaffe. To remedy both these problems the government decided to set up a 'shadow factory' for Spitfire production at Castle Bromwich, near Birmingham. The aim of these factories was to be specialist centres that were managed generally by a company with no aircraft experience but with extensive production capability to shadow the parent company and to provide bulk production.

While Supermarine in Southampton were contracted to build the Mk I Spitfire, the main difference in the order placed by the Air Ministry was for 1,000 Spitfire Mk IIs to be built at the Castle Bromwich shadow factory by the Nuffield Organisation, which had been chosen by the government to build and equip a factory for the construction of the aircraft. However, the work to build the factory did not start until 12 July 1938, mainly due to the Rearmament Programme creating a great upheaval in British industry. The Nuffield Organisation also had problems trying to train their skilled engineers, whose experience was building cars, by studying the work at Supermarine in order to gain experience in the production of the new air-craft. There was also a delay in getting the necessary machinery installed to build the Spitfires.

The Air Ministry, aware that the Nuffield Organisation were not finding it easy to transfer their automotive building skills to that of the construction of aircraft, decided to instruct Vickers to undertake the management of Castle Bromwich, and Supermarine were asked to assist the Nuffield Organisation with their manufacturing and assembly of Spitfire Mk II aircraft. In his lecture to the Royal Aeronautical Society, Southampton branch, on 6 March 1976, Stan Woodley remembers the time when the decision was made to transfer him to Castle Bromwich, where he was to remain until the end of the war:

> I was in the office in Woolston when the telephone rang and the General Manager Wilf Elliot looked up and said, 'Woodley, have you got your car?' I said, 'Yes.' He said, 'Go home and pack a bag. We're going to Castle Bromwich, and I don't know when we will be coming back.'

Supermarine Design Representative

Jack Rasmussen joined the Supermarine design team from Blackburn in 1931, just at the time of the early design of the Spitfire, as a senior section leader design draughtsman. When production was started at Castle Bromwich, Smith chose Rasmussen as design representative to iron out the many design and production queries that arose. Rasmussen's job was to travel to Castle Bromwich every two weeks to spend three or four days on the queries and then to return to Hursley to have the solutions to the queries embodied in the master drawings.

Murry White knew Rasmussen well, both as a friend and colleague, and remembers him as a great personality who quickly became a good friend of the general manager Bonner Dickson, so much so that he was soon staying in his home, rather than the local hotel. Murry comments: 'Jack did most valuable work in getting the Castle Bromwich Spitfire into production.'

Weight Engineering

Barrie Bryant was looking for a job and, although he did not have any special interest in aviation, he was fortunate that Harry ('Trem') Tremelling arranged for him to have an interview with Alan Clifton (Cliffy) who engaged him as a junior technical assistant. From his appointment on 12 October 1939, Barrie was to be a long-serving member of the Supermarine team.

Among the tasks assigned to junior members of the pre-war technical office were the keeping of weight records, weighing parts, measuring the weight and centre-of-gravity position of complete aircraft and preparing loading instructions for test flights. Draughtsmen had long had the responsibility for calculating the weight of each part and sub-assembly they designed, but to Barrie this became sporadic from about 1936, possibly due to the pressures of the development of military fighters and armaments. Where no weight was shown on the drawing, the value had to be calculated in the technical office by the 'weights men'. He was at first supervised by two other junior technical assistants, Murry White and Doug Scard, under Ernie Mansbridge's general control. By the mid-1940s, Murry was fully engaged on flight tests and Doug was involved in stressing, leaving Barrie as the only one in the weight section:

> That left me as custodian of weight & balance records and recipient of growing weight work on Walrus, Sea Otter and Spitfire in its many variants, experimental and production. I learned by being inquisitive, watching and listening. A year later I acquired an assistant, the first of an eventual 30-strong Weight Section. Our duties eventually included the prediction, calculation, verification and monitoring of weight, balance and moments of inertia of aircraft from conception to operational use; initiation of weight reductions; preparation of loading data; development of prediction methods; training design staff.
>
> The tasks of predicting, estimating, forecasting, calculating, measuring and recording such data were handled in the British industry by various ad hoc arrangements until wartime environments imposed increased uniformity upon Ministry of Aircraft Production contractors. National differences were revealed in the 1950s by which time the Society of Aeronautical Weight Engineers (founded in America) had international membership. Through membership of the Society of British Aircraft Constructors' Weight Control Panel and later SAWE I learned that developments were similar but not identical.

Charles Labette remembers the problems that began to occur before the war when the pressure was on the production of the Spitfire. Up until then it was usually the responsibility of the draughtsman to calculate the weight of the parts he had drawn, but the need to get the drawings more speedily to the production departments became essential to increasing production:

> Supermarine designers were very aware between the 1920s and 1930s of the importance of weight control, especially Alan Clifton who was dedicated to weight saving and the lightest possible design to sustain a sound resulting product. However, when the 1930–40 decade came to a close there was greater pressure on design office staff from production staff to get drawings out to the shops where production of the aircraft was vital. Then it was more 'estimates of weight' and also 'estimates of material'. These were frequently overlooked and its control became a shambles. That is until Barrie Bryant started to sort the shambles out.

When Barrie started in 1939, the small weights team had to spread itself over the range of Supermarine aircraft, including the Stranraer, Walrus and Sea Otter, but with the concentration on the production of the Spitfire the team's work became more focused:

> Spitfire developments and production dominated our work from 1940 until 1945 but not to the total exclusion of other types. Spitfire and later Seafire variants in profusion were devised, chiefly in the Supermarine design office. Prototypes were built or converted, usually in our Experimental Department, and flown at our Flight Test Unit. Before each prototype undertook its first flight the weight and centre of gravity position had to be measured and loading instructions issued.

Barrie became the section leader in the technical office for weight and centre of gravity, and remained working at Supermarine until dispersal in June 1958.

Learning on the Job

One of the benefits for the Supermarine apprentices in their quest for knowledge and experience was the help and support given by the design office, and 'learning on the job' became paramount to their eventual success in the aviation world. Barrie Bryant comments:

> With very few exceptions, I recall people ready to provide assistance, answer questions, share experience, satisfy curiosity, indeed to co-operate in

a friendly and constructive manner rather than erect departmental barriers. My work, but sometimes just my inquisitiveness, took me into many activities outside the technical office but I hardly remember an occasion when I was rebuffed or on my return being questioned about what I had been doing. I know that Joe Smith in his role of Chief Designer and Alan Clifton in charge of the technical office encouraged us to employ curiosity constructively. They were willing to listen, even to junior staff, and made communication easy. They fostered outward-looking personal responsibility and self-checking. This may have been a key contribution to the firm's remarkable productivity. As complexity grew through the 1940s novel situations arose. It was then usual for someone who had already shown ingenuity to be assigned the fresh task, and then largely left to get on with it. Appointment notices or job specifications were rare. Overlaps appeared from time to time but were usually resolved without conflict. Under-lapping could have more serious consequences so that individuals who spotted gaps and tried to bridge them were rewarded with extended responsibility, if not always financial compensation!

The Supermarine Design Team

At the beginning of the Second World War, the design team basically consisted of men who had been chosen initially by Mitchell. However, the team had worked together so closely and had so much professional confidence in each other's attributes that they were able to continue working effectively under the guidance and leadership of their new chief designer, Joe Smith.

Alan Clifton (Young Alan) comments that it was a small team in the early days, and they would all address each other by their surnames, except for Smith, who was always called Joe; the others were all 'Old something' – 'Old Clifton', 'Old Faddy' and so on. They were all scattered about during the war, living in outlying places.

Judy Monger remembers that her father became very busy with the flight-testing of the Spitfire, which meant him spending most of the time at the flight tests on various airfields: Worthy Down at first, High Post, and then Chilbolton:

Joe Smith was the team leader with a team that were all well qualified; all experienced and worked together just like a big family. As children we played with the Smiths, the Cliftons and the Faddys. Arthur Shirvall only lived up the road from us and travelled to work with my dad each day.

Vickers-Armstrongs Ltd Supermarine Design Staff Annual Dinner

The whole team working together just like a big family also extended into their social events, such as the design staff dinners, and examples of the menus are from the collection of Judy Monger from the time her father, Ernie Mansbridge, joined the team in 1924. The early menus are interesting because they have a collection of autographs of those attending the annual dinners in 1924, 1925 and 1926, and range from twenty to thirty signatures as the team grew. They include Mitchell, Smith, Clifton, Holroyd, Kettlewell, Gedge, Shirvall, Lovell-Cooper and Simmonds. The front cover of the 1930 menu was headed 'The Supermarine D.O. Annual Binge', but there is little evidence that the annual dinners continued after this, possibly due to the pressure for the designs and production for the new day and night fighter but also from the onset of Mitchell's serious illness that led to his death in 1937.

However, the next example of the staff dinner was in 1938, held on 16 December at the Dolphin Hotel in Southampton, and the front cover was headed with the more formal 'Vickers-Armstrongs Ltd Supermarine Design Staff Annual Dinner'. It is significant that the autograph list contained thirty-one signatures but sadly missing, of course, is Mitchell's. It appears that this was the last signed list, possibly due to the increasing size of the design team.

The 1939 design office dinner. *Judy Monger*

There was also a change in the format of the illustrations on the front cover, which tended to relate to work in the design office or to significant events, but were mainly caricatures of the chairman for the evening, often portrayed with humour. Spitfire production problems were humorously portrayed on the cover of the 1938 menu. It showed an angry Spitfire resisting any attempts by the design team to pull it along by ropes.

At first, the entertainment at the annual dinners was provided by professional entertainers who had been booked for the event, but this gradually changed to the design staff planning their own entertainment in-house. On the inside cover of the 1938 menu was quite a formal entertainment list of compère artistes: Messrs Arnold, Kettlewell, Humphrey, Laidman, Tong, Noble, Cox, Morgan, Vincent, Wherley and Weymouth, all members of the design team. This was to change over time to quite lively entertainment programmes, with the characters listed in a very humorous style.

After the outbreak of the Second World War, the annual dinners were set aside but when the drawing office dinners recommenced towards the end of the war, all the entertainment was completely home-grown. Members of the design team demonstrated their talents and skills in playing musical instruments, taking part in sketches, and a range of solo and group singing. The cover of the 1944 Vickers-Armstrongs Supermarine design staff dinner was a good example of the humorous and lively entertainment that was to follow. The chairman, Alan Clifton (Cliffy), is shown standing at the head table and making a speech to the staff members, saying, 'Need I say, Gentlemen, how pleased we are to have the management with us this evening,' while the illustration shows a number of inebriated gentlemen who were no doubt enjoying themselves! The 1945 cover represented a painting in a frame of Joe Smith with the title 'The Old Master'. The chairman was Lovell-Cooper, and the evening was a celebration of Smith having been awarded the CBE in 1945.

By this time, the staff at the dinners eagerly waited for Smith to deliver his annual speech. The 1946 Supermarine design staff dinner was held at Hursley Park on Friday, 13 December, and the chairman for the evening was Arthur Black, head of research. However, in an article written about the evening, reference was made to Smith's invitation to make a speech: 'During his opening speech the chairman remarked that no Supermarine function would be complete without a few words from their Chief Designer, and asked him to deliver his promised "words of wisdom".' Smith admitted that his reactions to these requests for a speech were always the same. First, he felt a sense of deep gratitude that he should be asked to speak at all; secondly, he invariably found himself without a single idea as to what to say; and lastly, he was always smitten with remorse because inevitably he made a resolution to prepare a speech

The 1945 cover of the design office dinner menu to celebrate Joe Smith receiving his CBE: 'The Master'. *Judy Monger*

The cover of the 1948 design office dinner menu with Ernie Mansbridge riding his famous wartime caravan. *Judy Monger*

specially written for the occasion but never managed to do so. Having thus made his apologies, he remarked on the magnificent spirit of the Supermarine team and proceeded in his inimitable style to poke some fun at his colleagues, which caused considerable amusement, particularly among the recipients.

From then on, each year the front cover had a picture relating to the chairman for the evening, starting with 'His Worship' Alf Faddy in 1947, then Ernie Mansbridge and his caravan in 1948, but in 1949 it was a special year being the 25th design staff annual dinner with Smith in the chair. The front cover showed Smith driving 'A Street Car Called Designer', powered by a jet engine on the roof with an added note, 'latest success'.

There were also Supermarine technical office parties held at the Court Royal Hotel, and examples of these were held in February and November 1950. The dinners continued, but in 1956, the year that Smith died, the chairman was E.J. Davis, with a picture and the menu added beneath on the same page. It was as though the spirit of Supermarine had begun to disappear, which in fact is what did happen over the next few years.

The annual dinner at Hursley House with senior staff sitting at the ends of each table. From the front, facing the camera: Arthur Shirvall, Len Gooch, Eric Cooper, Joe Smith at the back. *Judy Monger*

The cover of the 25th anniversary design office dinner menu in 1949, entitled 'A Street Car Called Designer'. *Judy Monger*

9

DEVELOPMENT OF PHOTOGRAPHIC RECONNAISSANCE

The arrival of the Zeppelin over Southampton, as mentioned earlier, had raised concern over the possibility that it was on a reconnaissance mission and taking photographs of the docks and the Supermarine factory for bombing attacks in a future war. The thought that Britain was undertaking similar missions was perhaps not in the minds of most people, and before the start of the Second World War photographic reconnaissance was not considered a high priority by the Air Ministry. But by September 1938, it had become obvious that Germany was preparing for war, and there was an urgent need to conduct some clandestine reconnaissance flights over German factories, airfields and other military areas.

At the time, Sidney Cotton ran the Aeronautical Research and Sales Corporation which was based at Heston aerodrome, and regularly flew in his own Hudson aircraft to the Continent. He was well known in the countries he visited, including Germany, and an ideal candidate to carry out the secret missions over areas of the Mediterranean, the Middle East and Germany.

Sidney Cotton's Background

Cotton was born in Australia but came to England at the age of 21 to serve in the RNAS in 1915. After learning to fly, he became a fighter pilot, but his skills as an inventor came to the fore in 1917 when his experience of the intense cold when flying at high altitudes caused him to develop the Sidcot suit, which kept pilots warm in their cockpits. It was so successful that the suit was still being used by RAF pilots long after the Second World War had finished. However, after being promoted to flight sub-lieutenant in 1917, his unconventional approach found him in conflict with senior officers, leading him to resign his commission shortly afterwards.

The Secret Intelligence Service (SIS)

It was in late 1938 that Cotton was recruited by Maj. Fred Winterbotham for the SIS, and at the same time he recruited Robert H. Niven who had come over from Canada to join the RAF as a pilot. Once in place, Cotton requested that a civilian Lockheed L-12A Electra be shipped from the USA to Southampton. The parts for the aircraft were brought on the steamship *Aquitania* in April 1939 and then taken to Eastleigh aerodrome where the aircraft was assembled by Cunliffe-Owen Aircraft Ltd.

On 11 May 1939, Cotton and Flt Lt Niven took off from Eastleigh in the Lockheed L-12A which had been registered as G-AFTL. The aircraft had been camouflaged in a light green, based on the experience of Cotton, who had seen an aircraft take off in a similar colour and disappear from his view once airborne. He therefore considered this a good camouflage colour for his photographic missions.

Once the aircraft had been fitted with cameras, the clandestine photographic reconnaissance operations were ready to begin. These were undertaken in June

The Lockheed L-12A was used by Sidney Cotton for his secret photographic missions before the war. *Alan Mansell*

1939, when they flew to Malta as a base to embark on photo reconnaissance covering Mediterranean areas including Sicily, Egypt and the North African coastline before returning to Heston in early July. From then on, photographic reconnaissance missions were undertaken from Heston to Europe, including Berlin and other German cities.

Cotton was very friendly and persuasive, and was able to invite and encourage important German figures to fly with him. Unbeknown to them, he photographed the military installations and airfields they flew over. This was demonstrated when Luftwaffe officer Albert Kesselring offered to fly the aircraft, and did so while Cotton secretly operated cameras from under his seat, photographing the German airfields below. He also took Hermann Goering for a flight while in Berlin in 1939, and continued with his photographic work secretly even while Goering was flying with him. Cotton claimed that his aircraft was the last civilian plane to leave Berlin before hostilities started.

Bombers Converted for Photographic Reconnaissance

The photo reconnaissance aircraft used by the RAF before the Second World War were bombers that had been converted for photographic work, but they retained their armaments because their slow speed made them easy prey for the Luftwaffe fighters. Bristol Blenheims were used for long-range photo reconnaissance and the Westland Lysanders for shorter photographic missions, but sustained heavy losses while flying over Germany.

The Air Ministry became interested in the benefits of photographic reconnaissance through the exploits of Cotton and wanted to know in-depth details of his aerial photographic work. Cotton was summoned to the Air Ministry on 12 September 1939 and asked if he could assist in the appraisal. Keen to prove how effective the photographic work was, he immediately took off that afternoon in the L-12A and photographed the whole of the Dutch coastline, and when he attended the next meeting, on 17 September, he showed the photographs to the senior Air Ministry officials. They were suitably impressed; he was commissioned on 22 September 1939 into the RAF with the acting rank of wing commander and put in command of the Heston Flight, which in fact was the No 2 Camouflage Unit, a cover name for the PDU (No 1 Photographic Development Unit). The cover name was given to keep the work of the group secret. When the No 2 Camouflage Unit received its Bristol Blenheims, Cotton was not happy because their speed was too slow to undertake effective photographic reconnaissance missions and return safely to Heston.

In August 1939, Flg Off. Maurice 'Shorty' Longbottom also recognised the need for photographic reconnaissance, especially for pre-planning bombing missions, but believed that the aircraft used should be able to 'fly high and fly fast'. He wrote to the Air Ministry to bring to its attention the versatility of the Spitfire, which could fly at high speed with a good rate of climb and was able to work at high altitude, thus avoiding the enemy defences. He considered that these attributes fitted the Spitfire for long-range photographic reconnaissance use. At the time, the Air Ministry declined because there were not enough fighter aircraft in production to consider diverting any for photo reconnaissance purposes.

From then on, there was combined pressure from Cotton and Longbottom to the Air Ministry suggesting quite firmly that airborne reconnaissance was better with small, single-seat aircraft which could maintain a fast speed at a high altitude and avoid the early detection that the slower Bristol Blenheims were subjected to. They asked if some Spitfires could be released for this work and have their armaments and radios removed so that two F24 cameras and extra fuel tanks could be fitted for long-range photographic reconnaissance work. Their requests were accepted by Fighter Command when they released two Spitfire Mk Is with the registrations N3069 and N3071. The aircraft were then converted by Heston Aircraft Ltd for photo reconnaissance, and to ensure effective camouflage, as recognised by Cotton, were painted with a special paint called Camotint which was a pale blue-green colour. Flying at high altitude was going to be a problem, so heating equipment was fitted on all photo reconnaissance aircraft to avoid the cameras freezing.

As well as the No 2 Camouflage Unit there was a section called the Special Survey Group (No 2 Photographic Development Unit) operating from Seclin in France, but this was renamed as 212 Squadron, again for security purposes, with the aim to confuse the Germans as to what the unit was actually doing. They remained at Seclin until the fall of France.

Flg Off. Longbottom flew the first operational flight of a Spitfire PR Mk IA from Seclin on 18 November 1939 over the area between the Siegfried and Maginot Lines. Teardrop windows had been fitted on each side of the cockpit to give better downward vision and the aircraft was also fitted with two vertical F24 cameras. On 22 November 1939, Longbottom again took off and photographed the Aachen area of Germany. However, low cloud restricted operations until 21 December when photographs were taken of Düsseldorf, Aachen and Cologne, which was so successful that it led to a whole series of PR variants with increased fuel loads and a variety of camera installations. Camera installations for the PR Mk IA to PR Mk IC included two vertical F24 cameras, and the other PR aircraft, including PR X, PR XI and PR XIX, had universal camera installations of either two vertical F52 cameras or two vertical F8 cameras, or two vertical F24 cameras and one oblique camera.

Wg Cdr Cotton and his 'Private Air Force'

Cotton was not one for red tape and would go his own way, resulting in the PDU becoming known as 'Sidney Cotton's Private Air Force', or 'Cotton's Club', or the not-so-complimentary 'Cotton's Crooks'! During his time leading the photographic unit, his efforts and skills created advanced work in photographic development and resulted in the PDU aircraft taking stereoscope photographs from high altitude and at high speed. However, his attitude to authority and the way he ran his 'private air force' became an embarrassment to the Air Ministry and, on 16 June 1940, a letter was sent from the Air Ministry thanking him for all his work with the PDU but informing him that his command was to be taken over by Wg Cdr Tuttle. The unit was moved to RAF Hendon under a new name from July 1940, as the PRU (Photographic Reconnaissance Unit) and was of great importance to target identification throughout the war.

Spitfire PR Development: PR Mk IA to PR Mk IG

Following on from the Spitfire PR Mk IA was the PR Mk IB, a medium-range version with a 29-gallon (131.83-litre) fuel tank behind the pilot and no armaments. It was first used in February 1940 to photograph German naval bases.

The PR Mk IC (PR Mk III) was a long-range version with a 30-gallon (136.38-litre) fuel tank under the port wing and a 29-gallon (131.83-litre) fuel tank behind the pilot, two cameras under the starboard wing and was not armed. It was first introduced into service in March 1940, and the recognition of the importance of photographic reconnaissance was demonstrated by the large numbers of this aircraft that were produced.

The PR Mk ID (PR Mk IV) was for very long range, carrying 57 gallons (259.12 litres) in each wing leading edge and a 29-gallon (131.83-litre) fuel tank behind the pilot, and had a rounded windscreen with bulged canopy and carried two vertical F24 cameras. Oxygen was available when flying high and it was unarmed. The aircraft entered service in October 1940 and was nicknamed The Bowser because of the amount of fuel it could carry.

The PR Mk IE (PR Mk V) was a medium-range version for low-level work, and there was just one conversion of Mk I (N3317). This aircraft was the first to be fitted

The PR Mk ID was a conversion of a Spitfire Mk I for photo reconnaissance. With extra long range and increased fuel capacity but no armaments, it later became the PR Mk IV. *Solent Sky*

P9453 PR Mk IV was based in France with 212 Squadron and used for experimental flights by Flt Lt Longbottom. In September 1940, the aircraft failed to return from a low-level sortie. *Solent Sky*

with an oblique camera mounted in the side to improve the low-level photography (vertical cameras were ideal for medium- or high-level photographs).

The PR Mk IF (PR VI) carried two F24 vertical cameras and was an extra-long-range variant with a 30-gallon (136.38-litre) tank under each wing and a 29-gallon (131.83-litre) tank behind the pilot. This was aimed at giving the aircraft the range to reach and photograph Berlin, which it did in March 1941.

The PR Mk IG (PR Mk VII) carried one oblique and two vertical F24 cameras. The use of the oblique camera for low-level photography placed the aircraft within range of German fighters and as there were no fuel tanks in the wings, the opportunity was taken to fit eight machine guns so it could defend itself from attack. The aircraft had a bullet-proof windscreen and a 29-gallon (131.83-litre) tank behind the pilot.

For some low-level PR aircraft there was a decision to use a very pale pink camouflage, which had the advantage of blending in with the clouds above and making the aircraft invisible when seen from the ground. This was most effective when the photo reconnaissance operations were conducted at sunrise or sunset, when the sun was low in the sky. However, there was a disadvantage if enemy aircraft were flying above the PR Spitfire because its pale pink camouflage clearly silhouetted it against the ground, whereas brown and green camouflage was more effective in these circumstances.

Murry White refers to the time when Cotton first conceived the idea of carrying fuel in the wing leading edges:

> It was a major step in Photographic Reconnaissance history. With the leading edges already assembled it was also very difficult to achieve and fuel leaks were a constant problem. This problem was partially cured by sealing components of the leading edge assemblies during manufacture and then employing a 'slushing' rig developed by Arthur Black and his boys in the laboratory. This wing became known as the 'D' Wing.

R7059 first flew in February 1941 as a Spitfire Mk I, but was converted to a PR Mk VII Type G and painted pale pink. Later, in 1943, the aircraft crashed due to engine failure. *Solent Sky*

Spitfire PR Mk IX

A number of PR Mk IXs were converted from the Mk IX fighter in November 1942, provided with a slipper tank under the fuselage to engage in long-range work.

Spitfire PR Mk X

The PR X variant had either a Merlin 64 or 77 engine powering it at 416mph (669.48km/h), with a range of 1,370 miles (2,204.8km) and a ceiling of 43,000ft (13,196.4m). This unarmed, high flying aircraft had a pressurised cabin and extra provision for fuel to give it a greater range, and universal camera installation. It came into service in early 1944, but only a small number were produced and it was in service only until September 1945.

Spitfire PR Mk XI

The PR Mk XI version had either a Merlin 61, 63, 63A or 70 engine powering it at a speed of 422mph (679.14km/h), with a range of 1,200 miles (1,931.21km) and a ceiling of 44,000ft (13,412.2m). It first flew on 21 November 1942, and 471 were produced, exceeding the numbers of any other PR variant. A number of PR Mk XIs were tropicalised for overseas service. The aircraft was in service from the summer of 1943.

Both the PR Mk X and PR Mk XI were long-range variants, each aircraft carrying 85 gallons (386.41 litres) in the fuselage and 133 gallons (604.62 litres) in the wings.

Spitfire PR Mk XIII

On 4 August 1942, the Mk IA that had been converted to a Mk VA flew to the Heston aircraft workshops to be fitted with a new Merlin 32 engine, one oblique and two vertical F24 cameras and four .303 Browning machine guns. This aircraft was designated PR Mk XIII and was in service in 1943, conducting low-level photographic flights. It was used in advance of the D-Day landings to take photographs of the Normandy beaches.

SW777 was ordered in April 1944 as a prototype F.21, but was completed as a PR Mk XIX at High Post in 1945. *Solent Sky*

Spitfire PR Mk XIX

This was the last of the photographic reconnaissance Spitfires, and was the only PR mark with a Griffon 65 or 66 engine powering a five-bladed propeller. The PR Mk XIX had increased tankage, with 82½ gallons (375.05 litres) in the fuselage and 133 gallons (604.62 litres) in the wings. It was tropicalised and had universal camera installation. With a pressurised cockpit and teardrop hood, its role was high flying reconnaissance, and it was noted as one of the fastest Spitfires with a speed of 446mph (717.76km/h). The Spitfire PR Mk XIX entered service in May and was the aircraft to fly the last sortie with the RAF in April 1954.

Fighter Reconnaissance

As well as the PR versions, some fighters were converted to fighter reconnaissance. The FR Mk XIV was converted in 1944, with a camera in the fuselage and an extra 34-gallon (154.56-litre) fuel tank to increase its range. The other aircraft converted was the FR Mk XVIII. This was powered by a Griffon 65 engine with standard wings. Armaments consisted of two 0.5mm machine guns and two 20mm cannons, with a camera installation of one oblique F24 or one vertical F52 and two vertical F24s, and it was tropicalised. The FR Mk XVIII had increased tankage, with 85 gallons (386.41 litres) in the fuselage and 25½ gallons (115.92 litres) in the wings.

The FR Mk XIV and FR Mk XVIII were low-level reconnaissance aircraft with a teardrop canopy that aided rearward vision for the pilot.

10

THE WAR YEARS
IN SOUTHAMPTON

With the threat of war looming in the late 1930s it became clear that if hostilities broke out, Southampton would be a high priority target for the Luftwaffe because it was the principal military port and a major commercial port with shipbuilding and ship repair facilities. It was also, of course, where the Supermarine works was based, where the Spitfire was being built.

The authorities prepared well with advanced air-raid precautions, including blackout rehearsals and bomb shelters identified for the public. Tony Kenyon lived in Chessel Avenue in the city, and with the panic of the war coming he can remember the scenes when trenches were being dug on The Common: 'Everywhere you went something was happening, such as making air raid shelters, informing about gas attacks, because everyone was certain that gas attacks would happen.'

In total, there were fifty-seven bombing raids on Southampton, especially Southampton Docks and the Supermarine factories, but one of the most tragic stories was the 500lb bomb direct hit on the School of Art in the Civic Centre. This was on the afternoon of 6 November 1940, when twelve bombs were dropped on the city. A total of thirty people were killed by the bomb on the Civic Centre and although not all children went to the air-raid shelter in the basement, it made very little difference as fourteen children were killed, as well as their teacher and many other adults. Only one child in the air-raid shelter survived. This was the start of Southampton's Blitz in the last weeks of November, and particularly on 30 November and 1 December when the city centre was almost destroyed and other bomb sites arose around the city centre and suburbs.

Despite the bombing, life still went on, and Lily Bartlett remembers the fun they had as young girls:

At the time we did not worry too much that it was wartime because we were young girls and had a lot of fun. I suppose because we were young we were a bit more daring in those days and I would go to the cinema and dances with my friends, despite my mum not being very happy. When we went to dances the band would keep playing if there was a raid. If they stopped you got out quickly, especially if there were incendiary flares landing. We were in the cinema the night a big raid started and we left and ran through the park with the shrapnel hitting the ground all around us.

When they bombed the High Street, Below Bar, it was complete devastation. My friend and I walked up the High Street just after the raid. It was terrible with the tramlines buckled and buildings collapsed, including the Palace cinema where we used to go. There was the glow and heat from the fires all around. It was so hot from the fires that it was like a very hot day in summer.

David Noyce also remembers that during the first year after war was declared, the bombing of Southampton took place both day and night but was fairly sporadic. He recalls having to go to the air-raid shelter at the bottom of the garden, but as an 11-year-old it was more exciting than frightening. David and his father would often stand outside, watching the searchlights sweeping the skies and looking for German aircraft. He also remembers seeing the special Supermarine lorry going up Peartree Avenue daily, taking the Spitfire fuselages to the Eastleigh factory for their final assembly and testing.

The Battle of Britain

After the German invasion of France in 1940, the British Expeditionary Force and Allied forces in Europe were compelled to evacuate from the Dunkirk beaches from 26 May to 4 June, under the code name Operation Dynamo. Luftwaffe airfields were then established just across the English Channel in France and air attacks on southern England became increasingly frequent, culminating in the Battle of Britain which came in three phases starting on 10 July and continuing until 31 October 1940. The three phases were as follows:

Channel convoys and ports
The Luftwaffe attacked and bombed with the aim to force Britain into a crisis caused by a lack of urgent supplies, including food, ammunition, oil and other materials for the war effort. They intended not only to attack and sink ships in the convoys bringing important supplies but also to put the ports out of action so they could not handle cargo arriving from ships that had survived the attacks.

Fighter Command and airfields

The aim was to destroy all means of air defence, including radar, command centres and airfields, with the destruction of hangars, aircraft on the ground, and RAF personnel working on repairs and maintenance of aircraft.

Aircraft factories and airfields

The focus was on attacking and destroying aircraft factories building the wartime fighters and bombers, and the airfields that were used for testing and delivering the aircraft to RAF bases.

The German offensive against Channel convoys, RAF Fighter Command airfields and aircraft factories was the start of a series of attacks to weaken the defence of Britain before Operation Sea Lion, the German code name for the invasion of Britain. The date chosen by Adolf Hitler for the invasion to take place was 15 September 1940.

'*Adler Tag*' or 'Eagle Day'

On 13 August 1940, the Luftwaffe launched '*Adler Tag*' or 'Eagle Day'. This was seen by the Germans as the day the Battle of Britain really began, and although airfields were attacked it appeared that the most serious bombing took place at Southampton and Birmingham where there were two important aircraft factories. At 16.23 hours major damage was caused to Southampton Docks, with many of the sheds bombed and several fires started. One of the most serious fires was at the International Cold Store, which caused many tons of butter to burn for days. There is a story that the building was set on fire by a German aircraft from a bomber group that had just attacked the Cunliffe-Owen aircraft works at Eastleigh aerodrome. The planes were flying away from Eastleigh and over Southampton when the Bofors gun crew on the roof of the International Cold Store decided to fire at the aircraft. One German pilot was not happy with this and circled around, dropping a bomb on the roof, which knocked out the gun crew and also set fire to the building. Tony Kenyon remembers that his father was working there when it was hit:

> My father had been a mariner, but was working as a superintendent in the docks when it was bombed. He was working at the Cold Store when it had a direct hit and caught fire. The bottom section, the basement of the Cold Store, was divided into four sections and my father looked in and saw people sat there up to their knees in rubble and who had all been killed by the attack.

A fireman came along and told my father, 'We've got to get you out of here.' They had hoses played on them as they came out, but there was no other attempt made to get back into the building.

Spitfires and Hurricanes Available for the Battle of Britain

The importance of getting as many aircraft ready for air attacks had been recognised. By 17 August 1940, RAF Fighter Command had 675 Hurricanes and 348 Spitfires available for the Battle of Britain. Owing to the delay in production, fewer Spitfires than Hurricanes that took part in the battle, thus limiting their involvement. However, because 603 and 609 Squadrons were flying Spitfires from their coastal airfields, they were able to score heavy successes against the German aircraft. The Spitfire was a popular aircraft with the pilots, but the guns were more difficult to keep on the target than those of the Hurricane which was a more stable gun platform.

The numbers of aircraft available to the Luftwaffe far outnumbered the British fighters, but with the British radar systems giving early warning of German aircraft crossing the English Channel it was possible to get many more fighters into the air in advance of the arrival of the bombers and fighters. This allowed the British fighters more time in the air and, because the attacks were over Britain, the opportunity for them to land in order to refuel, rearm and get back in the air to continue the battle, something the German fighters could not do. The overall success of the Spitfires and Hurricanes in the Battle of Britain prevented the Luftwaffe gaining air superiority prior to launching an invasion of Britain.

On 11 September 1940, German aircraft dive-bombed Eastleigh Naval Air Station without causing any damage but, more seriously, eight Bf 110s also dive-bombed the Cunliffe-Owen aircraft works that day. After the sirens had sounded, many of the workers made for the shelters but some made the decision to make for the woods which were further away. Barrie Bryant remembers the raid well. At the time, he was in the flight shed at Eastleigh measuring the weight and centre of gravity of P9551 (the first Type 'D' Spitfire, later called the PR Mk IV), but was interrupted by a spell in the shelter. The casualties after the attack were recorded as twenty-eight killed and seventy injured due to a shelter being hit.

The Luftwaffe attacked London with two large formations of bombers on 15 September, the day Adolf Hitler had chosen for the invasion of Britain (and now known as Battle of Britain Day), but were heavily defeated by the RAF. Hitler then cancelled the planned invasion of Britain and turned his attention to attacking Russia. Although the daytime air raids were to continue over London and the south of England into October 1940, the Germans were losing more aircraft than they could repair or replace, forcing them to change to night-time raids.

It was during the Battle of Britain that the Luftwaffe realised the importance of the Spitfire when in conflict with their aircraft, their overall aim being to gain air superiority which would then enable the invasion of Britain by German forces to take place. However, the British Government proved it had made a sound decision in building the Castle Bromwich 'shadow factory' because the Supermarine Woolston and Itchen works were attacked and destroyed by German aircraft on 24 and 26 September 1940, and the dispersal across the south of England for continuing production of the Spitfire began.

Spitfire Floatplanes

Prior to the invasion of Norway by Germany in 1940 under the code name Operation Weserübung, Britain and France sent an expeditionary force to support Norway, and although the conflict lasted from April until June 1940, the outcome was eventual withdrawal. Supermarine were asked to convert a Spitfire to a floatplane for operation in the sheltered waters of the Norwegian fjords.

Type 355 Mk V W3760 floatplane, converted by Follands and capable of 324mph (521.43km/h). *Solent Sky*

In the spring of 1944, it was planned to convert Mk IX MJ892 to a floatplane for use in the Pacific war. Following tests it was reconverted to a land plane. *Solent Sky*

One Mk I Spitfire (R6722) was used and, due to the limited amount of time available, Blackburn Roc floats were fitted. The floatplane was completed on time, but owing to the fall of France, and the subsequent German attacks on the Continent, the Norwegian campaign was suspended. With the urgent need for fighter aircraft for the Battle of Britain, R6722 (a Type 342) was reconverted back to a standard Spitfire.

Later, in 1943, the Admiralty saw the need for floatplanes to combat and disrupt German transport aircraft operating in the Mediterranean and requested that a Spitfire Mk VB be modified to use as a floatplane fighter. The work was carried out by Follands and a modified Mk VB Spitfire, W3760, was converted along with two other floatplanes, EP751 and EP754, and dispatched to be based at the Great Bitter Lake in Egypt. In 1944, one Spitfire Mk IX (MJ892) was converted to a floatplane for possible use in the war in the Pacific, but this came to nothing and MJ892 was reconverted back to a Spitfire.

11

SUPERMARINE PREPARES FOR WARTIME CONTINGENCIES

The Spitfire had gained much international attention by 1939, and in the first half of the year a number of countries, including Estonia, Greece and Turkey, had placed export orders with Supermarine. Only a small number of the Spitfire orders had been delivered before the outbreak of the Second World War, which brought an end to any further contracts for export orders. Furthermore, Spitfire production in the south of England at the start of the conflict was a concern to the Air Ministry. This was a crucial time for Britain because of the necessity for building up an effective fighter aircraft force to meet the increasing air attacks on southern England, and the building of the Spitfire fighter was urgently required to defend the country.

In 1939, Jeffrey Quill met Charles Lindbergh, the first aviator to fly solo across the Atlantic in 1927, and showed him around the Supermarine factory after he arrived in his own aircraft. Lindbergh had previously been to Germany, having been invited by Hermann Goering, and had been very impressed with what he regarded as a highly advanced aircraft industry. Quill commented that Lindbergh appeared less favourably impressed with the Supermarine factory buildings than he was with the very modern German factories.

Advance Preparedness by Supermarine in Identifying Dispersal Sites

Supermarine had been fully aware of the possibility of the Luftwaffe bombing their factories. They decided to initiate a dispersal plan to maintain production should the factories be attacked and damaged or destroyed. In November 1939, with greater concern over the threat of attack, the Accounts Department of Supermarine was moved to Deepdene House in Southampton.

Leonard Gooch was a young engineer who had first started his career in engineering working for the Southern Railway at Eastleigh. In November 1935, he joined Supermarine, working at first in Alan Shirvall's project office, which was responsible for new manufacturing techniques. In December 1939, Gooch was appointed works engineer, responsible to the production manager John Butler, and given the job of planning a complete production line of suitable premises in the Southampton area. He was also to plan and organise the transportation of the Spitfire parts from the dispersal sites to Eastleigh aerodrome for final assembly and then flight-testing.

Gooch started on the initial planning and delegated Gilbert Olsen to put the plans into operation. Olsen was a young foreman with effective organisational skills which he put to good use creating a system of dispersed workshops in which the Spitfire parts could be constructed. Despite many of the workers employed to build the aircraft not having the necessary skills of an experienced aircraft engineer, they were able to adapt to the job through this well-organised system. Other senior management assisted in the planned dispersal and were successful in identifying a number of locations that would be suitable, including bus depots, laundries and garages; in fact anywhere that could be used for production of the Spitfire in order to avoid such a large-scale loss in any future attacks on the factories.

The sites identified in Southampton included Hendy's Garage at Pond Street Lane, Seward's Garage and Sunlight Laundry in Winchester Road. Both the garages had two floors, the upper floor being reached by a ramp. Another garage earmarked was Lowther's Garage in Shirley, and it was planned that the important jig borer, which was temperature controlled, would be situated here. The requisitioning of the sites was not really a problem for the garages as their trade in selling cars to private motorists had virtually disappeared. The First World War Rolling Mills at Weston became the base for the production of the aircraft tanks and for the work of the coppersmiths.

Supermarine's preparedness ensured that the new dispersal plan was completed and in operation by 20 September 1940, just days before the attacks on the factories began and in advance of the order given by Lord Beaverbrook for dispersal of production across the south following the bombing of the Supermarine factories on 24 and 26 September.

Shelters Built for Supermarine Staff

Supermarine set about arranging for the construction of bomb shelters for their staff, and Arthur Black, chemist and metallurgist, was given the responsibility of being air-raid precaution officer. The main shelters for the staff from both the Itchen and Woolston works were built on a railway embankment on the opposite side of the railway lines. The problem was that the shelters were quite a distance from the factories; when the siren went, the workers had to go under a narrow brick railway bridge to reach them. It was quite possible that the walkway under the bridge could become a dangerous bottleneck when the workers were hurrying to get to the shelters.

Shelter allocation numbers were issued and practice evacuations took place without notice, but it soon became clear that if Supermarine kept to the system as advised, which was for all workers to leave the moment the sirens were sounded, a lot of production time would be wasted. The decision was made to leave it to the observers on the roof, who would only switch on the warning sirens when they saw the German aircraft approaching. However, this left many workers with little time to get out of the factory; when they did, some of them still had to run at least 500 yards (457.2m) and through the railway arch before they got to safety. The time at which the sirens went off could make all the difference as to whether workers could get to the shelters or not. The first warning that the Luftwaffe were aiming for the Supermarine factories was on Sunday, 15 September 1940 when approximately fifty enemy aircraft flew over the Isle of Wight and attacked Southampton. The bombers flew over the Woolston area and dropped their bombs, creating substantial damage to houses and buildings surrounding the Supermarine Woolston and Itchen works but not causing any damage to the factories. However, that was to come just over a week later, on Tuesday, 24 September.

The Bombing of the Supermarine Factories

The decision to delay sounding the sirens until the raiders were seen approaching the factories was to prove a disaster because, just four days after the completion of the dispersal plan, the Luftwaffe attacked the Supermarine factories. It was at 13.30 hours on 24 September that the Observer Corps post at Sandown on the Isle of Wight reported seeing hostile aircraft at 15,000ft (4,572m) flying towards Portsmouth. The formation of Messerschmitt Bf 110 bombers turned away from their Portsmouth heading and flew up Southampton Water and then overland to attack the Supermarine works on the River Itchen. Although there had been a warning from the Observer Corps on the Isle of Wight, no sirens were sounded in the factory, and the warnings were given only after the bombs were released by the Luftwaffe.

The guns opened up and a Messerschmitt was shot down, but there were no direct hits on the works, just near misses that blew in the windows and took off a roof, causing damage to some of the Spitfire fuselages. However, the most tragic thing about this attack was the direct hit on an air-raid shelter where many aircraft workers were killed or injured. One of those killed was Olsen, the young foreman who had been tasked to organise the start of the dispersal units in Southampton, and who Murry White had got to know quite well when Olsen had taken over the Itchen works. Fortunately, quite a few of the workers were not happy about having to go to the designated shelters and made other arrangements, which for some was a wise decision that day, because they were either too late to make the shelters or had left the works for other shelters away from the factory.

Lily Bartlett, who was in the factory but was unable to get to the shelters in time, remembers one plane flying over before the bombing started and being told that it had been taking photographs. It was when the planes went over that the sirens started, so they could not get out of the factory in time. Lily saw the bombs leave the aircraft, describing them as 'big and black', but found it funny when one girl held a metal dustbin lid over her head! It was fortunate for Lily that the sirens went too late for them to leave, because they would have gone to their allotted shelter:

I think the bombs hit the shelter we were supposed to go in and where many people were killed, so we were lucky. We would have been in the shelter if the sirens hadn't been late. It was unlucky for those that worked in the Itchen factory that was nearer to the shelters because they were the ones that were bombed.

Jessie Mason had a similar experience to Lily when the factory was bombed on 24 September 1940:

We could not get out to make for the shelters and I remember I was down on my knees with my sister who also worked at Supermarine and everyone was singing 'Somewhere over the Rainbow' while the bombing was going on.

For those working in the office block at the Woolston works it was a matter of getting out of the building as quickly as possible once the sirens sounded. Murry White remembers he was working with Sammy Hughes on the fourth floor of the office block when the siren sounded. They rushed out down the steps but by the time they got outside, the aircraft were overhead and machine-gunning. Someone shouted, 'Get Down!' and when the aircraft had passed over they had to run along to Shelter No 1. The shelters were about 500-600 yards (460-550m) away, and Murry recalls that when they got there, the shelter they had been allotted had received a direct hit, killing everyone who had managed to get there from the Itchen works:

> Sammy and I weren't sure what to do, but there was a Bofors gun in the corner of the field and so we thought we would go over and got in a ditch. We stayed there until the 'all clear' went and then we went back to the office at the Woolston works which hadn't been hit, but the only thing that had been damaged was the sawmill and that was going up in smoke.
>
> The next day a reconnaissance aircraft came over and we didn't know where to go so we rushed down to the boiler house, which was the most ridiculous place to go because we would have been scalded to death if the boiler house had been hit!

Alf Faddy was another who survived the Woolston factory bombing that day. David Faddy says that his father declined to go into the shelter to which he was allocated and instead drove his car to Peartree Green above the cliff into which the shelters had been built. It was the very shelter that Faddy was allocated that the bomb hit and almost everyone inside was killed. Not only did he survive the shelter bombing, but his house in Eynham Avenue received a direct hit by an incendiary bomb while he was asleep. The result of the bombing made the house inhabitable so he went to lodge with the mother of one of his team, Charles Labette, in the lodge of Longwood House, near Owslebury.

Following the attack on 24 September, the nightshift was cancelled and work commenced the next day on salvaging as much as possible. A Dornier Do 17 had subsequently flown across the Isle of Wight and over the Supermarine factories; obviously on a photographic mission to check on the damage. The Luftwaffe, having studied the photographs the next day, realised that more needed to be done and attacked again on 26 September.

The Supermarine Factories are Destroyed

Enemy aircraft were at first seen on the new radar screens at the Chain Home stations leaving France. Immediately warnings were given of an impending attack. As the Luftwaffe aircraft crossed the Isle of Wight at the Needles, it was estimated that there were a substantial number of bombers and fighters intent on destroying the Supermarine factories, and at 16.00 hours the sirens were sounded. The aircraft passed over Hythe, crossed the water and flew directly over the River Itchen, and with a massive 'carpet bombing' completely destroyed the Woolston works and what was left of the Itchen works. This attack did not go unchallenged. It was reported that a series of 'dogfights' took place in the skies overhead, with the shooting down of German aircraft but also the loss of some of our own Hurricanes and Spitfires.

Jessie Mason and some friends had been told to get out of the factory as the dope shop was on fire. They ran out as fast as they could to the shelter on Peartree Green. As they got near the shelter, they were machine-gunned but managed to make it safely. Eric Lovell-Cooper remembers looking out of his office window and seeing the bombs dropping from the German aircraft. The staff watched the planes flying so low that they could see the pilots waving at them as they went by!

Joe Smith managed to rescue the plans for the Spitfire from the raging fire started by the incendiary bombs. However, he was unable to retrieve the B.12/36 bomber plans, and both bombers under construction were destroyed by the fire.

Getting Away from the Factory

Murry White and his colleagues made arrangements to leave the factory when the air-raid siren sounded, intending to go to the house of George Nicholas who was living on Peartree Green, a quarter of a mile up the hill. Supermarine had made it a condition that nobody was allowed to move their cars out of the car park after an air-raid warning had sounded, so Murry agreed to leave his car at Peartree Common on the top of the hill. When the air-raid warning went, he and Sammy Hughes together with George Nicholas rushed to the car and drove to the house, which was not far away:

> ... when we got to his house his sweet little wife came out, saying that she had made the tea. We then got in the Anderson shelter in the garden with our tea!
>
> When it was all over we went back and found the factory and the offices had been hit. We went to see what was happening and Ernie Mansbridge gave me petrol coupons and folders of calculations which he told me to put in my car and take up to the Southampton University where I would find a chap there who would tell me what to do with them. So that is what I did, and I did it for most of the afternoon and the early evening, and the next day. I did it continually all the time.

Barrie Bryant who had taken over the weights department went past my house and called in to tell my mother that I was alright and that I would be late home. I thought that was so jolly nice of him, and I have never forgotten it. My mother was in tears when I went home, but so grateful to Barrie for doing that.

Fred Veal also remembers the attacks on Southampton. The Supermarine workshops were in the Itchen valley, and the bombers came across at a right angle to the line of the buildings. On the hill there were houses, and the bombs started to hit them until the Germans changed their tactics and destroyed the works:

I remember I never liked the shelters because it was a long time to get to them, and you could be in danger walking along the road, under a railway bridge and I didn't like it. I used to keep my cycle just outside the works and near to where I was working, and when the siren went, instead of heading for the shelter I would get on my bike and ride home because I only lived in Sholing which was only about five minutes away on a cycle. The siren was for the whole area, so when I had cycled home to my parents I waited for the 'all clear' and then cycled back to work! Eventually when the factory had been destroyed there was no place to go back to.

When the sirens sounded on 26 September, the workers started to leave the factory, but this time Cyril Russell from the wheeling squad got his bike and cycled with Fred to his home in Sholing, not far from the factory. The guns opened up when they arrived, so they promptly joined Fred's mother and brother in the Anderson shelter in the garden. Just after the 'all clear' was sounded a single German aircraft flew over the works to photograph the damage, but while flying over Exbury on its return trip it was attacked and crash-landed on the Isle of Wight.

Fred would also go up onto Peartree Green and watch the fighters and bombers coming in. There were several anti-aircraft balloons around the city, and he remembers on one occasion seeing the German fighters coming in and shooting them down, and also seeing the bombers going in and bombing the docks. However, the closest experience he had with the bombing was not at the works. He was cycling to Pinegrove Road and looked up just as the bombers were going in:

I saw them release the bombs and saw them coming directly towards me, so I threw myself off my cycle and into the gutter. When I stood up they had hit the houses nearby and there was brick dust all over the place. That was

Serious damage caused to the Woolston works after bombing on 26 September 1940. The barrage balloons were no protection from the attacking Luftwaffe who came up the River Itchen. *Solent Sky*

Woolston and Itchen works after bombing. Behind the Itchen works is the railway embankment with the tunnel under. The bombing of the shelters can be seen on the other side. *Solent Sky*

the closest I came to danger, but there were people killed at Supermarine. I remember seeing one girl dead, and she was the girl Cyril Russell was friends with, and had taken her out a few weeks before. It was very sad as her body was covered up on a stretcher.

The next day the many casualties killed and injured were listed. It was also on that morning that Cyril was informed by his foreman, Bill Heaver, that a girl he knew had been killed the previous day. Cyril writes in his book *Spitfire Odyssey*:

He knew that a few weeks previously I had quite a crush on her, and we had gone to the Grand Theatre together. Her name was Peggy, and a lovelier girl one could not wish to know. Now she was dead, and how grateful I am that I was not the one who found her – but what a waste.

Spitfire Production Spreads Across Southern England

After the factories were destroyed on 26 September, Lord Beaverbrook, Winston Churchill's minister responsible for aircraft production, arrived at Southampton to discuss the problems and to initiate the organisation and establishment of a new recovery programme. After viewing the bomb damage to the Southampton factories, his decision was to disperse Spitfire production over southern England and along the South Coast away from Southampton. Among those sites identified that were further away from Southampton were Reading, Winchester, Chandler's Ford, Hursley, Newbury, Salisbury, Hungerford and Trowbridge.

While the dispersal was a good idea, it caused delays in production and initially it was difficult to ensure that all the parts for each mark of Spitfire were delivered to the correct site in time. This took some time to rectify. Supermarine appointed area managers for each of the dispersal sites, but one of the problems was finding accommodation for the workers who would be required to transfer from Southampton to work in the various sites.

Fred Veal remembers the dispersal made him slightly unpopular with the amount of room his wheeling machines took up. After the Supermarine works had been destroyed, other works premises were taken over and all equipment was removed in order for the machinery for the Supermarine workers to build Spitfires to be installed:

I worked in a garage in Winchester Road where there was a ramp going up to the top of the building. The dispersal extended further out from Southampton and one place I went to work was at a place called Southwick.

That was a place that produced heavy machinery, and they just threw all the machinery out into the fields and they installed all the machinery necessary for us to move in and work. I spent most of my time wheeling and producing the skins for the fuselage. That required a wheeling machine and the number of people working on it that took up a fair amount of room.

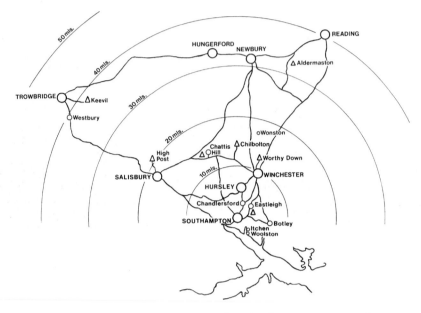

Dispersal map ranging out in concentric circles from Southampton every 10 miles to 50 miles. *Solent Sky*

Cyril and Fred were friends and both moved out of Southampton to work in Trowbridge. From there, they were transferred to Grove Street Garage in Salisbury where they worked for a while. However, when the Home Guard started, Fred was not keen on going on duty on Sunday mornings and decided to volunteer for the RAF. It was suggested by the RAF officers that, due to his skills gained from working at Supermarine, he should be working on their aircraft, and that is exactly what he did for four years. After the war ended, Fred returned to Supermarine but recalls that one of the best places he had ever worked at was Hursley Park. He was amused when he got there by being asked by the foreman if he had done any wheeling:

I then found myself working on the Attacker and the Swift. I really liked wheeling and spent the rest of my working life doing it. Until a few years ago I was self-employed, still doing wheeling, and both Cliff Colmer and I have worked in America helping in aircraft restoration.

Sunlight Laundry was used for detail fitting and sub-assembly. *Solent Sky*

Weston Rolling Mills

One of the sites that had been identified for dispersal was the Weston Rolling Mills on the shore at Netley, and it became the base for the tank and pipe fabrication unit. Lily Bartlett was among the workers sent there, where they continued their work and also made the metal fuel tanks. She thought it was a good place to work because 'the men working there were real coppersmiths' and 'we were a happy crowd'. Their working hours were from 7.30 a.m. until 7.30 or 8 p.m., with just a half hour for dinner.

The Main Spitfire Testing Sites in the South

The main sites for the building, testing and delivery of Spitfires to the RAF were centred on four towns: Southampton (including Eastleigh aerodrome); Salisbury (including airfields at High Post, Salisbury and Chattis Hill, near Stockbridge); Trowbridge (Keevil aerodrome); and Reading (using Henley and Aldermaston aerodromes). The factories would then send completed Spitfires

Weston Rolling Mills fuel tanks became the base for the tank and pipe fabrication unit. *Solent Sky*

Anna Valley Motors, Salisbury, was used for sub-assembly. *Solent Sky*

on the large Commer 'Queen Mary' low-loader trucks to the airfields to be assembled, flight-tested and then delivered to the RAF squadrons. Supermarine also used Worthy Down airfield from December 1940 to March 1944 for the flight-testing of the Spitfire.

In addition to the dispersal sites throughout the south, there were the other firms connected to Supermarine that took on construction of aircraft, including Saunders-Roe at Cowes, building the Walrus and Sea Otter aircraft; Westland, based at Yeovil, building the Spitfire and Seafire; Cunliffe-Owen at Eastleigh, building the Seafire; and the 'shadow factory' at Castle Bromwich, that had a large output of Spitfires throughout the war.

Hursley Park

After the destruction of the factories, the design staff moved to Southampton University and the management to the Polygon Hotel. Murry White worked at the university for a while until transferred to Hursley Park:

> Ernie Mansbridge and I got on with the performance work and we were in the billiard room at Hursley Park to start with, but it was very crowded. At the time Ernie Mansfield was having to share an office with Alan Clifton, but eventually a butler's pantry became available and it was just big enough to hold Ernie, myself and one other person, although it was only Ernie and I for a long time. We set up our operation there and it was very successful.

The Experimental Department

Prior to the development and production of the much-needed wartime Spitfire, Supermarine had been heavily engaged in experimental work when orders for the aircraft production were much lower. With the more urgent need for increased production of aircraft, the experimental work was not deemed as important by some on the management side, but to others there was a more urgent need to have an Experimental Department that would be able to build and test new aircraft designs and modifications. However, due to the urgent need for completed Spitfire fighters and the requirement at the end of each week to submit figures to the Air Ministry on how many aircraft had been built and tested, much of the experimental work was left to weekends. The frustration of not having a dedicated Experimental Department focused Joe Smith's attention on getting something done about it.

Wessex Motors, Salisbury, was used for assembly of fuselages (stage 2). *Solent Sky*

Short's at Winchester was used as a machine shop. *Solent Sky*

Jeffrey Quill was very interested in the experimental test flying and states in his book *Spitfire: A Test Pilot's Story*, 'Had it not been for experimental flying and the urgent need to increase the performance capability of the Spitfire, and Joe Smith's evident determination to do so, I should have left the firm to return to the Royal Air Force.'

Alan Clifton (Cliffy) comments on this in his lecture to the Southampton branch of the Royal Aeronautical Society in 1976:

Once the orders for the Spitfires arrived from the Air Ministry the works concentrated on production, and the work on prototypes lagged far behind. To remedy this Joe Smith sent a rather strong note to our manager H.B. Pratt, asking for a separate organization to deal with experimental work. It was not until some years later that we got an experimental department at Hursley Park. The Experimental Department was responsible for prototype construction.

After the factory was destroyed, the drawing office was at first relocated within Southampton and then finally to Hursley Park. Various buildings were constructed for the drawing office as well as the Experimental Hangar in the grounds. The new Experimental Department was formed under Joe Smith's control, and Frank Perry, one of his draughtsmen, was delegated to run the new department for him.

In early 1940, Barrie Bryant got to know Perry when he had just been appointed manager of the Experimental Department. He was assisted by two recently finished apprentices, Dion Houghton and Gordon Eldridge, and was based in a small office in the workshops:

They seemed to operate as progress chasers for parts and assembly work in connection with prototypes and experimental. When we had moved from Woolston to Hursley Park an outbuilding in the stable block was used for experimental work under Perry. A substantial hangar was later built in the Hursley Park grounds near the Southampton entrance. Perry worked hard and eventually had a large Department.

The aim of the Experimental Department was to build and test the experimental aircraft. To support their ongoing work the department made a request to have their own lathes and other equipment to enable them to produce their own parts and not be reliant on the main workshops. This request was not supported by Wilf Elliot, who thought the machines would not be used to their full capacity and that those components needed would be better produced in the main workshops. However, after further discussion and consideration, Elliot eventually agreed to the Experimental Department's request and they were then able to work more efficiently under the leadership of Perry.

The Research Department

When the Research Department moved to Hursley Park in 1940, a special section was set up to carry out development work on fuel, oil and electrical and cooling systems. Harry Griffiths comments in his book *Testing Times: Memoirs of a Spitfire Boffin* that it was, 'a far cry from our early "Heath Robinson" efforts of the Schneider Trophy days'. In Hursley House the laboratory occupied the linen room, which had one wall completely covered with cupboards used for storing chemicals, the photographer was put in the wine cellar, and the mechanical testing equipment was situated in the stables. Arthur Black became head of research and development, controlling the chemical metallurgical, photographic and systems functions through the section leaders.

The Effects of the Bombing on Supermarine Families

From 1937, Alf Faddy and his family lived in Peartree Avenue, but for the period of the 'Phoney War' the family moved to Alton, later returning to Eynham Avenue in Southampton where they began to experience the German bombing of the area. David Faddy remembers the Blitz in Southampton and comments that his father hated to be confined, insisting that they all crouched under the dining room table, which he was convinced was the safest place, while he stood outside on the lawn. Concerned for the safety of his family, he sent them to Roundhay in Leeds in May 1940 to stay with his mother and sister while he remained at Eynham Avenue. During their stay in Leeds, David's sister Jennifer was born, but this period at his grandmother's house was not a happy time for David. The family were later reunited, first at Hungerford, near Newbury in Berkshire for a short time, and then at Monks Barn in Twyford, near Winchester, on 5 December 1941. David writes:

> Monks Barn had a trapdoor in the sitting room leading to a network of underground tunnels which were also accessible from a brewery yard outside and so served as an air-raid shelter for several of the nearby houses. We moved on 22 January 1943 to 'The Mount', Twyford where we remained until 1954.

Alan Clifton (Young Alan) recalls being on holiday in Highcliffe in a chalet, and has a very clear memory of his father coming home from work on the night of Sunday, 3 September 1939 and telling him and his older sister Ann to put on their pyjamas and get in the car. They were driven to Bournemouth and handed over to a family who they had never met or heard of before, as an escape from Southampton:

> This was not for long because by Christmas we were in a house in the New Forest and were there for a few months until my father found the house at Awbridge, near Romsey, where we moved to in May 1940.

He describes his father as very thoughtful and analytical, but strict in morality terms, and of enormous integrity. His favourite story about his father concerns an incident that occurred before the war:

> One Christmas he dug up a Christmas tree from a plantation and got caught by a policeman putting it back! I think that sums him up. When he took it he knew he was going to put it back so he looked after it, but unfortunately got caught by the local copper, and possibly getting a telling off. He had an enormous sense of humour and was a terrific fun lover.

Barbara Harries, although then very young, remembers the war years:

> We had troops all camped around us prior to the D-Day landings. I went to the Sherborne House School private school and the American soldiers used to give us chocolates and cigarettes to take home to our mummy. I also remember my father would come to my school to watch me play lacrosse; he was an interested dad.
>
> I remember the bombing, and I don't know how true it is, but I was told that the Germans were aiming for our house on one of their raids. A whole stick of bombs came down our main road and they got the Smiths four houses down. I can remember being bundled into the car and having to sleep on the floor sometimes.

It is possible that Barbara was taken to Alan Clifton's (Cliffy's) house to sleep on the floor on some evenings as 'Young Alan' remembers that during the war a lot of friends and relations used to come and camp on the floor, have breakfast and then go back to work in Southampton in the morning. This was in order to escape the Blitz, and he can remember coming down stairs and finding people lying around who he had never met before in his life, although some of them were friends of Supermarine staff:

This was part of life in those days. However, I think my mother was struggling at the time because she had a handicapped sister who she was looking after as well as my grandfather who was living there at the time.

He also recalls having four wonderful years living at a Tudor farmhouse in Bridestowe, Devon, where his school had been evacuated during the war. American troops were stationed around Bridestowe at that time and it was the US Army that built the bypass to the north of the village, and local memories were of General Eisenhower signing some important papers in the Nissen hut that was the village hall until 2002.

Judy Monger remembers their father taking them to the shops in Woolston, and she recalls going into the offices with him at weekends, and that there was also an occasion when their house got land-mined and the ceilings came down and the windows caved in. The family then went to live in a caravan at Farley Mount, near Hursley, so that her father could easily get to work at weekends:

> There was also a shortage of petrol so you couldn't get around a lot. At the time we were at kindergarten school just around the corner. In 1940 I started school in Southampton and at weekends we all went out to the caravan on our bicycles, which was something like a 12-mile ride on a bicycle. My father worked long hours and we had a telephone put in because of the work, and they would talk at all sorts of hours in the night.

Barbara Harries remembers the Mansbridge family caravan and her visits there with her father at weekends when he would have a meeting with Ernie Mansbridge:

> They lived in the caravan throughout the war near Hursley. I remember I was tickled pink because the caravan had a bath in it. Recently I asked Judy if they still had the bath, and she told me that it was now in the garden as a pond!

Ann Crimble (née Fear) has a clear memory of the war starting and the bombing of Southampton. She went with her family to stay with an aunt in Bath but it was also heavily bombed, so they moved to another aunt in Bristol. Ann's father, Bill Fear, was still living in Woolston and they saw him mainly at weekends. However, the bombing became worse in Bristol, so the family moved to Hursley Park and stayed in rooms in the Saddlery in 1940. To Ann it was good because at last the family were all together.

Bill Fear got to know Sir George Cooper, the owner of Hursley Park, who let the family use his bathroom at the top of the house. They used to walk to the house with their washing gear and towels in the evenings:

When you entered the main door there was a stairway with beautiful blue carpet leading upwards. Around the toilet, sink and bath there was a lovely pattern of blue flowers. This was luxury to us because in the house where we had rooms there was no water laid on and every day the water you needed had to be fetched from the water pump 50 yards along the road in a pail. The toilet was up the garden in a shed. Very dark at night too! Obviously a bucket job and its contents were disposed of in the garden. No wonder the flowers grew well in that garden!

Ann's father, along with most of the men in the village who had not been called up into the services, was in the Home Guard and she remembers that he kept his rifle at home, by the fireplace. At the time, Joe Smith had an office in South End House, Hursley, a house opposite the pub which had been taken over mainly for administrative offices but also had a social club:

They had lovely gardens and when we were kids at the age of about 6 or 7 we used to play in there, but we were told to keep very quiet outside of Joe Smith's office. He was someone special so we had to be quiet.

Hursley House was the base for Supermarine's Administration, Commercial, Design and Experimental departments. *Solent Sky*

Hursley Park on 1 April 1944. From left to right, back row: Eric Cooper, chief draftsman; Arthur Black, metallurgist; Joe Smith; –?–; –?–; Leonard Gooch, production manager; Frank Perry, Experimental Hangar manager; Ken Knell, resident technical manager; –?–; Ernie Mansbridge, flight test manager; –?–; Alan Clifton, chief technician; Arthur Shirvall, project chief. Front row: Wilfred Elliot, general manager; Vice Admiral Mackintosh of Mackintosh; Hew Kilner; Sir Stafford Cripps; Sir James Bird, managing director; Mrs Perkins; Gp Capt. Max Perkins, overseer. *Judy Monger*

During the war, Barbara Harries would also go with her father to Hursley Park when his office was in Hursley House:

> All through wartime we used to go to Hursley Park every Sunday because it was the only time dad could get his letters signed. I used to sit in his office doing my scribbling and drawing while he did all his correspondence. He used to cut me off some tracing paper in the drawing office so I could trace some of my pictures while he was doing his work. His office was a large room and it always amused me as a youngster that there was the large safe in his office. After he had finished his work in the office we would then go into Hursley Park, down to the factory, seeing what the men were doing. There was quite a bit of woodwork and wood turning, and a lot of completed work was then sent to garages and different areas. I remember watching one of the men turning an egg cup for me. A few years ago I managed to get permission from IBM to go into dad's old office and it was how I remembered it. The carpet was still the same one that I remembered!

Joe Smith would have to make frequent journeys to London during war-time, often by rail, and with this came a certain amount of danger due to possible agents of Hitler targeting people of importance to the war effort. Barbara recalls:

> I remember the story of when my father was returning from a meeting in London on the train and was moved out of his compartment because there was someone on the train who was carrying a knife and intended to attack him. I don't know whether it was the secret service or the police that moved him into another compartment for protection. If he was in charge of getting out the Spitfires then Hitler didn't want him around.

12

The Spitfire in the Second World War

Sad End to K5054

The Second World War began on 3 September 1939, and on the following day the original prototype crashed on the grass at the RAE, Farnborough. The cause was thought to be a misjudgement on the part of the pilot, Flt Lt 'Spinner' White, the aircraft having nosedived and landed on the cockpit which was crushed, killing the pilot. The investigation resulted in modifications to the Sutton seat harness. Ernie Mansbridge found on examining the wreckage that the harness anchor cables went under the platform of the RT antenna mast so that the mast was forced down, thereby killing the pilot. The simple solution was to lead the anchor cables over the platform.

Second-year apprentice Highton was told a few days later to dismantle the aircraft carefully and list all parts. He was helped by another apprentice, B.J. Smart. They organised the equipment needed to be able to dismantle the aircraft and then began to take the aircraft apart, starting with the propeller, then the engine block and the other parts, leaving just the fuselage and pilot's seat. The wings were removed after taking off the wing bolts. The dismantled aircraft was sold for scrap, but both apprentices kept a wing bolt each. As these were made of toughened steel, they made two hammers, and that is all that remains of K5054. One of the hammers is now in the Solent Sky Museum collection in Southampton.

On an earlier occasion, on 22 March 1937, K5054 had had to make an emergency landing when engine problems forced Flg Off. McKenna to make a belly landing on a test flight out of Martlesham Heath. Fortunately, on that occasion the pilot had landed safely and was unhurt.

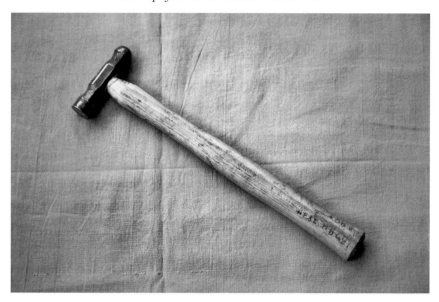

A hammer made from the wing bolt of K5054 after it had crashed and was written off.
Alan Mansell

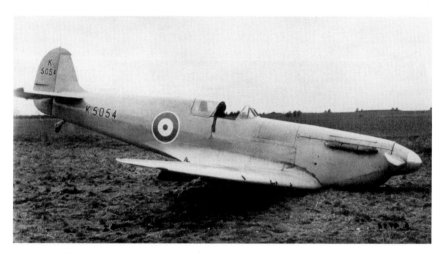

During performance trials at Martlesham Heath a major oil leak forced K5054 to make a belly landing on 22 March 1937. After repairs, the aircraft continued with the trials. *Solent Sky*

The First Spitfire Successes Against the Luftwaffe

On 16 October 1939, the first Luftwaffe attacks of the Second World War on Britain began when Junkers Ju 88s of I./KG 30, led by *Hauptmann* Helmuth Pohle, started attacking the warships in the Royal Naval Base at Rosyth on the Firth of Forth. Spitfires from 602 (City of Glasgow) Squadron at RAF Drem and 603 (City of Edinburgh) Squadron at RAF Turnhouse were scrambled to meet the attacking Ju 88 bombers. Three Spitfires from 603 Squadron attacked Pohle's aircraft, causing it to ditch into the sea off Scotland's east coast. Pohle was the only survivor and became a prisoner of war. While this was happening, other Spitfires from 603 Squadron shot down a Heinkel He 111 whose task it was to photograph the results of Pohle's raid, and later on that day another He 111 was shot down by the same squadron.

Development of the A–E Wing Types

During the early days of the Spitfire in action, it was found that the armaments were not suited to current combat situations and it was therefore necessary to design different wing types for the armaments that were to be carried in the Spitfires. These came in the A–E wing variants.

The original armament carried in the A wing were eight .303in Browning guns carrying 300 rounds of ammunition. Although this was sufficient initially, it soon became necessary to provide more hitting power when attacking enemy aircraft, as a result of the increasing armour being put into German fighters and bombers. Therefore, in July 1939, the Air Ministry started to test the 20mm Hispano cannon. The results proved that the explosive shells from two Hispano cannons were far more destructive to enemy aircraft and other targets than the solid bullets fired from several machine guns. However, this conversion was not easy to carry out as only sixty rounds of 20mm ammunition could be carried in a drum-type magazine, and further work had to be done on modifying the wing structure of the Spitfire A wing before the cannons could be fitted. This was achieved by adding blisters to the wing surfaces to accommodate the ammunition drum – and this became designated as the B wing. The conversion was accomplished on the Spitfire Mk IB, resulting at first in two 20mm Hispano cannons and later two cannons and four .303 (7.7mm) Browning machine guns. This version had projecting gun barrels and blisters in the wing surface.

The third type of wing, the C wing, also called the 'universal wing', allowed mixed armament options of either A or B type or up to four 20mm Hispano cannons. A later development was the Hispano belt-fed cannon which had a larger capacity for the ammunition, carrying up to 120 rounds per gun. With the Mk IIB (Type 329) the armaments were two Hispano cannons and four .303 (7.7mm) Browning machine guns which projected from the wing and a blister in the top wing surface. The later Mk IIB (LR) (Type 343) was a variant of the Mk IIA but was built as a long-range fighter able to carry an extra fuel tank under the port wing, and including an enlarged oil tank in a deeper nose.

The D wing was used to carry extra fuel, mainly for the long-range reconnaissance aircraft which were unarmed. The E wing, similar to the C wing, appeared in late 1944, having either four 20mm cannons or alternatively two 20mm cannons and two 0.5mm Browning machine guns, the machine guns being fitted inside of the cannons which took the outer position.

Increasing Fuel Capacity

The original Spitfire was designed as an interceptor, operating from home bases and attacking German aircraft when they flew over the coast on the way to their pre-planned targets. At that time, the Spitfire carried a fuel capacity that allowed a limited time in the air, but being able to land in order to refuel and rearm and then be back in the air to continue the battle served its purpose. However, as well as the requirement for increased armaments there was now a need to carry extra fuel for increasing the range of the fighters. This was gained by creating space for carrying fuel in extra tanks behind the cockpit, and also carrying fuel in the leading edges of the wing together with the use of a drop tank.

In the later versions of the fighter, extra fuel tanks were carried in self-sealing tanks in the wing root leading edges. These should not be confused with the PR variants. It is helpful to recall that the nomenclature of the PR variants had no relation to the fighter variants; for example, the PR Mk IV was basically the F Mk I or later Mk V, whereas the Mk IV was the prototype of the Griffon engine installation and became the production Spitfire F Mk XII. The two Griffon engine installations in the Mk III airframe were numbered DP845 and DP851 and were given the nickname by the test pilots as the 'leaner backers' due to their very high rate of climb.

The Guinea Pig Club

One of the dangers was that the Spitfire had a fuel tank directly in front of the pilot, between the engine and the cockpit, and a direct hit on the fuel tank could ignite the fuel and fill the cockpit with flames. Many pilots suffered horrific burns when this happened, but new treatment was being developed for such severe burns at the Queen Victoria Hospital in East Grinstead by RAF surgeon Archibald McIndoe. The Guinea Pig Club was formed by his patients and met regularly until the last annual reunion was held at East Grinstead after sixty-six years, in 2007.

The author accompanied a BBC reporter to a meeting of the Guinea Pig Club at the Marchwood Priory Hospital, near Southampton, in the 1990s and met a number of its members. Talking to them, it was interesting to hear of their bravery during the war and the author was impressed by their friendliness and cheerful nature, despite the horrific burns they suffered and the descriptions of how it had happened. Murry White became a friend of Geoffrey Page who was a member of the Guinea Pig Club and author of the book *Tale of a Guinea Pig*. He became a test pilot after the war, and later was also part of the Supermarine sales group.

Air Ministry Specification F.18/37

Supermarine Types 324, 325 and 327 were designs for twin-engine fighters with tricycle undercarriages and twin Merlin engines. Armaments for Types 324 and 325 were twelve Browning machine guns, six in each outer wing, and for the Type 327 were six 20mm Hispano cannons, three positioned in each wing root. However, the Type 325 was designed for a pusher engine, while Types 324 and 327 used the tractor engine.

The Air Ministry specification F.18/37 (1937) was for a 'Heavily armed interceptor armed with 12 x 0.303 machine guns and capable of at least 400mph [643.73km/h]'. To meet this specification, Supermarine submitted the Type 324 under company specification No 458, a tractor design, high-speed, single-seat fighter. The Type 325 was of a pusher design under company specification No 459 to meet the same Air Ministry requirements.

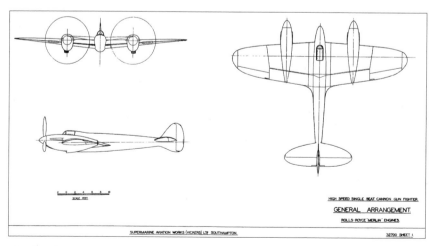

Plan for a high-speed, single-seat cannon gun fighter with Rolls-Royce Merlin engines. *Solent Sky*

Company specification 458 highlighted the following:

The twin-engine types offered better performance, and with oppositely rotating aircrews the swing on take-off in formation was reduced. The aircraft would have a higher maximum speed by 20mph [32km/h], tricycle chassis for easier landing, can get home if one engine is out of action, has a better take-off and utilizes existing well-tried design of engines.

The aircraft would be powered by twin Merlin engines and have a maximum speed of 450mph (724.2km/h). However, the specification states that the company had considered making the aircraft suitable for alternative Bristol Taurus engines. It would be of aluminium construction with an elliptical wing area that would be just 20 per cent greater and with a fuselage of similar size to the Spitfire. This was gained by the use of Fowler flaps which gave 10 per cent greater lift than other types, and would be a simple and efficient construction. The armament would be for twelve machine guns, six on either wing, and each unit, complete with ammunition, could be quickly removed for work on the gun on a bench.

Cannon Gun Fighter

Supermarine Aviation Works (Vickers) Limited also produced a company specification No 460, dated 26 August 1938, for a high-speed, single-seat cannon gun fighter. This aircraft would also have twin Merlin engines with a maximum speed of 465mph (748.34km/h), achieved mainly due to keeping the aircraft dimensions to a minimum. This arrangement was made possible by the use of Fowler flaps and a tricycle undercarriage. The undercarriage supported safer landings and also reduced take-off and landing distances compared with other fighters at the time. There would be a simple and efficient construction due to 'well-tried and efficient methods of construction' developed by Supermarine over time. Two groups of three 20mm Hispano cannons positioned in the wing roots would be easily removable for servicing and repair. The specification gives an alternative of replacing the six Hispano cannons with twelve Browning machine guns, six positioned on each outer wing. Further protection for the pilot against armour-piercing bullets was provided with a 7mm bulkhead of armour plate and also a shell covering of 4mm armour around the cockpit. Similar to Types 324 and 325, consideration was given to alternative engines with Bristol Taurus instead of Rolls-Royce Merlins. The project was discontinued due to the developments of the Spitfire using Hispano cannons, and also because the single engine speeds of the Spitfire fighter had increased.

Spitfire Mk I

The Supermarine Spitfire Mk IA was the first production version of the Supermarine Type 300 and had eight machine guns, as did K5054 to which they were fitted later in its life. The tail skid was replaced by a tailwheel and at first the aircraft had a Merlin II engine powering a two blade fixed-pitch wooden propeller. This was later changed to the de Havilland three blade variable-pitch metal propeller. However, when the Merlin II was changed to a Merlin III

A busy workshop engaged in Spitfire production.
Solent Sky

Final assembly of Spitfires at Eastleigh aerodrome.
Solent Sky

engine, the propeller was changed to a three blade constant-speed propeller powering the aircraft at a speed of 367mph (590.62km/h). To ensure greater protection for the pilots, there was an armour-plated seat and a bullet-proof windscreen. Although the earlier versions of the aircraft had a straight-topped cockpit, this was later changed to a bulged cockpit.

Problems occurred over the construction of some of the parts. Fuselage, engine and tail units were easily produced, but the wings were not as easily constructed due to a special design feature. To help with the production, twelve sets of wing assembly jigs were provided at the Woolston works in April 1938, the first production Spitfire, K9787, flying on 15 May 1938, piloted by Jeffrey Quill, with the second, K9788, flying on 12 July. Eventually the first Spitfires were sent for trials at the Martlesham Heath Experimental Establishment. On 4 August 1938, Quill delivered K9789 to No 19 Squadron at Duxford, Cambridgeshire, which was the first RAF squadron to be equipped with the Spitfire.

No 19 Squadron at Duxford was the first RAF squadron to receive the Spitfire Mk I. *Solent Sky*

An example of an early Spitfire Mk I cockpit. *Solent Sky*

The 'Speed Spitfire'

It was in late 1938 that the 'Speed Spitfire' made its appearance. One Mk I Spitfire (K9834) was modified with a Merlin II engine of 2,150hp powering a four-bladed propeller to give a speed of over 400mph (643.73km/h) and with a shorter wingspan and streamlined windscreen for an attempt on the world speed record. This aircraft was known as the N17 'Speed Spitfire' and first flew on 11 November 1938. However, even before it could make an attempt on the record, a Messerschmitt Me 209 set a record in excess of N17's capabilities. Furthermore, by the time all the developmental work on N17 had been completed, the Second World War had broken out.

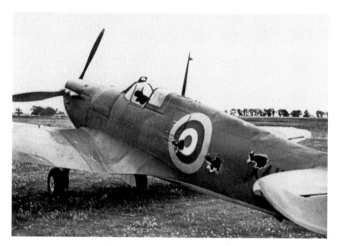

In August 1940, Flt Lt J. Dunlop Urie took off in a newly delivered Spitfire Mk I, X4110, but was quickly shot down by a Bf 109. The aircraft did not fly again. *Solent Sky*

Before the war a Spitfire was being developed for an attempt on the world air speed record, but a Me 209 extended the record beyond the limit of the 'Speed Spitfire'. *Solent Sky*

Dave Glaser's father was an ex-First World War pilot who kept The Bugle pub at Hamble, which was also Jeffrey Quill's local. Dave flew as Jeffrey's No 2 in 65 Squadron during August 1940. *Solent Sky*

The 'Speed Spitfire' (K9834) was a static display at the Salon de l'Aéronautique, Brussels, in the summer of 1939. *Solent Sky*

Murry White was involved with Ernie Mansbridge with the 'Speed Spitfire' and one of their tasks was timing the aircraft along a straight railway embankment for a measured mile. They did not have the equipment that is around today and relied on two stopwatches:

> We only got the measured mile vaguely right, but the aircraft flew quite a bit, and we had to take the radiator out of it. It had a boiling tank in the place of a top fuel tank and the water only had a short duration–short fuel and short water! It took off, did a run and then went back again. It never really did anything because war came along and it was converted back into a semi-standard Spitfire.

The aircraft was then fitted with a Merlin XII engine and used for high-speed photo reconnaissance duties instead. However, the important message was that the 'Speed Spitfire' demonstrated to Joe Smith the power that could be achieved with the Merlin engine. By 1939, the Merlin II engine, combined with a supercharger, achieved enormous boosts in power and was proving to be the way forward.

Smith had great faith in the Spitfire design and its development. With war approaching, he felt that it was not the time to consider new designs because of the years it would take to fully develop, and he was determined that the Luftwaffe would be challenged at every level. With the Rolls-Royce Merlin and Griffon engines he set about leading his team through the many marks that commenced with the power of a Spitfire Mk I with a Merlin 1,050hp to the Seafire 47 with a Griffon 2,350hp, and speeds from the Mk I at 362mph (582.58km/h) to the Mk 24 at 450mph (724.2km/h).

Demonstrating the Speed of the Spitfire

In November 1938, one of the early production Spitfires was flown to the Salon de l'Aéronautique International in Paris. Quill and Mansbridge planned the 200-mile (321.86km) route in order to challenge the Croydon to Le Bourget speed record. The plan was to use the Spitfire's best climbing speed to a height of 18,000ft (5,486.4km), fly level at full power and then descend to Le Bourget at a steady calculated rate to avoid damage to the engine. The flight took 40 minutes going out and 41 minutes return, successfully breaking the record and creating prestige for the Spitfire as the press acclaimed its performance.

Spitfire Mk II

By mid-July 1940, there were a total of nineteen RAF squadrons equipped with Spitfires Mk Is. It was soon after the Battle of Britain and into the winter of 1940 that these aircraft started to be replaced with the Mk IIs in RAF service. The Mk Is were then used in the OTUs (Operational Training Units).

The first Mk II Spitfire flew on 24 September 1939, but it was not until August 1940 when 611 Squadron at RAF Digby received its first Mk II. There were two variants, IIA and IIB, depending on the type of armament used. The Mk IIA used eight .303 Browning machine guns whereas the Mk IIB had two 20mm cannons and four .303 Browning machine guns. Some Mk IICs were used for air-sea rescue (ASR) and in 1942 they were designated the ASR Mk IIC. These aircraft carried survival packs which would be dropped to airmen who had ditched in the sea. The speed of development and replacement of the different marks of Spitfire found the Mk IIs being replaced in March 1941 by the Mk Vs, at which time the Mk IIs were also sent to OTUs.

A Spitfire Mk I was fitted with a 30-gallon asymmetric fuel tank under the port wing and undertook trials in the summer of 1940. *Solent Sky*

P8088 IIA 'The Borough of Lambeth'. When stationed at RAF Ibsley the aircraft was flown by Alec Lumsden who named it 'Bette'. The aircraft finally crashed in 1944, killing the pilot. *Solent Sky*

Spitfire Mk IIB P8327 was with No 308 'Krakowski' Polish Squadron. The aircraft was shot down on 24 July 1941 over France, the pilot surviving to become a PoW. *Solent Sky*

Jeffrey Quill Returns to RAF Service

After the fall of France in 1940, Quill felt it was his duty to return to a fighter squadron and despite the anticipated opposition from Vickers (naturally reluctant to release him from his test flying operations) he eventually succeeded in arguing the case for gaining combat experience in the Spitfire as a fighter pilot. In this he was helped by the intervention of Air Vice-Marshall Keith Park, and was posted on 5 August 1940 to the RAF 65 (Fighter) Squadron at Hornchurch. During this attachment he shot down a Messerschmitt 109 and a Heinkel 111. Throughout the posting he kept in close contact with Joe Smith by writing or telephoning regular reports suggesting modifications and improvements. These included changes to the design of the windscreen side panels and canopy to improve rearward vision for the pilot, as well as improvements in aileron control at high speed. Smith was thus able to issue ongoing instructions to the design office to work swiftly on these suggestions.

From his combat experience Quill recognised the need for more powerful armaments, such as cannons, which would do more damage to enemy fighters and bombers than machine guns: 'We needed better hitting power and the sooner cannons could be made to work and be introduced into regular services the better.' He was just settling into his role as a Spitfire combat pilot with the squadron when, on 24 August 1940, he was instructed to return to Supermarine because his services were required for test flying the Spitfire Mk III. That evening he reflected on his experiences in combat and his recommendations to Smith for improvements to the Spitfire. He decided that it was important to get back to Supermarine to report to Smith so that the necessary improvements could be put in place as speedily as possible for Spitfire squadrons, and then perhaps he could return to his combat role with the squadron. Quill's combat experiences had taught him that fabric-covered ailerons were impossible to use at high speeds and he promptly reported this to Smith, who then focused efforts to improve aileron control. This resulted in replacing the fabric-covered ailerons with metal ailerons, which brought about a huge improvement in control at high speed.

Spitfire Mk III

In the early design stages of the Merlin-engined Spitfires the Supermarine design team, led by Smith, worked on an experimental prototype of the Mk III variant (N3297), powered by the Merlin XX 1,240hp engine with a two-speed supercharger and first flown on 16 March 1940 by Quill as a test aircraft. It had clipped elliptical wings that were adapted to take either eight .303 machine guns, four

N3297 was the first Mk III prototype with a Merlin XX engine. It was first flown by Jeffrey Quill, who remembers that when he flew DP845 the Mk III had been cancelled. *Solent Sky*

Hispano cannon or a combination of both, a retractable tail-wheel, increased armour and a bullet-proof windscreen. Despite the improved performance, the Air Ministry did not take it up and only two aircraft were built. This was because the Merlin XX engine was needed as the powerplant for the production of the Hurricane II, and the Mk III aircraft became the basis for the Spitfire Mk IV.

Spitfire Mk IV

Smith was constantly looking for new ways to develop the Spitfire even further and was fortunate to gain early information about a new Griffon engine being designed and tested by Rolls-Royce that could take over from the Merlin. The new engine was a development of the old 'R' engine that had been used in the Schneider Trophy races by the Supermarine S.6 and S.6B, and using this knowledge Smith was quick to move forward on design work to use the new engine. He has been quoted by Quill as saying, 'the good big 'un will eventually beat the good little 'un'. He knew that it would not be easy to put a Griffon engine in a Spitfire, but with his stubborn determination he persevered and succeeded. This was a surprise to those who thought that it would be an impossibility. It was in October 1939 that Smith submitted a design proposal under Supermarine specification No 466 for the Mk IV powered by the new Griffon engine which was able to reach 420mph (675.92km/h) and climb to 15,000ft (4,572m) in only 4½ minutes.

DP845 was used as a test aircraft to compare with the German Fw 190. *Solent Sky*

Decisions regarding what possible armaments to use on the later Spitfires led to Smith suggesting a six-cannon for the Mk IV, which Quill flew in mock-up form in DP845. *Solent Sky*

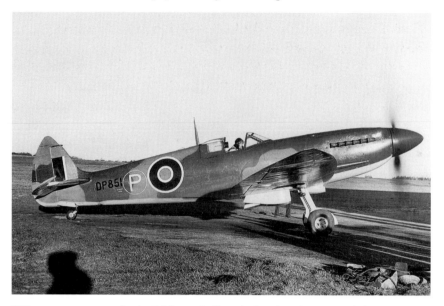

DP851 was a prototype for the F Mk 21. Quill crashed with undercarriage failure in May 1943 while flying DP851 from Blackbushe airport to Worthy Down. *Solent Sky*

The Air Ministry issued the specification F.4/41 for a Spitfire with Griffon engine and Supermarine responded with the two prototypes, DP845 and DP851, both designated Mk IV. However, in order not to confuse the aircraft with the PR Mk IV, these aircraft were redesignated Spitfire XX. DP845 was first flown in November 1941, and was to become the prototype for the F Mk IV and F Mk XII, while DP851, first flown in August 1942, became the prototype for the F Mk 21.

One of the advantages in changing over to the Griffon engine was that it was possible to lower the nose of the Spitfire and improve the pilot's view forward, especially when taking off. The Air Ministry was impressed with the test results at Boscombe Down and announced its plans to introduce the Mk IV as the Mk XII.

Spitfire Mk V

At about the same time the Spitfire Mk IV was being developed, the Mk V was being designed. From the successful results of the trials of a Mk I carrying a new Merlin engine the Air Ministry ordered production of the Mk V and this commenced at Castle Bromwich in March 1941. During its service the Mk V had the Merlin 45, 46 and 50 engine, the low-flying Mk V aircraft using the Merlin 50M or 55M. The Mk V carried 85 gallons (386.41 litres) of fuel in the fuselage. This was the most numerous mark of Spitfire.

Rolls-Royce had developed the Merlin 45 series and Supermarine fitted a Merlin 45 to X4922, which was first flown by Quill in February 1941. Murry White remembers these early trials because this aircraft achieved a better top speed by a few miles per hour, confirmed by Boscombe Down, than Supermarine or Boscombe Down were ever able to achieve on any other Mk V aircraft.

There were to be four major variants of the Mk V; these included the Spitfire Mk VA, VB and VC fighters, all similar and with a Merlin 45 or 46 engine giving a speed of 369mph (593.84km/h) and a ceiling of 37,000ft (11,277.6m). The differences between these three variants were mainly in the armament fittings and wing design. The Mk VA carried eight .303 Browning machine guns, whereas the Mk VB carried four .303 Brownings and two 20mm Hispano cannons. However, the Spitfire VC was fitted with a universal wing that could accept either the VA or VB weapon fitting. The fourth variant was the Spitfire Mk V (LF), a low-flying aircraft, and to help the pilot and improve the handling at low level the wing tips were 'clipped' (squared off).

EN854 LF Mk VB was first with 401 Squadron RCAF (1943), then Belgian 350 Squadron RAF. The aircraft crashed during a dive but the pilot bailed out and landed safely. *Solent Sky*

Spitfire Mk VC ER810 'Inca' had a strengthened airframe, repositioned chassis, bullet-proof and faired-in windscreen, universal wings, extra protection for the pilot and alternative forms of armament. *Solent Sky*

The Mk V was the first Spitfire to be fitted with a drop tank, at first with a 30-gallon (136.38-litre) capacity and later with an 80-gallon (363.68-litre) capacity, thus enabling it to increase its range. Some Mk Vs were equipped to carry 250lb or 500lb bombs. When first introduced in 1941, the Mk V was a good match for the Messerschmitt 109, the Spitfire being more manoeuvrable and faster at low level. However, the Me 109 had the advantage in the climb and was also somewhat faster at higher altitudes, but when the Focke-Wulf Fw 190 appeared late in 1941, the advantage the RAF had with the Mk V disappeared.

There was also a need to develop a Spitfire that could intercept and attack high-flying Junkers Ju 86 reconnaissance aircraft over England during 1940–41, because at this time no British fighter had been developed whereby the pilot could patrol and fight at 40,000ft (12,192m). It was necessary to pressurise the cockpit as a matter of urgency, so a prototype was constructed by modifying one Mk V Spitfire, R7120, which was fitted with a special high-altitude Merlin 47 engine, two airtight bulkheads and a specially designed sealed canopy with a Marshall cabin blower. The aircraft was flight-tested at 40,000ft (12,192m).

Up until the development of the Mk V, all Spitfires had been used solely for the defence of the UK, but now they started to be sent overseas. Where Spitfires were operating in the desert environment, such as in North Africa, sand filters were fitted.

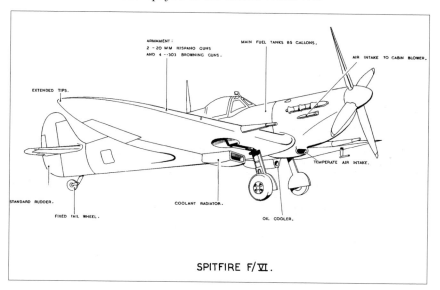

The F MkVI's changes in design from the MkV.B were the Merlin 47, four-bladed Rotol airscrew, extended span wings, pressurised cabin and non-sliding hood. The pilot could fly higher with increased efficiency. *Solent Sky*

Spitfire MkVI

It was the concern of the Air Ministry that the Germans would use their fighters to attack Britain at different altitudes, including both high-flying and low-flying aircraft. To counter that threat, Spitfires were designed to meet all possibilities. It was found that the result of 'clipping' the wing tips improved the characteristics for the low-flying aircraft, and attention was then switched to improving the characteristics for their high-flying counterparts. This was solved by increasing the wingspan of the MkVI by extending its wing tips. The cockpit was pressurised for high flying, a Merlin 47 engine was fitted, powering a four-bladed propeller, and the aircraft carried 85 gallons (386.41 litres) of fuel in the fuselage. The armaments included two 20mm cannons and four .303 machine guns. The service ceiling was 40,000ft (12,192m).

Spitfire MkVII

The Type 351 was the prototype MkVII (AB450) and had a Merlin 61 engine with a four-bladed Rotol propeller and an increased speed up to 410mph (659.83km/h). It was the first two-speed, two-stage supercharged engine to be used in the Spitfire and gave a better performance at high altitude. It had

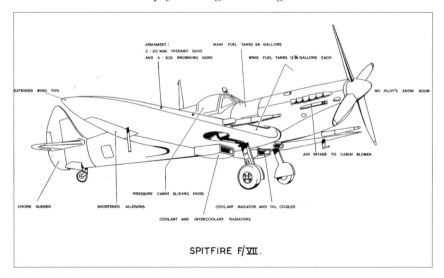

The F MkVII's design changes from the MkVC were the Merlin 61, four-bladed Rotol airscrew, strengthened airframe, retractable tailwheel, increased tankage, pressurised cabin and double-glazed hood. Its maximum speed was 410mph (659.83km/h) and it could fly at a higher altitude. *Solent Sky*

extended wings and a pressurised cabin with a sliding hood, but no pilot's hinged entry door. The fuel capacity in the fuselage was increased to 95 gallons (431.87 litres), and wing fuel tanks totalled 25½ gallons (115.92 litres) in both tanks. A second variant was the HF MkVII (JG204) which was powered by a Merlin 70-series engine. Both aircraft were also provided with extended wing tips and pressure cockpits for flying at high altitudes.

Meeting the Might of the Luftwaffe: Spitfire MkVIII

The Spitfire MkVIII was similar to the MkVII, but was unpressurised and came in three versions. It had either standard, clipped or extended wing tips, depending on its role. The SpitfireVIII was the fighter-bomber with a Merlin 61, 63 or 63A engine powering at 408mph (656.61km/h), with a range of 660 miles (1,062.16km) and a ceiling of 43,000ft (13,106.4m). There was a low-flying fighter version of the Mk VIII powered by a Merlin 66 engine at 404mph (650.17km/h), with a range of 660 miles (1,062.16km) and a ceiling of 41,500ft (12,649.2m). This version sometimes operated with 'clipped' wing tips. The high-flying fighter version had extended wing tips, a Merlin 70 engine powering at 416mph (669.48km/h), a range of 660 miles (1,062.16km) and a ceiling of 44,000ft (13,412.2m). The F MkVIII, LF MkVIII and HF Mk VIII all had an increased fuel capacity of 95 gallons (431.87 litres) in the fuse-

Spitfire F Mk VIII JG204. The hand-built wing was first fitted in July 1944, with the aim of improving the pilot's view and reducing drag, but with little success. It was easier to produce because it was unpressurised. *Solent Sky*

EN172 Mk IX RF-J with 303 Polish Squadron. On 6 July 1943, the aircraft attacked and damaged a Fw 190 over the Pas-de-Calais and later took part in the D-Day landings. *Solent Sky*

lage and 25½ gallons (115.92 litres) in the wings. There were 1,658 produced, but most of these aircraft finished up in the Far East and Australia.

By the end of 1941, the new Fw 190 fighter was making its mark in its capacity to challenge the Spitfire squadrons and cause increasing numbers of losses to the RAF, highlighting the need for a new fighter to replace the Spitfire V which was proving no match for the German fighter. The outcome was to be the Spitfire IX, and the first operational station to receive it being No 64 squadron at Hornchurch, in June 1942. During the war this was the pilots' favourite Spitfire variant.

Operation Airthief

In early 1942, one of the problems for the RAF was that it had no in-depth knowledge of the performance or capabilities of the Fw 190 to compare against the operational Spitfire Vs. Quill became acquainted with Capt. Philip Pinckney, a troop commander in No 12 Commando, who was stationed near where he lived in the Southampton area. In a conversation about the problem of the Fw 190, the officer had a germ of an idea which he put to Quill. The idea was for a commando raid on a French airfield to capture a Fw 190, and for Quill, who would be with the commando team, to fly the aircraft back to an RAF station in England. The idea got official approval and Quill was to prepare for the operation. As well as some time at the RAE gaining information about the German cockpit instruments and labels, he also trained in a Folbot canoe, which he and Pinckney (the only commando to be on the operation) would paddle to the shore. This training often took place after he had done a full day's test flying.

The raid never actually took place, much to Quill's relief, but it was a great disappointment to Pinckney who had been keen to undertake the operation. The reason for its cancellation was due to a Luftwaffe pilot, *Oberleutnant* Arnim Faber, landing his Fw 190 at Pembrey in South Wales on 23 June 1942. Faber had been in combat with Spitfires, was short of fuel and believed he was landing on a Luftwaffe airfield in France. The aircraft was taken to the RAE at Farnborough where all the information required was gained, as well as testing it against the Spitfire IX in simulated combat trials. Quill had the opportunity to fly the Fw 190 and concluded that if the raid had taken place he would have been able to fly the captured aircraft back to England. Sadly, Pinckney was killed in 1943 while leading an operation behind enemy lines in Italy.

The Focke-Wulf Fw 190

The Fw 190 came into its own on the Dieppe raid by the British in 1942, despite the Allies having more numbers of aircraft in the air than the Germans. The raid took place on 19 August, with a landing force of approximately 6,000, including 5,000 Canadian troops. However, it failed and many troops were killed or captured.

The Allies considered that air cover was essential to the success of the raid over Dieppe in order to draw the Luftwaffe into combat, and this was down to the RAF Spitfires and Hurricanes. During the raid forty-eight squadrons of Spitfires were in action, forty-two of which were equipped with Spitfire Mk Vs, two squadrons with the Mk VI and four squadrons with the Mk IX. Other aircraft involved included American Spitfires and British and American bombers. However, the Luftwaffe attacked with their Fw 190s which outclassed many of the fighters in the air battle, with the exception of the Spitfire Mk IX which put the RAF pilots on a more level par than the earlier marks.

The largely Canadian force attempted to deal a heavy blow to German forces occupying Dieppe, but the raid was a military disaster. On this one day, 907 Canadians were killed.

During this time Spitfires began to be supplied to the Americans in significant numbers and were also used in Operation Torch, the Allied landings in North Africa. With the Japanese threat in the Far East it was considered necessary to send Spitfires to the area for combat duties.

Spitfire Mk IX

The Mk IX Spitfire was a development of the Mk V. Murry White explains how this was achieved:

> When the Merlin 60 series was envisaged flight experience was required. Rolls-Royce at Hucknall installed an experimental Mk 61 two stage engine in the Spitfire Mk III [N3297] that they had and gave us a Mk 61 engine which we installed in a Mk I airframe, R6700, on which Supermarine continued their modifications for a production airframe. I was working closely with Jeffrey Quill on the performance reduction which showed a spectacular increase in speed, rate of climb and ceiling over the Mk V.

Quill started flying the R6700 from Worthy Down from 7 January 1942, while N3297 had gone to Boscombe Down for performance tests. The results of these tests showed a great improvement on the Mk V, including an increased speed to 427mph (687.18km/h) and an increased altitude ceiling. The Mark IX and XVI airframes were identical, the latter having Packard-built motors instead of Rolls-Royce. Both were delivered to varying modification standards, including cut-down fuselages with extended rear-view canopies.

Spitfire Mk IX 'Edmonton II' RK889 was built for high altitude and served with 313 (Czech) Squadron and later with the Royal Danish Air Force, but was scrapped after crashing in 1954. *Solent Sky*

Spitfire Mk IX BR592 joined 64 Squadron in July 1942, but was shot down by Fw 190s near Dunkirk in October that year. The pilot was captured and became a PoW. *Solent Sky*

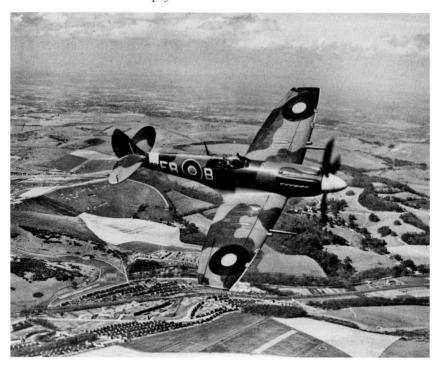

MB882 EB-B Mk XII was built in Southampton, with final assembly and flight-testing at Chattis Hill. It joined 41 Squadron and later transferred to the Fighter Leaders' School at Milfield. *Solent Sky*

EN224 EB-L Mk XII joined 41 Squadron in April 1944, but was damaged when it was hit by EN221 while landing. The present owners have contracted Air Leasing Ltd to rebuild it. *Solent Sky*

Spitfire Mk XII

This was the first Griffon-engined Spitfire fighter to enter service, having either a Griffon III or IV engine. The Spitfire XII was built with 'clipped' wings for a low-level role, the engine powering a four-bladed propeller, and it carried 85 gallons (386.41 litres) of fuel in the fuselage. However, in order to do so, the nose of the Spitfire had to be lengthened to accommodate the engine. The Mk XII was significant in its introduction because it was powerful enough to challenge the Fw 190 flying at low level. Its armaments consisted of four .303 machine guns and two cannons. One hundred of these aircraft were produced.

Spitfire Mk XIV

By 1943, the Spitfire's deployment was extending to the Far East and Australia, and its role increased as a fighter-bomber. The Spitfire Mk XIV fighter-bomber had a Griffon 65 engine of 2,050hp powering a five blade propeller at 400mph (643.73km/h) and carried 85 gallons (386.41 litres) of fuel in the fuselage and 22½ gallons (102.28 litres) in the wings. Its armaments consisted of four .303

RB140 Mk XIV was the first production model flown by Jeffrey Quill in October 1943. Operational with Nos 616 and 610 Squadrons, it crashed and was destroyed when landing at Lympne on 30 October 1944. *Solent Sky*

RB141 Mk XIV served with 322 (Dutch) Squadron (1944) preparing for the D-Day landings. It engaged V-1 flying bombs, but went missing from a patrol off the Isle of Wight on 3 May 1944, with the loss of its pilot. *Solent Sky*

machine guns and two cannons. As well as the firepower the Mk XIV could carry either a 250lb or 500lb bomb under the fuselage, and two 250lb bombs under its wings, making it a very effective attack aircraft. It first came into service in 1944, and gave aerial protection to the Allied armies for D-Day and the invasion of Europe.

Another important attribute of the Mk XIV was its speed in order to catch and destroy the V-1 flying bomb, otherwise known as the 'Doodlebug'. However, it was found that by firing at the V-1, the ensuing explosion could be very dangerous for the pilot. The technique of flying alongside, positioning the Spitfire's wing under the wing of the flying bomb and tipping it over was much more effective, as it caused the flying bomb to lose control and crash. How this was developed is explained by Murry White. In July 1944, Ernie Mansbridge asked him to go to 610 Squadron at Friston in Sussex, who were equipped with the Mk XIV. At the time, it was out of bounds to all personnel but Mansbridge arranged for a special pass which got Murry into the prohibited area:

> Their major occupation was chasing V-1 bombs, the 'Doodlebugs'. They had shot down 54 for the loss of two pilots who had lost their lives as a result of damage sustained when the bombs exploded in midair. The method of tilting the bomb with the Spitfire wing tip was the preferred method, which the engineer officer and I managed to achieve by replacing the Spitfire wing tip with a piece of angle iron which gave the aircraft a slight speed increase and saved damaging the wing tips! I also talked to the pilot who had used this method successfully three times.

Although Murry had driven to the squadron base in his car, he needed his special pass to get through all the roadblocks and into the prohibited area. However, he observed that all the local help on the base travelled by train where, of course, there were no road blocks. As he was staying locally, he hatched a plan to get his girlfriend down for a weekend:

> For me this was a special occasion. My girlfriend came without any trouble by train and we got engaged. In due course we got married and after producing two great children, [my family] later came to America with me. Of course, the real purpose of the visit was to rectify a few engineering problems that [the company] were having which I managed to achieve without much trouble.

Repairs to Spitfires Following the D-Day Landings

The RAF was keen that once the Normandy landings had taken place and the Spitfires were operating in Northern France that aircraft damaged in battle could be repaired 'in the field'. Murry remembers that as D-Day approached, Smith was asked to provide a reliable design engineer to make rapid on-the-spot repairs to Spitfires in the field. It did not take Smith long to choose Jack Rasmussen for this important role, as he had great confidence in his work as an engineer and in his skills in RAF liaison:

> I think Jack was given the rank of Squadron Leader and put into a special RAF uniform, provided with the Jeep and all the necessary passes for him to travel to France on D+6. Again he did most remarkable work in the field. The Spitfires were repaired and he made many sketches, some of which were eventually incorporated in the Spitfire repair manuals. His efforts greatly enhanced the service life of many damage Spitfires. I remember that the first time he reappeared in the office in his uniform he was greatly admired for his courage and skill.
>
> Jack told me that he had to sleep under canvas, so he took the semi-circular 106 Alclad fairing from a crashed Spitfire's fuel tank and slept under it to keep the shrapnel from injuring him.
>
> Again Jack's personality came into play when they advanced into Belgium. He met a well-placed Belgian citizen, who took him in, introduced him to the local golf club, played a round of golf with him and later after the war he invited Jack and his wife Margaret to spend a holiday with him at a Belgian coastal resort.
>
> Jack did sterling work in France and Belgium and right up into Germany. After VE Day he went to the Far East and Burma for the RAF. He was eventually returned to us and was awarded an MBE for his bravery and skill.

RW396 LF Mk XVI was with the Central Gunnery School at RAF Catfoss in April 1946. It was written off following a forced landing on the shoreline at Skipsea in January 1949. *Solent Sky*

Mk XVIII final assembly at Keevil. The first aircraft on the left, TP218, was part of the Far East Air Service. Its undercarriage collapsed on landing at Seletar, Singapore, in 1951. *Solent Sky*

Spitfire Mk XVI

The Mk XVI was a low-level fighter/fighter-bomber with a Merlin 266 engine powering a four blade propeller at 400mph (643.73km/h), a range of 434 miles (698.45km), and a ceiling of 40,000ft (12,192m). The designation 266 was given because it was the American Packard version of the Merlin engine. Its armaments consisted of two cannons and two .5mm machine guns. The aircraft carried 85 gallons (386.41 litres) of fuel in the fuselage, and later versions had a rear-view hood fitted. Some of the American-built Merlin engines were delivered to Castle Bromwich for installation in the Mk IX airframe which then was known as the Spitfire Mk XVI.

Spitfire Mk XVIII

This variant was based on the Mk XIV with standard wings, was powered by a Griffon 65 engine and had increased tankage, carrying 85 gallons (386.41 litres) in the fuselage, 25½ gallons (115.92 litres) in the wings and 66 gallons (300.04 litres) in the rear fuselage. It was tropicalised and had a rear-view hood fitted. Armaments were two 20mm cannons and two .5mm machine guns.

Spitfire Mk 21, Mk 22 and Mk 24

The second Mk XX, DP851, first flew in August 1942 and was at first powered by a Griffon II engine, but later in the year it was fitted with a Griffon 61 engine and redesignated as the prototype for the Mk 21 fighter.

There was a change from Roman to Arabic numerals when the Spitfire 21 (Type 356) was introduced in 1945. The Spitfire Mks 21, 22 and 24 were redesigned aircraft with two-speed, two-stage Griffon 60-series engines, modified fuselage and strengthened wings which, while retaining the elliptical form platform, bore little resemblance to the Mark I wing. These three variants differed mainly in wing design, on which Jack Davis was to have a great influence, changing from the elliptical wing to a new wing which was stronger and could carry four Hispano Mk II cannons. The 20mm Hispano cannons used on the Mks 21, 22 and 24 were found to be the most effective weapon against the Luftwaffe. With a redesigned fuselage, the aircraft were much heavier and work had to be done to design a stronger undercarriage. The engine was the Griffon 61 or 64 with a five blade propeller, but some were fitted with a Griffon 85 and required contra-rotating blades, two sets of three blades rotating in opposite directions. The F Mk 21 carried 84 gallons (381.87 litres) of fuel in the fuselage and 36 gallons (163.65 litres) in the wings.

The Spitfire Mk 22 was similar to the Mk 21, but had a teardrop canopy. It was armed with four Hispano 20mm cannons and carried 85 gallons (386.41 litres) of fuel in the fuselage and 36 gallons (163.65 litres) in the wings. The larger tailplane also helped to improve its handling.

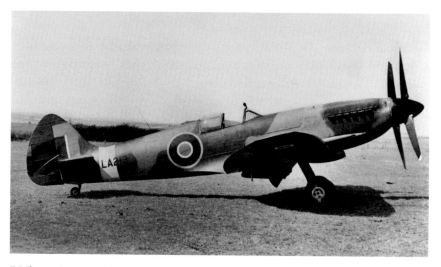

F Mk 21 LA213 was built in 1944 and had two three-blade contra-props. It was eventually sold for scrap in July 1954. *Solent Sky*

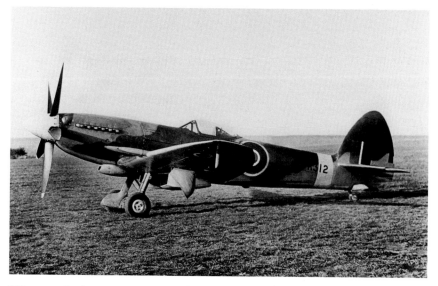

PK312 was the first production Mk 22 and went to the A&AEE for metal elevator installation, Rotol contra-props and a 'Spiteful' tail unit. Design changes from the Mk 21 included a cut-back rear fuselage and teardrop canopy. *Solent Sky*

The design of the Mk 23 was to produce a Spitfire with a laminar flow wing, but as this type of wing fitted to a single Mk VIII did not prove to be of any great advantage over the later Spitfires it was never produced, and therefore the Mk 23 suffered the same fate.

It was in the middle of 1944 that the Mk I and Mk II Spitfires were finally withdrawn from service, and the last Spitfire, the Mk 24, left the production line on 20 February 1948. It was a ground attack fighter with a big 'Spiteful' tail that had been first delivered at South Marston on 13 April 1946. The main difference from the Mk 22 was that it had a strengthened undercarriage and additional fuel tanks with 85 gallons (386.41 litres) of fuel in the fuselage, 36 gallons (163.65 litres) in the wing and 66 gallons (300.04 litres) in the rear fuselage behind the cockpit, and was also fitted to carry rockets. It was armed with four short-barrelled 20mm Hispano cannons which did not protrude forward of the wing. Fifty-four Mk 24 Spitfires were produced and were in service with the RAF 80 Squadron, initially based in Germany before going with the squadron to Hong Kong's Kai Tak airport from 1949 to 1952. It is thought that these Spitfires were bulldozed into the sea when the land reclamation took place to lengthen the airport runway.

The highest altitude ever recorded was on a survey flight over Hong Kong in 1952, when the pilot, Flt Lt Ted Powles, flying a Spitfire PR Mk XIX, reached a recorded altitude of 51,550ft (15,712.44m). However, he had to descend rapidly

Sqn Ldr Derry took F Mk 24 VN479 up for its first test flight of 15 minutes. It served in the Far East Air Service from 1948. *Solent Sky*

before he became a victim of hypoxia (lack of oxygen). Powles put the aircraft into a dive to get to a safe height but the plane suffered from compressibility effects and he lost control, not regaining it until reaching the altitude of 3,000ft (914.4m) and eventually landing safely.

Elsewhere, it was quite a contest in the Arab–Israeli war in which both sides had Spitfires – the only occasion when Spitfires fought against each other in a war situation. Spitfires were also used against the communist guerrillas in Malaya.

Both Mitchell and Smith had been concerned about the safety of the test pilots who flew Supermarine aircraft for the first time, but during the war Smith was acutely aware that for 24 hours of every day Supermarine aircraft would be flying somewhere in the world, whether land-based Spitfires, or Seafires taking off from aircraft carriers. Jeffrey Quill and others who knew Smith well were aware that this was to be a constant worry for him. Reports that Quill regularly gave him about the Spitfire's performance and any accidents that occurred, regardless of the reason, whether pilot error or technical faults, were taken personally by Smith. It was Quill's belief that the heavy responsibility he felt on hearing such news made him ill. In Quill's book *Birth of a Legend: The Spitfire* he writes:

> For there were a total of 22,759 Spitfires and Seafires built, equally worthy of the highest praise on the achievements of Mitchell's successor at Supermarine, Joseph Smith and his assistants, together with the design team at Rolls-Royce under Ernest Hives, who successfully developed both airframe and engines to a level undreamt of by R.J. Mitchell in the early Thirties. Their success kept the Spitfire in the forefront of piston-engined fighter development throughout the war.

The Impact of the Spitfire from the Luftwaffe Perspective

It must be remembered that although the Spitfire was Mitchell's original design, it became the basic starting point from which Smith began to develop the aircraft. He and his design team worked consistently throughout the war years to meet every threat thrown at the aircraft from the Luftwaffe, developing the prototype Spitfire right through to the deadly and much feared fighter. So much so that when the German pilots identified the attacking Spitfires they would shout, '*Achtung! Achtung! Spitfeuer!*'

13

Wartime Apprenticeships

Gordon Monger was keen to leave school early and had been made aware by the School Attendance Officer of a job opportunity as a 'handy lad' at the naval air station HMS Kestrel at Worthy Down, where the Supermarine experimental flight tests had moved after the bombing in the Southampton area. As Gordon had always been interested in aircraft, he rushed off the next day on his bike, had an interview, and was asked if he could start the next day:

> When I arrived the next morning it was 4 January 1941. I was met by a naval policeman at the gates of HMS Kestrel which was based at Worthy Down. I discovered my clock number was 13 and the hours of work were 7.30 a.m. to 7.30 p.m. There was little electricity, no heating and it was dark and freezing, but there were a number of glorious Spitfires and other aircraft in the hangar.

However, Gordon was not happy after a few weeks as a 'handy lad', so applied for a Supermarine apprenticeship and was accepted. As an apprentice he worked at Worthy Down for some time, but found it incredible that young apprentices aged 16 were changing propellers, often helped by a 14-year-old. He remembers an RAF pilot who landed at the other end of the airfield after having trouble with his Spitfire which was vibrating excessively in flight, causing him to consider baling out. He had come straight from a raid and wanted to get back to base. When Gordon approached the Spitfire he saw that one of the propeller blades had been damaged and was the probable cause of the vibration:

> I replenished the air but you could hear it leaking badly. I had a look around the Spitfire and saw bullet holes in the fuselage and one especially through the linkage fairing to the rudder so there could not have been much holding the rudder. I tried to persuade the pilot not to take off, but he wouldn't listen and I wondered if he ever survived the flight back. We had other Spitfires land

with battle damage but the pilots could never be persuaded to stay and always wanted to continue home.

The flight-testing was moved from Eastleigh to Worthy Down, High Post and Chilbolton, and experimental aeroplanes would be found there as well as bimonthly samples from production deliveries. These were diverted for checks on weight, balance and flight characteristics.

From 1941, Barrie Bryant was at Worthy Down, and later High Post, on a weekly basis for checks on weight and centre of gravity, and also for the bimonthly rota of production Spitfire/Seafire variants flown in from the Supermarine dispersal areas, Castle Bromwich, Westland and Cunliffe-Owen. Barrie recalls:

I thus became acquainted with Edgar Woolridge, fitters, labourers and inspectors, and eventually some of the pilots. Since each part, component and modification can affect weight and balance my 'need to know' was wider than other members of the design staff, save only Joe Smith. That gave me licence to inspect mock-ups and prototypes in the Experimental Hangar, structural and system test rigs as well as enquiring about current work in all DO [design office] and TO [technical office] sections. By 1945, I was leading a section of about half-a-dozen which grew to around thirty as the scope of our tasks widened during the following decade. Such was the mode of my education in the science of aeronautics and the art of management. While the war lasted I had no way to learn of practices elsewhere and assumed that other aircraft firms behaved similarly. However, in 1945 the SBAC formed a 'Weight Control Panel' whose membership gave me a broader insight.

Barrie also went to Westland Aircraft at Yeovil in Somerset a few times, and remembers his first airborne experience when Supermarine test pilot Frank Furlong flew him from Worthy Down to Westland's in the company Miles Monarch.

Gordon Monger remembers that production Spitfires after their flight test would sometimes land at Worthy Down where post-flight checks would be undertaken, the propeller tightened and items fitted that had not been supplied during production. He also recalls that some exciting but dangerous events occurred from time to time. One hot summer's day after the armourer had disarmed an aircraft, he got the inspector to clear the job before the aircraft was taken into the hangar. The aircraft was pointing up to the control tower and the inspector decided to check by pressing the gun button. There was still one round in the breach of each of the eight guns. Gordon had never seen anyone move so fast as the men sunning themselves on the tower balcony! Another memory was of flights in the prototype Supermarine Type 322, 'Dumbo', which was a single-engine wooden naval aircraft with a fully slatted, fully flapped and variable-incidence (plus 15 degrees from setting) wing, which also folded:

> It could fly very slowly and we fitted a special ASI [air speed indicator] that we turned on at 75 knots; the lowest indicated speed that I saw was 18 knots. When it stalled you knew it; the starboard wing fell to 90 degrees, which occurred once in the flair, but it had a strong starboard undercarriage to survive. There were other excitements which would frighten me today.

The Supermarine 'Dumbo' was the Air Ministry specification S.24/37 for a naval torpedo bomber and reconnaissance aircraft to replace the Royal Navy Albacore biplane. Supermarine came up with their Type 322 with a variable-incidence wing designed to be adjustable to reduce take-off and landing distances. It was especially suitable for carrier use and carried a crew of three. Only two prototypes were built, R1810 and R1815, the first prototype powered by a Merlin 30 engine and the second by a Merlin 32. This aircraft was mainly of a wood construction and the first prototype flew on 6 February 1943, with a maximum speed of 280mph (450.61km/h). However, the aircraft did not enter production.

Gordon found it interesting working in the experimental flight hangar because there was always something new. He later transferred to Hursley Park's Experimental Hangar, where the prototype Spitfires and Seafires were built, to continue his training. As an apprentice he worked in the various shops including detail fitting, machine, erection, precision layout etc. This also included a period in the production machine shop at Winchester:

> I remember when I worked in the experimental hangar at Hursley Park, Joe Smith would come in every morning at 10 a.m. to look around and see how things were progressing while sucking away on his pipe. 10 a.m. was the time for our tea break, and the ladies in the canteen must have been watching for when Joe Smith left because as soon he did they came out immediately into the workshops with the tea trolleys.

After completing his studies at Southampton University College, to gain more experience Gordon moved to the drawing office at Chilbolton designing aircraft parts, and then to the technical office at Hursley on high subsonic and transonic aircraft. One job in the drawing office was the starboard console for the two-seat prototype trainer which had a lever system for the undercarriage and fuel cock linked to both cockpits:

The undercarriage lever was forward and the fuel lever was aft beside the seat such that you could only operate it before you did up your harness. One pilot had taken off and had by mistake turned off the fuel cock instead of raising the undercarriage. Everything went very quiet. A test pilot happened to be in the control tower and guessed the problem. He radioed the pilot to warn him. The engine started again just in time as it was so low and would have certainly crashed in a field.

Gordon then went on the two-year course at the College of Aeronautics at Cranfield before returning to the Supermarine flight-test technical office where he worked on Swift and Scimitar handling, tropical trials and terrain-following in Libya, TRS2 programming flight and instrumentation requirements. Later he worked on the VC10 and BAC 1-11 automatic landings for some years and was invited to Heathrow to see the first flight of the VC10 with passengers to test the landing system. After this, he worked on Concorde, and then the Chevaline strategic missile programme.

Getting an Apprenticeship in 1944

Tony Kenyon's interest in aviation was stimulated by the Imperial Airways flying boats that regularly took off from Southampton Water. This was after Imperial Airways had inaugurated the Empire flying boat services from Southampton Docks in 1937. His father, who had been a superintendent at the docks in Southampton, was transferred to Wales, where Tony attended Swansea Grammar School, staying on for a further year, at his father's suggestion, to improve his grades in order to help him get an apprenticeship at Supermarine. At the time, it was a choice of either doing National Service or taking on an apprenticeship, but as his brother worked at Supermarine it seemed natural for him to apply there. Tony travelled from Wales for his interview at Supermarine, then based at Hursley Park, and was told to report to Sunlight Laundry in Winchester Road at 7.30 a.m. on 2 October 1944 for his first day of work as a 'handy lad'. Tony's first day was quite a shock and a memorable event for him. It felt like the longest day of his life, spending the whole time filing metal sheets for the fuselage sections.

When the apprentices were new they would have tricks played on them. One was the 'struggling bar'. The apprentice would be sent with some metal with the instruction to go and see a certain person to get a hole put in it. He would be then be passed from one person to another, and this would go on for some considerable time until being told, 'You can go back now!'

After Sunlight Laundry, Tony moved to Eastleigh aerodrome and worked on putting the fuselages together, which included using big iron jigs to bolt on the wings, before moving on to the section where they were flying Spitfires in for reconditioning. When a Spitfire landed, the apprentices would be told that they had to get out as much oil from the glycol coolant as possible while it was still hot. They also had to get the fuel out and collect it in drums using large funnels. From there he went to Lowther's Garage in Shirley, which had been requisitioned and was where the tool room machine shop relocated. His next move was to Shaw Works at Newbury, a MAP (Ministry of Aircraft Production) specially built factory with a shop packed full of machines:

> I found it quite frightening because you had machines like milling machines; you had to do up a big nut at the top. If someone forgot to take the spanner off, the spanner would come hurtling across the shop. I remember a buffing wheel came off and went right along the ceiling. From there, with great relief, I was sent to the experimental hangar at Hursley Park that was just inside the main gate. It is now just an open space like a car park, but then it was built amongst trees for camouflage.

For a time Tony worked in the drawing liaison office where any mistakes a draughtsman made on a drawing would be corrected. After this, he went to the main drawing office, starting at the query section which was under Ron Vere:

> He was quite a disciplinarian, especially if you misused his stapler! I was then moved only about five boards along to the modification squad (the Mod Squad), so that when the modifications came out you had to write a set of directions on how to fit it.
>
> From the drawing office the query note would go in and you would see all these people with slide rules, calculators with handles and rotating slide rules, working away like fury. The management was upstairs. All during wartime about 10 buses used to come in from all over Southampton. They would hide them during the day and then rush home at night with the bus driven by a foreman bus driver.

At Hursley there was a special glass partition at the end of the drawing office where all the high level work went on, and Tony can remember Smith as a dynamic man, charging through with his entourage and disappearing into the glass house before rushing back out again:

The drawing office was sunk in the ground so that you wouldn't get any shadows. One of the big things on reconnaissance flights is that shadows give things away. It also had camouflage netting over it.

The canteen was in the maids' quarters in the main house and that was where we had our lunch. The house had loads of oak panelling and the ball-room for the tracers, and there was T.O. [tracers' office] North and T.O. South. We also had an apprentice school up there and we used to go up there one afternoon to learn drawing.

Tony also recalls the prefabricated hutments at Hursley, where the key people's families lived. These were also hidden amongst the trees:

The stables were taken over as the test house, so they had test rigs in there, the metallurgy department led by Arthur Black, and Sandy Stewart who used to run the hydraulics and machine systems. When you came to the jet age

A Spitfire carrying beer kegs for ground crews working on dusty airfields in France where drinking water was suspect. It was carried on modified bomb pylons and called 'Triple X Depth Charge'. *Solent Sky*

everything became more complicated. They built a variable-incidence wing Seagull which was all metal. Three were ordered, but only two flew, but they had a very tricky undercarriage designed by H.T. Tremelling who was in charge of landing gear.

One particular story that amused Tony was the period after the D-Day landings when a Spitfire was used to undertake very important missions to the front-line troops. These were the 'beer keg missions' when a Spitfire would take off to fly to France in order to supply the servicemen with beer. The excuse was that the troops were advancing at a faster rate than the water supplies, so the Spitfires flew over with beer kegs on the wings and a slip tank underneath which was also filled with beer!

14

AIR TRANSPORT AUXILIARY FERRY PILOTS

Until the start of the Second World War, the peacetime role of the RAF pilots had been ferrying production aircraft to maintenance units where armament and other operational equipment were installed. Machines were then stored until required. However, with the outbreak of war there was an urgent need for trained pilots to engage in a combat role. This was a problem that needed solving because otherwise who would deliver the production aircraft from the factories?

In August 1939, it was decided to set up a pool of civilian pilots to take on the job of ferrying new and repaired aircraft between aircraft factories and maintenance units and so the Air Transport Auxiliary was formed. At first the ATA was administered and financed by British Airways Ltd. However, this administration was short-lived, as in 1939 the AMSO (Air Member for Supply and Organisation) took over the control of the ATA. By the end of the year it was decided that the command headquarters of the civilian ferry pool would be based at White Waltham near Maidenhead in Berkshire. At first it was envisaged that male pilots would be used, but the government made the decision that women pilots with similar experience could be enrolled in the ATA. It was in August 1939 that Pauline Gower was appointed to the job of organising the women's section of the ATA.

The first male pilots of the newly formed ATA were beginning to arrive at a base in the west of England for vetting and training in September 1939, and by the spring of 1940 they had started to ferry urgently needed aircraft such as trainers, fighters and bombers from factories and stores to the RAF stations. Ferry pools based near the aircraft factories were gradually formed in different parts of the country, each one having some Fairchild Argos four-seat aircraft and Avro Ansons to ferry the pilots to the various maintenance units and factories in order to deliver the operational aircraft to the RAF stations. Ferry pilots would fly only during daylight hours, did not have any radio communication and often there was no heating in the aircraft.

Gordon Monger clearly remembers an occasion in his early apprenticeship days when a group of six smart young ladies alighted from an Avro Anson and he was shocked to discover that they were ATA ferry pilots who had arrived to deliver the Spitfires to their destination airfields. However, this was only one of several surprising incidents involving ferry pilots, and he recalls the time when one Saturday afternoon he had been asked to wait for an ATA pilot to come and take one of the Spitfires for delivery:

> I waited quite a time and eventually saw a man walking up the road wearing a trilby hat, wearing a riding mac and carrying a 12-bore shotgun and holdall. He came in the gate and walked over to me, and turned out to be the ATA pilot. He had his parachute in the holdall and got into the cockpit. I tied the holdall up and put it in the cockpit as they had no radios at that time and slid the 12-bore alongside him. He still had his trilby hat on and I closed the hood otherwise when he took off it would have blown off with the wind. He started up the engine and I pulled the chocks away and away he went.

He also recalls that on another occasion a young lady pilot went across the airfield on take-off and passed very close to the control tower and over the signals area:

> The 'T' went up into the air behind the Spitfire. Having known an ex-ATA pilot in recent years, I now understand that they did exceptionally well considering how little training they had for the different types of aircraft they had to fly.

Today, Gordon belongs to the same Spitfire Association as ATA ferry pilot Joy Lofthouse.

Joy Lofthouse

Now living in the Cotswold town of Cirencester, Joy regularly gives talks about her ATA experiences, and on 20 May 2011 she attended the 'Women in Aerospace and Aviation' half-day seminar, along with three other veterans: Molly Rose, Margaret Frost and Mary Ellis. She has appeared in a number of BBC television programmes about the Spitfire, including *The Spitfire: Britain's Flying Past* in which John Sergeant introduced the 75th anniversary of the Spitfire and focused on MH434, which is still flying today, and *Spitfire Women*, the story of the ATA ferry pilots.

Joy Lofthouse, ATA ferry pilot, ready to ferry another Spitfire assembled at Eastleigh aerodrome to an RAF squadron airfield. *Joy Lofthouse*

Joy was completing her school examinations when war broke out and got her first job at the local Lloyds Bank, thinking she would stay there until she was old enough to join the forces, but the area where she lived was surrounded by RAF initial training schools and most of her first boyfriends were from the RAF. Her only interest then was in flying, and after reading a news item in *Aeroplane* magazine that the ATA were inviting applications for initial training, she applied and was offered a place. Joy was thrilled, but the bank manager would not release her and it was not until December 1943 that she was able to join the ATA. The first ATA training school was in Thame, and Joy attended a fairly basic nine-day technical training course consisting of meteorology, theory of flight and basic navigation:

> Although we did map-reading we didn't do navigation because we had no contact with the ground and didn't use radio. After the nine days' training we had a practical exam which I staggered through! Then we saw our first aeroplane. We were trained on Miles Magister, not on the Tiger Moth like the Royal Air Force used. However, we did go into a Tiger Moth for 'spinning experience' and learnt how to come out of a spin. You were allocated an instructor and we did circuits and bumps. Then the big day when you were ready to go solo. After that you did twenty-four cross-countries which was drawing a line on a map and plotting a compass setting.

After the cross-country flights the new ATA pilots were fitted with their uniform and wings and Joy transferred to RAF Cosford for six weeks to gain experience. She mainly flew the Fairchild Argos taxi aircraft as she was only qualified to fly training aircraft. When Joy returned to Thame, she converted on the Harvard, which was the first aircraft she had flown with a retractable undercarriage. The course was very similar, with mainly the same basic instructors, solos and cross-country. After the course on the Harvard had been successfully completed the next aircraft was the school Spitfire, if the instructors thought the trainee was capable:

> There were no dual trainers, just the single seat in those days. You just got in and did a few circuits and were then regarded as fully trained to fly Class 1 and Class 2 aircraft, all single-engined aircraft.

Joy was very pleased when she was posted to Hamble for two years, because it was one of the two all-women's pools, the other being at Cosford. The women became well known as the 'ATTA' girls. The ATA had increased its number of pools across the country, mostly close to aircraft factories, because its main job was picking up aircraft from factories and flying them to the maintenance units to have the armaments and radio fitted and then flying them on. However, they also flew any aircraft movement that allowed the RAF to do operational duties.

For the ATA ferry pilots at Hamble most of their work was out of the Supermarine aerodrome at Eastleigh. Joy flew about fifty Spitfires during her time as an ATA ferry pilot, which she saw as 'nothing compared to our senior girls who by the end of the war had flown over 200 Spitfires'. She enjoyed her time at Hamble and got used to the routine very quickly. If she had to pick up a Spitfire at Eastleigh there was transport provided, but she found that there was a lot of sitting around waiting for suitable weather to fly:

> You could only fly your category of course. They would say, 'Joy, you haven't flown a Hurricane yet, would you like to try? You then opened your little copy of ferry pilot's notes on every RAF and Fleet Air Arm aircraft to check the information you needed such as landing and stalling speeds and off you went.
>
> My longest time was at Hamble, but after VE Day of course there was little work so the ATA was closing some pools, but I never wanted to leave.

When Hamble closed, Joy moved to a pool near Leeds and was pleased to be able to do a few more hours' flying due to quite a few Fleet Air Arm Fairey Barracudas going up to Scotland:

> The Americans were still fighting their way across the Pacific, and we thought the Barracudas were going on to carriers and out to the Far East. Then when VJ Day came there was no work for us so I was demobbed in the September of 1945.

There was always the possibility of emergencies while flying, and Joy had her fair share:

I didn't break anything, but had a few nail biting moments. The most memorable was when I flew my first Spitfire from Eastleigh with a Griffon engine. The senior girls were helpful and told me to open up slowly and full rudder to counteract the swing. I did everything I was told but I was still making for the Southampton barrage balloons. It was only a second or two, but it felt like minutes. Once you got up into the air stream you could regain control and straighten her up. That was my first Griffon.

Once when flying out of an airfield in the Midlands I lost the hood of the Spitfire. You always took off with the canopy open until you got to the cruising speed; I put up my hand to close the hood and it flew away, but thankfully the controls told me it hadn't hit anything so I landed back on the airfield. The log book showed that they had had lots of canopy trouble which they had tried to repair, but hadn't succeeded in resolving the problem, so I didn't have to go through a Court of Inquiry for that one.

The third hair-raising incident was once when flying up to Scotland I got into a Scottish mist over the Firth of Forth, and of course it is like flying in cotton wool. With no instrument rating at all I had to guess a 180° turn and make for an airfield in Northumberland. Thankfully that time I was in a Barracuda because in a Spitfire you don't have so much time to think. In the Fairey Barracuda if you let the flaps and undercarriage down you could practically go backwards!

The one thing all the Hamble ATA ferry pilots remember was the lead-up to D-Day. From the air they could see all the mechanised vehicles piling up in the roads in Hampshire. 'You could have walked across to the Isle of Wight on the landing barges!' The German reconnaissance aircraft would have been able to see the build-up in Southampton and the surrounding area, but the indication was that the invasion fleet would be landing at the Pas-de-Calais. They had no idea that the D Day invasion force would take the longer channel crossing and attack Normandy:

Then on the morning of June 6 1944 from the air we saw the Solent was empty and we thought of all those chaps on the beaches. That was one of my wartime memories.

The Air Transport Auxiliary had another name – Ancient and Tattered Airmen – because the male pilots were much older, too old to be in the services, including one ex-First World War pilot who flew with one arm and one eye, and another who flew with just one arm. Many of them were bank managers, solicitors, businessmen, and all pre-war flyers:

> I flew eighteen different types of aircraft altogether because you had to fly anything that came on the books in your category. In February 1945 I went back to White Waltham, Maidenhead, to do my conversion to fly the Oxford, Anson and Dominie. The Anson was used as a factory aircraft and we could fly around and pick people up. If the war had continued I would have gone back and converted on a Hudson, and then you could fly all the fast twin engines, the Mosquito, Beaufighter and the Blenheim. About ten of our ladies flew multi-engines and I think the RAF converted them.

The ATA pilots who flew the multi-engined aircraft also had one other member of crew, the flight engineer:

> On some twin engine planes the pilot needed a second pair of hands, but not necessarily a qualified flight engineer, so every pool had one or two ATC cadets and they would fly as the second pair of hands when needed. One or two pools were on operational airfields, but mostly they were on little grass airfields such as Hamble.

The Spitfire was the favourite aeroplane amongst the ladies, and Joy found it had a compact cockpit and:

> … was the nearest thing to flying oneself and was very light on the touch. In fact a friend of mine, who belonged to the same local Spitfire Association as I did but has since passed away, was Gordon Mitchell, the son of Reginald Mitchell. I said to Gordon it was a 'ladies' aeroplane', and he replied, 'Joy, I don't think dad had that in mind when he designed it!'

Although the Spitfire was good in the air, it was not so friendly on the ground. Because it had a long high nose, the pilot had to weave to taxi:

> I loved flying the Spitfire, but it did have wheel brakes, actuated by compressed air which could be a bit fierce which made you careful otherwise you could tip on the nose.
> It had quite a narrow undercarriage and you had to be careful when landing cross-wind. If you landed into the wind on a grass airfield they could always put the windsock into the wind, but if you were landing on an airfield

with a runway and they couldn't have it exactly into the wind you had to try to land a three pointer, because otherwise you could be blown sideways.

I also had a sister in the ATA and she broke a Spitfire once when she came in cross-wind, tried to wheel it in but a tyre burst and one leg collapsed. She did what we called a ground loop, like looping the aircraft on the ground! My sister was eighteen months older than I. After an accident you would go to a Court of Inquiry and they would call that pilot error. My sister said, 'The only thing I broke was my finger nails!'

The ATA ferry pilots were provided with only enough petrol for their flight and Joy remembers that in 1945, while she was still at Hamble, they were experimenting with the Meteors in the Cotswolds and the pilots were told that if they tried to land and got a red they should keep well out of the way because the Meteor jets did not have a very long air time, and at the time they were monitoring the fuel consumption:

To take off you had to line up on the duty runway, whether it was a runway or grass and there was the caravan at the end of the flight path. It gave you green to take off or red to stop. The same for landing when you flew around and saw where the caravan was you could only land on a green. If red it was because someone else was landing.

Joy did not continue with flying after the war, and there were no opportunities for the senior ATA lady pilots who flew the multi-engined aircraft due to the numbers of men leaving Bomber Command who had far more experience. It was just a wartime job which Joy thoroughly enjoyed and felt very fortunate to be allowed to do, but after six years of war she was more than happy to settle down to marriage and children.

Giles Whittell wrote *Spitfire Women of World War II* in 2007, and a BBC documentary based on his book was broadcast on 18 September 2010. It was only when Scottish MP Nigel Griffiths brought to the attention of Prime Minister Gordon Brown that no recognition had been given to the work of the ATA pilots that a veteran's badge was presented to the remaining fifteen women and 100 men at No 10 Downing Street in 2008.

15

TEST PILOTS

The work of the test pilots was very important to the development of the Spitfire because it was from their test flights that Joe Smith received the reports that would influence the ongoing design work and further highlight any problems or issues that needed dealing with urgently.

It was well known during the war that the pilots fighting for the defence of Britain were constantly in danger, and many were killed or injured. It was so traumatic that in the evenings, after the day's flying, they would often let their hair down and get up to many escapades and pranks to take their minds off the events of the day. Sometimes they were required to test up to twenty aircraft in a day, all with the potential for problems such as engine failure or other aircraft mechanical failures and all with the possibility of having to bail out or crash-land the aircraft. Yet many of these pilots would still perform stunts to entertain the workers or visitors to the factory.

Alex Henshaw

Alex Henshaw, the chief test pilot at Castle Bromwich, had started to learn to fly in 1932. He became involved in air racing and won the King's Cup in 1933 and again in 1938. Just before the war, he purchased a Percival Mew Gull, G-AEXF, a single-seat racing aircraft, as he wanted to attempt the record for England to Cape Town and back, and had the aircraft modified and adapted to increase its speed and range for the attempt. He took off from Gravesend on 5 February 1939, completing the flight in 40 hours including refuelling stops. After just over a day in Cape Town he undertook the return flight, landing on 9 February after a flight of 39 hours and 36 minutes, successfully breaking the record on both trips. He was so exhausted that he had to be lifted out of the cockpit and carried away from the aircraft.

Alex Henshaw was the chief test pilot at the Castle Bromwich 'shadow factory'.
Alan Mansell

Later Henshaw became well known in Castle Bromwich for performing daredevil stunts in the Spitfire he was testing, keeping many of the workers' eyes glued to his impromptu displays. He was often required to demonstrate the Spitfire's capabilities to visiting dignitaries, including Winston Churchill. Henshaw once caused a sensation when he flew the length of Broad Street, Birmingham, at low level, and was also credited as the only pilot ever to perform a barrel roll in a Lancaster bomber.

It was very dangerous work as Castle Bromwich was often blanketed in fog, yet Henshaw was known to have taken off on flight tests in such conditions. Jeffrey Quill describes him as a 'real master of aerobatics', and also praises the way he managed with adverse weather conditions, in which he flew with no 'aids'. There were times when the engines failed, and once he was forced to crash-land within a built-up area: he aimed the Spitfire between two rows of houses which took the wings off, with him still sitting in the cockpit, amazingly with only minor injuries. On another occasion, the engine of his Spitfire blew up and he had to bail out, but had serious problems with his parachute which was badly torn. However, he landed safely and survived. It was claimed that he would fly low over his house to indicate to his wife that he was ready for his tea.

George Pickering

Another daring test pilot known to have been involved in various exploits was George Pickering, as his daughter, Jennie Sherborne, explains:

My father was an extrovert and he did mad things, and one time he flew the Spitfire under the bridge near Winchester which then became known as 'Spitfire Bridge'. He came home and told my mother what he had done, but of course he could have got into serious trouble for this exploit. It is now called 'Spitfire roundabout' because they demolished the bridge. There has been some controversy because some say it was a Canadian pilot in a Typhoon that was the only one to fly under the bridge, but other pilots are thought to have done the same. However, my father did do it and we were brought up to believe that, otherwise how else would the bridge be named Spitfire Bridge?

Pickering was known to purposely fly low over the Itchen floating bridge in order to scare the crew and passengers. Another of his daring stunts was to loop-the-loop in a seaplane at the Hendon Air Show, and it is thought that he was possibly the first and the last to do so. If, after a flight test on a Walrus, Pickering flew at 300ft (91.44m) over the workshops and did a loop-the-loop, this signalled to the aircraft engineers below that everything was OK; if not, he would just land on the water and they would know that further work needed to be done. However, a cause for concern over his safety was raised after he failed to return after a test flight. A search was conducted and the Walrus was found floating on the Solent with a fishing rod sticking out of the cockpit and the pilot, Pickering, fast asleep!

Jennie remembers her father's sense of humour and talks about when they lived in a 'lovely thatched cottage' near Fordingbridge after being evacuated from Southampton before war broke out:

> My father would fly over, you would hear him, he would come over in a Spitfire and fly very low and we would go outside. He would come back and drop a little silk parachute carrying a note inside.

Denis Webb describes Pickering as a truly great character, full of wisdom and tact, and remembers an incident where his wisdom was used to great effect. This related to two young pilots' enthusiasm and competitiveness concerning a decision to fly in bad weather on a particular day. Those pilots were Quill and Henshaw. Pickering told them that it was no weather for flying and mentioned that even the birds were walking, adding that it was not his intention to be the best pilot in the world, but the oldest. That did the trick!

Pickering's Spitfire Disintegrates

While testing Spitfire AA876 on 25 October 1941, Pickering had a serious accident. Jennie explains that her father was in a steep dive, going at 520mph

(836.85km/h), when the aircraft disintegrated. His parachute did not open properly at first and he landed in trees. Pickering wrote in his log book, 'Aircraft disintegrated after pulling out of a dive of 520mph trial. Landed by parachute, breaking arm and losing two fingers of left hand.'

Webb remembers Pickering telling him that when the aircraft disintegrated the next thing he knew he was flying through the air unaided! Pickering tried to find his parachute release, but was unable to because his harness had somehow got twisted, and remembered subconsciously counting the cloud layers as he went through them, thinking 'there's one more to go' when he found the release and pulled it. He was so low that the parachute had barely deployed before he hit the top of the tree, which being fairly tall, probably saved him. The parachute chords were tangled in the tree and he started shouting for help. Pickering was then rescued and taken to hospital where his left hand was found to be very badly damaged.

It was Ernie Mansbridge, with Murry White's help, who solved the problem that caused AA876 to break up:

I knew George very well. He was a very tough individual, but had a bad accident in a Spitfire. He was diving and determined to get to the maximum diving speed at the time which was 450mph [724.2km/h]. He survived, but could remember that everything fell apart. I checked around with Ernie and he got hold of a damaged Air Speed Indicator which showed an imprint of the needle at 400mph [643.73km/h], 50mph [80.46km/h] below the authorized maximum diving speed. I found it was an instrument manufactured by a company who also manufactured car fuel gauges.

I obtained three or four new instruments from the stores and found on calibration that those manufactured by the same company as the ASI fitted to AA876 all had stops in them at the 400mph position. George had tried to push the ASI to the maximum diving speed and had achieved much higher aircraft speed than the official diving speed of 450mph [724.2km/h].

As he was in a dive when the aircraft pulled out, probably on its own due to compressibility effect at lower altitude, the aircraft exceeded its maximum strength and fell apart. We stopped this particular instrument from going into aircraft from then on. These instruments were all manufactured by different companies but we continually random checked their performance by calibration.

Jennie comments that between the time that the Spitfire went into full production in 1938 and this accident in 1941, her father was averaging about thirty-six test flights a month and during this period he had tested more than 1,100 Spitfires as well as other aircraft:

He was off for about two years before he was told he could test fly again. However, in the meantime my father assisted in the testing of the Spitfires from the ground and also delivered communication aircraft, but was not considered fit enough for testing the Spitfires in the air.

At this time he was flying the Oxford AB649, Monospar X9331 G-AFSA, Miles Falcon G-ADTD and Miles Magister to take test pilots to and from the various airfields, including Eastleigh, Chattis Hill, Worthy Down and Boscombe Down, and also on flights to Henley, Aldermaston and Hornchurch. Joe Smith was a frequent passenger, and one particular flight in October 1942 was from Eastleigh to Hucknall and then on to HMS *Merlin* at Donibristle in Fife, which was then flying Supermarine Seafire IICs. Smith was at Donibristle for twelve days before returning in the Oxford to Eastleigh.

Pickering finally went for his medical on 1 June 1943 in Oxford and passed to test Spitfires again. He spent the night with his sister who owned the King's Head pub in Ivinghoe, Bedfordshire, and while celebrating passing his medical he met Irish Guards Officer Capt. Desmond Kingsford whose regiment was training in the Chilterns. By the end of the evening it had been decided, with much encouragement from Pickering, that Kingsford would give him the opportunity of driving a Bren gun carrier, as Jenny explains:

> The next morning they were negotiating the sheer face of Ivinghoe Beacon when the Bren gun carrier stopped, unable to go up the steep gradient, and while trying to turn round, the open topped carrier turned over and my father was killed. My aunt was also in the Bren gun carrier, but was thrown clear and survived. My father was only 38 years of age. Desmond Kingsford was unharmed apart from suffering from deep remorse. He really never got over it.

Kingsford, who as a Cambridge graduate had taken part in two Oxford and Cambridge boat races, and had also represented Great Britain in the 1936 Berlin Olympics, was sadly killed in August 1944, one week after being awarded the Military Cross for bravery in action.

Jeffrey Quill and the Team of Test Pilots

All production Spitfires were flight-tested before delivery. From 1938, Quill took charge of Spitfire development and production flying, and by the Second World War he was Vickers-Supermarine's chief test pilot, in charge of the flight-testing of all aircraft types built by the company. Working closely with Joe Smith, Quill devised the standard testing procedures, with variations for specific aircraft designs, which became operational from 1938. He also oversaw a group of ten to twelve pilots responsible for testing all development and production Spitfires built by Vickers-Supermarine in the Southampton area.

The team of pilots involved in the testing of Supermarine aircraft included his close colleague George Pickering; Alex Henshaw, who was in charge of the Spitfire testing at Castle Bromwich; George Errington; George N. Snarey, his former colleague in the Meteorological Flight; Pat Shea-Simmonds; G.J. Home; J.W.C. Judge; Guy Morgan; Frank Furlong; Peter Hillwood; Johnnie Wakefield; Don Robertson; Les Colquhoun; and John Derry.

As well as the Supermarine test pilots, a number of RAF and Naval pilots were attached to the team. Sadly, among those killed while testing aircraft were Johnnie Wakefield, who had been a racing car driver but was killed while flying a Spitfire PR Mk IV, and Frank Furlong, who had ridden the winner 'Reynoldstown' in the Grand National in 1935, and was killed while testing a prototype Spiteful in 1944.

When Quill retired from his test flying career in 1947, Mike Lithgow took over as Supermarine's chief test pilot. Lt-Cdr Lithgow had served in the Fleet Air Arm from 1939 until 1945 and after leaving the service in January 1946, joined Supermarine as a test pilot and undertook many test flights on the Supermarine Attacker, Swift and Scimitar.

Test pilots Jeffrey Quill, G.P. Shea-Simmonds and Mike Lithgow. *Solent Sky*

Spitfire MkVB AB910 was part of 133 (Eagle) Squadron based in Lympne, Kent, that provided air cover in Operation Jubilee in which Allied forces tried unsuccessfully to capture the port of Dieppe. *Solent Sky*

As a small child in the 1950s, Sarah Quill remembers her father flying over their house in a Spitfire or other aircraft, sometimes on the way to an air show. Sarah and her sister Virginia would be waiting outside in the drive so that they could wave as he flew over. The sound of the Spitfire engine was unmistakable:

> From about the age of eight, I remember being taken to air shows where he was flying. Occasionally there would a mock battle, with my father flying the Spitfire AB910 and Bill Bedford flying the Hurricane. I think the first time I flew with him was as a child when I was taken up in an Auster.
>
> In 1962, my father drove the power boat 'Tramontana' [designed by his friend Peter Du Cane] to win the Daily Express Offshore Powerboat Race from Cowes to Torquay. His co-driver and navigator was Don Robertson, a colleague and former test pilot with Supermarine. I used to be taken on the trial runs, which were hard on the back when we were against a head-on sea. But it was rough weather on the day and that helped Tramontana win the race, as she was a heavy boat. She was later bought by Gianni Agnelli, who had taken part in the race in his boat 'Ultima Dea'.
>
> Although my father was extremely busy and much preoccupied with work, he was always a kind and affectionate parent, and even as a child I was aware

of the regard in which he was held. But he was modest about his achievements, and as tends to happen, I discovered much more about them after he had died. I had not realised, for instance, until I researched his log books that the aerobatic flying sequences in 1941, shown at the end of the film *The First of the Few* [known as *Spitfire* in the USA and released in 1942], were made by him from Northolt on 1 and 2 November 1941 in a Spitfire Mk II, presumably painted to resemble K5054.

At an air show in about 1958, Virginia and I were allowed in turn to sit in the cockpit of a Spitfire [most probably AB910]. I remember being astonished that the aircraft was so much smaller than I had always imagined it to be, and wondered how tall pilots had managed to cram themselves into it. JKQ was not very tall – and just as well for him, I thought!

16

WORKING CLOSELY
WITH JOE SMITH

Barrie Bryant did not really get to know Joe Smith until the end of the war, covering only the final decade of his life, when the team expanded from 350 to 700 members. Barrie viewed him more as a manager than a designer, but realised the huge responsibility that Smith had in heading up the design team. Smith was very much a man to consult and discuss important design matters before making a final decision:

> Frequently he would adjourn such a discussion, lead the group to the Design Office, collect Eric Cooper or Alf Faddy and repair to the board of some senior draughtsman to inspect current schemes. Seated at that draughtsman's stool, with half a dozen of us standing around, he sketched with a soft pencil in the manner ascribed by various authors to R.J. Next morning we would probably learn what Joe had decided.

Murry White also recalls Smith's belief in consulting with the senior design and technical team before making his final decision on design matters:

> By 1943, Ernie Mansbridge was Joe Smith's right hand man. I believe that Joe would never make a decision without consulting Ernie first. Alan Clifton was also consulted as he was absolutely the key pin there. Alan Clifton was the structural man and Ernie was the performance man. Ernie Mansbridge was certainly a great help to Joe Smith.
>
> Ernie Mansbridge came into me one day and told me that he had been talking to Joe who was very unhappy as he wasn't getting enough information on what was happening and thought he would make me into a sort of 'wandering minstrel' to walk around and find out what the chaps were doing in the field. I told him that I would like that very much, and he said that

we would talk about it a little more later on. Eventually by November 1943 I became Joe's technical assistant.

Working as Joe Smith's Technical Assistant

The Supermarine Sea Otter prototype was first flown on 21 September 1938, and was the last biplane flying boat built by Supermarine. The Sea Otter was an amphibian biplane and was a development of the Walrus but built for long-range service. There was one major difference between these aircraft: the Walrus had a rear-mounted pusher propeller configuration whereas the Sea Otter had a forward-facing engine with a tractor propeller configuration. The aircraft was used by the RAF, the Royal Navy and the Royal Danish Navy.

In 1943, the Walrus Mk II was built with a wooden hull, whereas the Mk I had a metal hull and was used for rescue and reconnaissance duties. The engine was a Bristol Pegasus VI and was built by Supermarine, later switching to Saunders-Roe who built the aircraft up until 1944.

Murry White recounts his work with the Royal Navy Trials Unit in Arbroath where his first job concerned the Sea Otter, a single-engine amphibian designed for catapult operations from cruisers. Although it had folding wings and lifting gear, it had no arrester hook, but the Navy wanted to use it on carriers for air-sea rescue. Due to incorrect loading by the Naval Trials

Supermarine Sea Otter JM885 ABRI, designed to carry bombs and depth-charges, was built under contract by Saunders-Roe. *Solent Sky*

The Sea Otter ASR II RD872 amphibian biplane replaced the Walrus for reconnaissance and general duties, including air-sea rescue. This aircraft was also built by Saunders-Roe. *Solent Sky*

Unit, the aircraft porpoised while trying to take off from the water. Mansbridge told Murry to go and sort it out. On arrival at Arbroath in November 1943, he measured the weight and C.G. of the aircraft and reloaded the aircraft with ballast, and asked the RNVR pilot if he could fly with him. After some difficulty, he was allowed to fly after signing a 'blood chit', and they did take-offs and landings for two weeks in all sorts of conditions. Then it was time to go on the carrier, but they had no hooks:

> I told them that it was essential to put new brakes and wheels on it and we flew over to Ayr, on the west coast of Scotland where the carrier was operating. I told the pilot I wanted to fly to the carrier with him, but he refused in case he went over the side. He wanted to make sure that if he did he could get himself out and not have to worry about me. I then went on board in an Avenger and the first thing that happened was hearing over the Tannoy that I had to report to Commander Air. The captain of HMS *Pretoria Castle* was Caspar John who was on the bridge. He looked at me sternly when I asked if he was Commander Air and he pointed to a man in the corner of the bridge. Incidentally, Caspar John was the son of the famous artist Augustus John.
>
> We got the Sea Otter on safely with new brakes and wheels which were in top condition. I recommended that we needed a hook, and they agreed. I returned to Joe and advised him that a hook would be a great improvement and was essential for the Sea Otter.

Getting to Know Alan Greenwood

Murry remembers Joe Smith mentioning that there was a member of the Weybridge team, Alan Greenwood, who would like to come down to look around. Greenwood was a personal assistant to George Edwards and Smith felt that he would be 'snooping around' to see what he could find out. He did not want him to get any wrong ideas, but wanted to know exactly what Alan Greenwood was up to, so asked Murry to look after him:

> Alan came down and he had been an apprentice like me, but at Weybridge, and was about four months younger than me. He had joined the Royal Navy at the beginning of the war, serving on the Russian convoys. I took him around the plant and we had a good day together. I told him what we were doing and what we hoped to do. I reported it all back to Joe and that was it.
>
> Alan phoned me up a bit later and said, 'I came down to look at your place; you had better come up and look at mine.' We became buddy pals and he was doing the same sort of job that I was. He was with George Edwards and I was with Joe Smith, the poor chap that died. Alan Greenwood was to become my greatest pal in the end, and the chap I was with mostly after Jeffrey Quill and Walter Gibb died. They were also my great friends too.

Royal Navy Seafires

Early in the war, the Atlantic convoys were at the mercy of the U-boats because shore-based aircraft could not maintain cover flights, and it became urgent to provide continuous air cover. The Royal Navy first responded in 1941 with CAM (catapult armed merchant) ships to catapult a fighter to defend a convoy. However, although the catapulting worked successfully, recovering the aircraft was impossible, with the pilot having to be rescued by other ships in the convoy. The decision to fit a flight deck to a merchant ship solved that problem and so the first escort carriers joined the Atlantic convoys to give support and maintain a continuous air cover role.

Towards the end of 1941, a Spitfire Mk VB was fitted with an arrester hook in the form of an A-frame hinged to the underside of the rear fuselage and was referred to as a 'hooked Spitfire'. Another machine, this time a Mk VC, was similarly treated and also given catapult spools. A number of both types were built, but their successful operation from carriers raised the much greater problem of wing folding in order to utilise to the full the available hangar space. The folding of such a thin wing presented problems, but was eventually resolved by the wing being hinged and raised vertically with a second fold near the wing tip joint turning downwards.

Seafires were first used in Operation Torch, the invasion by British and American forces of French North Africa, on 8 November 1942. When the war ended in Europe in 1945 and attention turned to the war in the Pacific, Seafires were sent to prepare for a planned invasion of Japan. However, this was not forthcoming as the atomic bombs on Hiroshima and Nagasaki ended the war with Japan.

The Seafire Series

The Seafire F Mk IB was the first naval development of the Spitfire, which was tropicalised and had a Merlin 45/46 engine, tankage for 85 gallons (386.41 litres), standard wing tips, deck arrester hook; slinging points and armaments consisting of two 20mm cannons and four .303 machine guns.

The F Mk IIC was also tropicalised and had a Merlin 32 engine, tankage for 85 gallons (386.41 litres), standard wing tips, a strengthened airframe and under-carriage, deck arrester hook, slinging points and catapult spools, and was armed with two 20mm cannons and four .303 machine guns.

The F Mk III, also tropicalised, had a Merlin 45 engine, tankage for 85 gallons (386.41 litres), four blade propeller and folding wings, deck arrester hook and armaments comprising two 20mm cannons and four .303 machine guns.

BL687 VB was converted to a Seafire Mk IB and became MB329. It served in North Africa, but returned to 731 Squadron in Scotland. The pilot was forced to belly land when unable to lower the undercarriage. *Solent Sky*

Seafire F Mk IIC of 889
Squadron based at RNS
Colombo, Ceylon, from April
1944. The squadron then
embarked on the escort carrier
HMS *Atheling* to protect ships
from Japanese attack in the Bay
of Bengal. *Solent Sky*

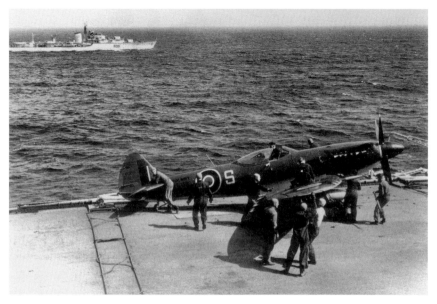

The Seafire F Mk XVII had strengthened wings, a reinforced undercarriage supporting
heavy landings on aircraft carriers, and a cut-down rear fuselage with an extra fuel tank and
bubble canopy. *Solent Sky*

The decision by the Air Ministry that the Royal Navy would use Griffon-
powered aircraft led to the prototype for the Navy Seafire being developed in
the Experimental Hangar at Hursley Park in late 1943. The Seafire F Mk XV
had a Griffon VI engine, strengthened undercarriage, a rear-view cockpit and
folding wings, and was armed with two 20mm cannons and four .303 machine
guns. It was tropicalised and could carry a 500lb bomb. Later models were fitted
with a sting arrester hook. The prototype, NS487, first flew in February 1944.
The production model, SR446, was delivered in September of that year.

The Seafire F Mk XVII was a modified version of the Mk XV, with a reinforced undercarriage that had improved shock-absorbing qualities (especially
advantageous for deck landings on aircraft carriers) and strengthened folding

wings for storage on carriers. It had tankage for 80 gallons (302.83 litres) of fuel in the fuselage and 20 gallons (75.7 litres) in the wings, a curved windscreen in front of the bullet-proof screen and rear-view hood and sting hook, and was armed with two 20mm cannons and four .303 machine guns.

The Seafire F Mk XVIII was similar to the Mk XVII, but with a Griffon 36 engine, although there is no confirmation of it ever being built. The Air Ministry did place an order with Cunliffe-Owen under Contract No Air/5128 for 250 Seafire Mk XVII/XVIIIs with serial numbers VA461-856, but it appears that the order, which included Mk XVIII serials VA661-VA694 totalling 163 aircraft, was cancelled.

The prototype Mk XVII NS493 was developed in 1945, too late for active war service. Some became fighter reconnaissance aircraft with cameras in the fuselage space designed for the extra fuel tank. *Solent Sky*

Seafire PK240 Mk XV took part in the deck landing trials led by Lt-Cdr Eric 'Winkle' Brown on HMS *Pretoria Castle* in November 1944. *Solent Sky*

Seafire Mk XVII SX283 served in 778 Squadron. A Seafire Mk XVII from this squadron achieved Mach 0.88 in a dive and was credited as the Fleet Air Arm's fastest aircraft. *Solent Sky*

Some Seafires, notably LR Mk IICs, FR Mk IIIs and F Mk XVIIs, were also fitted with two F24 cameras, one vertical and one oblique, to carry out a reconnaissance role.

Seafire F Mks 45-47

When the Seafire was needed for attacks on the Japanese mainland, it was necessary to upgrade its role from the low-level work defending the British fleet or supporting the troop landings to a more powerful high-level fighter. The engine was therefore changed from the single-stage engine to a two-stage Griffon 61 powering a five-bladed propeller and raising the speed to 442mph (711.33km/h). This fighter was the Seafire Mk 45 which had tankage for 84 gallons (381.87 litres) in the fuselage and 36 gallons (163.65 litres) in the wings. It was tropicalised, but did not have folding wings which caused problems for storage on aircraft carriers.

With such power from the Griffon 61 engine and the five-bladed propellers, the pilots found the Mk 45 difficult to fly in a straight line. Smith and his team therefore came up with a solution with the three-bladed contra-rotating propeller for the Seafire Mk 46 which helped keep the aircraft flying straight.

Seafire Mk 45 TM379 prototype. It was originally designated LA193 and undertook trials from HMS *Pretoria Castle* conducted by Eric 'Winkle' Brown in July 1945. *Solent Sky*

While landing on HMS *Illustrious* in March 1947, this Seafire Mk 46 hit the barrier, causing slight damage to the aircraft. *Murry White*

Seafire Mk 47 VP483 was built at South Marston in 1947, then flown to RNAS Anthorn in Cumbria (HMS *Nuthatch*). In August 1948, it embarked on HMS *Ocean* for service in the Mediterranean. *Solent Sky*

The variant was similar to the Mk 45 but had a few minor changes such as a teardrop canopy.

The Seafire Mk 47 had folding wings operated by hydraulics and a Griffon 85 engine powering contra-rotating propellers giving an increased speed of 452mph 727.42km/h). There was also increased tankage, with 84 gallons (381.87 litres) in the fuselage, 36 gallons (163.65 litres) in the wings and 33 gallons (150.02 litres) in the rear fuselage. The aircraft served with the Fleet Air Arm Squadron 800 on the light aircraft carrier HMS *Triumph* in the Korean War, but was withdrawn from Fleet Air Arm front-line service in 1951.

The Seafire FR Mk 47 was also used in a reconnaissance role and was fitted with two F24 cameras, one vertical and one oblique.

Carrier Trials

In June 1941, HMS *Audacity* (D10) became the first Royal Navy escort carrier. It was originally the German merchant vessel MV *Hannover*, which had been captured in March 1940, and after two further name changes was converted for use as an escort aircraft carrier. The design as an escort carrier had not included space for a lift and hangar, 802 Squadron's six Grumman Martlets

(Wildcats) being stored on the deck and open to the elements. The main role of the squadron was to protect convoys from the threat of the Luftwaffe Fw 200 Condor reconnaissance bombers, and a number of the bombers were shot down in the ship's short career.

On the OG 76 convoy to Gibraltar Sub-Lt Eric 'Winkle' Brown shot down his first Fw 200 Condor, and on the return convoy, HG 76, he shot down another, just two days before HMS *Audacity* was sunk by *U-751*, commanded by Gerhard Bigalk, on 21 December 1941. There was a heavy loss of life, but the 22-year-old Brown was one of two 802 Squadron pilots to survive. Following the sinking of HMS *Audacity* the squadron was disbanded and not re-formed until February 1942. Brown, who was noted for his experience of deck landings, was then posted to the RAE at Farnborough where he became involved with the Supermarine Seafire deck landing tests:

> I was with my squadron on HMS *Audacity*, the first Royal Navy escort carrier that was built, and it was a very small ship indeed. We had been flying Wildcats there, but the ship was torpedoed and sunk by a U-boat.
>
> After the sinking, when I returned to the UK I was told that I was going to be asked to land a Seafire on a small aircraft carrier. A full-size carrier had a deck about 800ft [243.84m] long, while a small carrier had a deck of about 300ft [91.44m] to 400ft [121.92m] long. It wasn't a Seafire, but the first converted hooked Spitfire VB. Even the name Seafire hadn't been chosen at this stage.
>
> I did the trials and although Joe Smith was very interested, I didn't meet him at the time. The trials were very successful and resulted in the Admiralty deciding to order the Seafire in large numbers.

HMS *Pretoria Castle*

On 2 October 1939, the Union Castle passenger liner *Pretoria Castle* was requisitioned by the Admiralty for use as an armed merchant cruiser in the Second World War. In 1942, the ship went into the Swan Hunter shipyards on the Tyne for conversion to an escort carrier, and was commissioned into service in 1943. HMS *Pretoria Castle* was then used as a trials and training carrier and was not involved in active service.

Barbara Harries remembers her father joining the aircraft carriers while the trials were being held. The clothes he wore were kept in his office in Hursley Park, and Barbara describes them as 'warm, fleecy lined trousers and jackets'.

Eric 'Winkle' Brown recalls the times he met and got to know Joe Smith on board HMS *Pretoria Castle*:

When landing on HMS *Pretoria Castle* in August 1945, the undercarriage of this Seafire Mk 45 collapsed. The sting hook below the tail attached to the wire is clearly shown. *Murry White*

We had a dedicated trials carrier called HMS *Pretoria Castle* and I was constantly on and off this carrier. Joe began to take a real interest in the Seafire as well as the Spitfire. He didn't see the Seafire as an odd job, but concentrated on helping the Navy. As he got deeper into it Joe decided he needed to know more about what actually took place on a carrier, and he asked the Admiralty if he could go on board for these trials, and of course they welcomed the idea.

When there was a major modification to prove on the *Pretoria Castle* Joe would come along. He was flown on board in something like a Fairey Albacore and dug in and spent the night on board. The captain, Caspar John RN, made sure he had a nice cabin for the night and Joe thoroughly enjoyed himself. In fact I think he began to determine that he wasn't going to miss this because he was enjoying it so much. He was very good company and we would chat in the wardroom. He was a quiet sort but he was a good conversationalist and we naturally talked mainly about the engineering aspects of the Seafire.

To have an ally like him on your side meant a lot and I respected him very much. Joe was very quietly spoken and very unobtrusive. I think Joe would have been happy to settle on a carrier for a long time. However, we found that the Seafire had two fundamental problems: It had a terrible view ahead because of the length of the engine. You could hardly see the deck unless you did a curved or crabbed approach. The undercarriage was built for the RAF and when they came into land on an airfield they came in much faster than we do on the carrier and floated before they touched down. They didn't have a very high vertical velocity on the undercarriage, about 7ft [2.13m] a second maximum. Whereas landing on the carrier we would sometimes get a double that vertical velocity, mainly about 10ft [3.04m] a second.

These were two problems for Joe Smith so he decided that he would get stuck in and do something about them. However, there wasn't too much he could do about the view, but there was a lot he could do about the undercarriage, mainly strengthening it by mainly using long stroke oleo legs. When Joe had the undercarriage changed I was asked to check the aircraft out. Of course it was much better for us.

Jeffrey Quill Joins the Fleet Air Arm and RNVR

There was a second spell of service flying when Quill was commissioned in the air branch of the RNVR in 1943–44, to assist in developing better carrier deck landings. With the introduction of the Supermarine Seafire, the Fleet Air Arm had suffered enormous losses in deck landing accidents on the aircraft carriers whose decks were 30 per cent shorter than those of the big fleet carriers. During five months of service, Quill made more than seventy-five deck landings, leading to modifications in the production of Seafires and the training of Navy pilots.

In 1944, Murry White was asked by Smith to be present on all the future carrier trials that he had lined up to develop the Seafire into what finally became the Seafire Mk 47:

Incidentally, the name Seafire was first suggested by Freda Clifton, Alan's wife, as a contraction of the name Sea Spitfire. It is one of Joe Smith's greatest achievements in producing the superb naval fighter, Seafire Mark 47 to be followed by the jet Attacker and the ultimate twin Avon engines Scimitar.

The Seafire I, II and III were very much stopgap efforts and did a memorable job under difficult conditions. In working up from the Seafire II and Seafire III, Joe Smith had to devise a vastly improved arrester hook, self stowing, catapult gear, hydraulically folding wings, RATOG and above all greatly improved shock absorbing undercarriage, all at an increased weight, while at the same time installing the Griffon engine and contra-rotating propellers. I was involved in all these trials from 1944 to 1956 as Joe's representative and reporter and eventually became the trials manager for the Supermarine party.

Design of the Sting Hook

The Seafire Mks I, II and III had a belly hook which dropped down from the rear fuselage and were already doing great work for the Royal Navy, but on engaging the arrester wires the aircraft tended to dip over on its nose unless the pilot was very careful. Eric 'Winkle' Brown was very familiar with this problem:

> The Seafire had its original arrester hook under the fuselage, but the problem with that was when it arrested it tended to make the aircraft dip forward and if it dipped too much the props would strike the deck. On the Wildcat there was a sting hook that came right out of the tail and I suggested that this was the way to go. Joe was enthusiastic about this idea and this was a major step forward.

Smith had asked Murry to rejoin HMS *Pretoria Castle* to observe the deck landings, and he returned with the recommendation that a hook designed on the thrust line was essential for the aircraft's deck handling performance:

> This was pretty obvious but was easier said than done. However, Alan Clifton, Ernie Mansbridge and Arthur Shirvall got together and offered the design of the telescopic hook on or close to the thrust line which would be accommodated by cutting off a portion of the rudder. Joe gave the go-ahead and the telescopic hook, subsequently known as the sting hook, was fitted to prototype Seafire XV PK245 which was proof tested in the wires at RAE Farnborough and I went back to HMS *Pretoria Castle* for carrier trials in June 1945.

Further reinforcing was carried out and increase clearances to the assembly were provided. The troublesome Dural rivets were replaced by high tensile steel rivets having shallower countersunk heads, and mild steel pins were replaced by high tensile steel pins. Before the trials were resumed, an improved arrester hook damper was fitted and the main undercarriage oleo legs were replaced by improved rebound damping oleo legs:

> When the trials were continued in August 1945 the arrester gear was proved satisfactory for production although we still had to make three minor modifications which were included on all future aircraft right up to the Seafire Mk 47.
>
> These carrier trials, together with proofing runs into the wires at the naval department at the RAE, occupied the period from early June to late August 1945 and involved a great deal of hard thinking on the part of the design staff and a great deal of skilled flying and testing on the part of the pilots.

HMS *Pretoria Castle* was operating out of the Clyde in Scotland and many nights were spent on the Glasgow night train by the Supermarine party, mostly Sunday night to start trials on Monday. They were great times!

Three incidents stand out in Murry's memory. The first incident was making the original sting arrester hook strong enough; the second was solving the problem of undercarriage shock absorption; and the third was when preparing for the deck landing trials of the Seafire Mk 47.

Incident 1

The initial sting hook trials were carried out on HMS *Pretoria Castle* which was far from ideal. At a speed of 18 knots it meant they had to find a steady wind speed of at least 8 knots with no sea. The ship's round down had a much tighter radius that the fleet carriers and, worse, had obstructions on it. These obstructions proved the cause of the problems. On landing the telescopic hook pulled out of its mounting or 'fixed part' on engaging the wire due to the rivets failing in shear.

> After a couple of reinforcing efforts, I asked for Alan Clifton [Cliffy] as Chief Structures to come on board. He brought Harold Smith, our then Chief Stressman and a man of remarkable practicality of 'know-how'.
>
> On the first attempt with all the reinforcing in the arrester telescopic gear, the hook pulled out. We were all dumbfounded, except Alan and Harold. I had obtained permission for them to watch the landings from the safety net close to the round down and they believed the hook had hit one of the obstructions. On close examination we found the imprint of the hook on one of the round down lights putting an unacceptable load on the arrester gear and the troublesome rivets.
>
> This would not have happened on a fleet or light fleet carrier because of the round down design and the spacing of the arrester wires, and so the installation of the sting hook was cleared and subsequently proved to be exceptionally reliable.
>
> After VJ Day we used firstly HMS *Illustrious*, some of the light fleet carriers and finally HMS *Ark Royal* and HMS *Eagle*. Of course, all the hard work was done by the pilots, firstly our Jeffrey Quill, Mike Lithgow and others followed by naval pilots for the RAE and STU [Service Trials Unit] while the design work and manufacturing was done by those back at Hursley Park.

Incident 2

A major problem arose regarding the original type of legs on a Spitfire which was proving unsuitable for carrier landings, and Smith was determined to ensure that the problem reached a successful conclusion. The development of the Seafire produced a major problem of undercarriage shock absorption. The Spitfire's original leg was fine for aerodrome landings and long or even short runways, but when the aircraft was arrested in the air and thrown onto the deck, the oleo legs were compressed rapidly and gave back its energy by bouncing the aircraft:

> The answer was to make the stroke of the legs longer and absorb the energy by hydraulic fluid which is uncompressible and not by air, using only a small air capacity as a spring to return the legs to the extended free position. Such long stroke undercarriage legs were developed for the Seafires and introduced on the Mark XV and Mark XVII aircraft.
>
> Carrier trials were required to examine these new legs, so with the Supermarine party I joined HMS *Triumph* [a light fleet carrier] to witness deck landings of two production Seafires Mk XVII (SX311 & SX314) fitted with long stroke legs.

The trials proved the excellent performance of the legs and almost 100 landings were made by the two aircraft. However, they had an accident, which is the reason these particular trials remain in Murry's memory. On one of the landings, the pilot made his approach too low, with the result that his port leg and hook hit the round down. The aircraft slewed sideways engaging a late wire, but the pilot was unable to avoid going into the catwalk. The aircraft sustained damage, but the pilot and the undercarriage were undamaged. It was generally accepted that the aircraft would not have engaged the wire and gone over the ship's side if it had not been for the great improvement in the rebound damping provided by the long stroke oleo legs:

> This is a great example of Joe Smith's determination of pursuing a problem to a successful conclusion. The long stroke legs were used in all Supermarine naval aircraft. When the Seafang and the Attacker came along and the leg stroke got longer a unique device of linkage enabled the legs to be partially shortened on retraction in the wheel arch. Joe never gave up!

Incident 3

This incident occurred during preparation in advance of the carrier trials for the Seafire Mk 47, when acceptance trials on the first production aircraft were about to be carried out. The aircraft was at the Service Trials Unit at RNAS Ford and was being flown by the C.O. Lt-Cdr Carver, practising aerodrome dumble deck landings (ADDLs):

> I was in the control hut watching. The aircraft was performing splendidly and had made about 6 ADDLs of a 10 batch when the pilot came on to say he had a red undercarriage light on his port leg.
>
> He tried all the manoeuvres in the book without avail. Finally, Lt-Cdr Carver said he would have to land on one leg as he was running out of fuel. He landed on the grass alongside the runway and did a remarkably good job, but not without severe damage to the wing, aileron and flap which I thought put us out of the trials and so I told Joe Smith on the phone.

This was a Friday and the team were due on the carrier on the following Monday. About some 40 minutes later, Murry was called to the phone and found Len Gooch 'full of fire'. He told Murry that he was taking the port wing off the next production aircraft and wanted details of all other items, saying he would be down that evening with a full squad to put the Seafire back into flying form:

> I was to inform everybody that the trials could proceed. I assured him I would do this and asked him to send Sandy Stewart, our hydraulics engineer, down so we could find out what was wrong. That is exactly what happened. Sandy Stewart found the problem, a loose sequence valve in its mounting. The squad worked all night and Saturday and a new squad took over and the aircraft was flying again on Sunday morning, much to everyone's delight and the admiration of Len Gooch and his team.

The trials in HMS *Illustrious* were a complete success, but Murry took Sandy with him on the carrier just in case!

Joe Smith's Reflections on the Development of the Spitfire and Seafire

'The Development of the Spitfire & Seafire' was the title of a lecture given by Smith to the Royal Aeronautical Society on 19 December 1946, when he looked back on the development of the wartime fighters. He raised a number of major points with regard to Spitfire development and its status as a front-line fighter throughout the whole period of the war.

First, Smith acknowledged that the Spitfire was originally designed by R.J. Mitchell in 1935 and first flew in 1936. However, with reference to the urgent need for efficient fighters for the war, he was aware that 'the hard school of war leaves no room for sentimental attachments and the efficiency of the machine as a fighting weapon is the only criterion. Judging the aircraft on this high standard, the firm's design team took the initiative which resulted in continuous improvement of the type.'

He then highlighted that there was a major debt to acknowledge to the Spitfire and all connected with it, referring to 'the whole-hearted co-operation of another design team, that of Rolls-Royce Ltd, whose magnificent series of engines, the Merlin and the Griffon, supplied the power for every Spitfire and Seafire, without which the developmental life of the aircraft might have been seriously curtailed'. The very valuable experience that had been gained from the design and manufacture of the Schneider racing aeroplanes resulted 'in a team whose outlook was essentially speed conscious, and who thought in terms of drag reduction by small size, thin wings and aerodynamic cleanliness. The natural outlet of for this was its application to high-performance fighter'.

Although there were thirty-three different marks of Spitfires and Seafires produced, Smith still felt that the progress in production was not altogether to his satisfaction, and went on to summarise how the Spitfire family was developed:

During the period 1938–1940 many extensive investigations were made by Supermarine on the problem of fighter development. In this work many factors have to be considered, and their relative importance and influence on the problems on the whole taken into account.

The more important of these he stated as follows:

Performance
It was obvious that with the country involved in a major war it would be essential to maintain technical superiority over the enemy enough fighter aircraft.

Armament and equipment
Service requirements were bound to change and the suitability of the aircraft to take heavier and more cumbersome equipment had to be considered.

Maintenance

Under wartime conditions this aspect was of primary importance, and the possibility of the machine being in use in climates with extremes of heat and cold, and thus needing special equipment, had to be assessed.

Production

For a proper appreciation of this aspect it is necessary to turn one's thoughts back to the situation as it existed during the 'expansion' period, and during the early days of the war. From the technical point of view, progress would have been made along the lines mentioned. The preparation of new designs which could never be brought into production in time was obviously useless. New designs were prepared and fully considered in relation to the above factors, but the conclusion reached was that it would be very difficult to improve upon the aerodynamic and structural efficiency of the Spitfire, and that the development of this type was the best course to follow from every point of view. By fitting new and more powerful engines, heavier armament, the cleaning up of the basic design still further, and by periodically strengthening the airframe it was thought that the machine could be kept abreast of requirements.

Smith saw the main line of development was the fighter type, but referred to the early introduction of the photographic reconnaissance aircraft, and later the introduction of the Seafire gave rise to other separate types. Furthermore, he mentioned that the introduction of the Griffon engine, replacing the Merlin, made a further main division, and finally mentioned the interim types:

> There existed several interim types which bridged the gaps between one mark and the fully developed and strengthened mark which followed. The most outstanding examples of the interim types were the Marks IX and XIV.

He then gave a breakdown of the main line of development: Mks I, II and V had Merlin engine changes and an increase in the power; Mk VI was a development of the Mk V, but with a pressure cabin and extended wing tips; Mk VII became a two-stage Merlin-powered aircraft with a strengthened airframe, redesign of the cooling system, improved pressure cabin and retractable tailwheel; Mk VIII was an unpressurised version of the Mk VII; and a Merlin 61 engine was fitted to a Mk V and this became the interim type Mk IX.

The design experience gained from Mks III and XX was used by Smith to introduce the Griffon-engined aircraft, first the interim Mk XII and, later, using the Mk VIII airframe, the Mks XIV and XVIII, followed by the completely redesigned Mks 21, 22 and 24. He also referred to the increase in power available and the efforts of Rolls-Royce, which resulted in more than doubling engine power – from a maximum of 1,050hp on the Spitfire Mk I to 2,350hp on the Seafire Mk 47. He commented, 'that such an enormous increase was accommodated without material alteration in the size of the aircraft constituted one of the main achievements and was only accomplished by the closest co-operation,' and that 'increased power necessitated increased cooling, culminating in the introduction of the two-stage engine, in the use of duplex radiators, one side combining glycol and oil coolers, and the other side glycol and intercoolers'.

In conclusion, Smith summarised the factors that solved the technical problems that had faced Supermarine over a period of ten very busy years. He commented on the several general impressions that had emerged:

1. The Spitfire was superbly served by its power plant, and full advantage was taken of the alliance of a new airframe with engines which were only at the start of their development life. Also the close co-operation between Rolls-Royce, the airscrew firms and ourselves, enable advance provision to be made for engine changes.

2. The sound basic design of the aircraft with its outstanding simplicity enabled major modifications to be incorporated without materially altering the original conception.

3. The continuous improvement in aerodynamic cleanliness, the maintenance of ease of control and structural efficiency were in the hands of a design team working continuously over a period of ten years on a type which they had originated.

4. The co-operation received by officials and officers of the Ministries and Services concerned was at all times whole-hearted and extremely helpful, and without it no progress could have been made.

17

POST-WAR DEVELOPMENTS LEADING TO JET AIRCRAFT

Replacement for the Spitfire

Throughout the war Joe Smith had continued with the development of the Spitfire and Seafire, including later designs for the Spiteful, Seafang and the first jet fighter, the Attacker, along with the Swift and Scimitar, the other Supermarine jet aircraft. By 1944, Smith had taken the Spitfire design to its limit, at double the speed and weight of the first prototype aircraft.

Capt. Eric 'Winkle' Brown reflects on the Joe Smith he had got to know by the end of the war:

> The pressure on Joe must have been immense because to keep the Spitfire in the front row of the world's fighters and at the same time keep the Royal Navy happy was very, very demanding indeed. Joe never stopped being the catalyst for anything new and the stress of this must have been very wearing for him.
>
> At the end of the war Joe must have heaved a very huge sigh of relief, having got through keeping the Spitfire and Seafire at the head of the tables. However, he didn't rest on its laurels because while he was drawing breath at the end of the war suddenly the Korean War [1950–53] cropped up. He did not have the same demand for the Spitfire, but he had demands for the Seafire because the aircraft carriers were involved in that war.
>
> He went back to the drawing board and changed it quite dramatically. The difference between the last Seafire at the end of the war and the Seafire 47 which went to Korea was huge. It had contra-rotating propellers and a sting hook. It was a very fast, powerful aircraft that I would describe as a thunderous aircraft, so powerful, and its vertical climb was ferocious.

Then it was the jet age and I think Joe was probably a little mentally and physically exhausted by this time, and I don't think he made his mark quite as well as he did with the piston aircraft.

Developments in the Post-War Aircraft

Alan Clifton (Young Alan) comments on how the development of aircraft following on from the Spitfire was achieved:

I think their approach was interesting. The single-engine series developed from the Spitfire by putting a new wing on it and calling it the Spiteful. This was a straight wing instead of the elliptical wing, and almost the same fuselage. They then decided they had to start building a jet aircraft, the first being the Attacker which had the Spiteful wing and a new fuselage. This then became the Swift which had virtually the same or similar fuselage as the Attacker, but with a new swept back wing and tail surfaces, i.e. fin and rudder. This was how they developed the aeroplane, by using the same or similar fuselage and bolting on a new wing, or new fuselage. This process went on through the 505, 508, 525 twin-engine series, culminating in the Scimitar which took them to the end of the Supermarine life which ended up in Swindon.

Spiteful prototype NN660, first flown by Jeffrey Quill after being fitted with a new wing, was the aircraft that crashed in September 1944, killing test pilot Frank Furlong. *Solent Sky*

The next stages of development were to be the Spiteful (1944) and Seafang (1946), produced to take over from the earlier Spitfire design. It was at this time that a change was made from the elliptical wing to the laminar flow wing and given to the Type 371 Spiteful (NN660). A laminar flow wing allows airflow over the wing to be smooth and uninterrupted in any way and is designed for minimum drag. However, if there is any form of interruption to the flow, then turbulence of the airflow is created, resulting in increased drag.

Jeffrey Quill flew the prototype first in June 1944, but despite appearing to be like the later Spitfires, it was a completely new aircraft. This was seen in the use of tapered wings with squared tips. It was more streamlined and with a larger tailplane, new fin and rudder assembly, and was powered by a Griffon 69 engine. This was the Spiteful NN660 flown by test pilot Frank Furlong when it crashed and he was killed on 13 September 1944. There was a second prototype (NN664) first flown by Jeffrey Quill in January 1945, which was followed by the first production Spiteful (RB515) in April 1945.

The Spiteful Mk XV had contra-rotating Rotol airscrews fitted to the Griffon 89/ 90 engine. This led to the Spiteful Mk XVI (RB518), powered by a Griffon 101 engine and achieving a speed of 494mph (795.01km/h) at 28,500ft (8,686.8m) during official tests at Boscombe Down. At sea level the speed was 408mph (656.61km/h), with a climb rate of 4,750ft (1,447.8m) per minute. It was the converted Spiteful F Mk XIV (RB520) that eventually led to the Seafang.

Spiteful Mk XIV RB520 was the only aircraft used for Seafang development. *Solent Sky*

Seafang Mk 32 VB895's first flight was in January 1946, and was demonstrated to the Royal Netherlands Navy later that year. It was flown by Mike Lithgow for deck landing trials on HMS *Illustrious* in May 1947. *Solent Sky*

The Seafang Mk 31 (Type 382) VG471 was an interim production variant built to the Ministry of Aircraft Production specification N.5/45 and was basically the navalised Spiteful developed for use on aircraft carriers. It was powered by a Griffon 65 engine with contra-rotating airscrews, and had an arrester hook but non-folding wings. However, although the order for 150 Seafang Mk 31s was placed, fewer than ten were built, the rest being cancelled.

The Seafang Mk 32 was the production version of the Mk 31, but this time with folding wings, increased fuel capacity and a Griffon 89 engine powering a Rotol contra-rotating airscrew, and was armed with four cannons. Two prototypes were built: VB893 and VB895. Seafang VB895 first flew in June 1946. It was later flown by test pilot Mike Lithgow in May 1947, for deck landing trials on HMS *Illustrious*, but was not considered any great advantage on the Seafire Mk 47. None of the aircraft went into production.

In tests, little improvement was found compared with the later versions of the Spitfire, causing the Spiteful to be cancelled by the RAF first, and then the Seafang by the Royal Navy. Furthermore, the design work being carried out by Smith on jet aircraft at the same time would have soon replaced these aircraft, but the wing design for the Spiteful was to be used on the Supermarine Attacker jet aircraft.

More Recruits Needed for the Technical Office

There was an urgent need to encourage more recruits to apply to work in the design and technical teams. In 1946, Alan Clifton (Cliffy) had perceived that traditional apprenticeships and graduate recruiting would not provide adequate intakes to the technical office and elsewhere in the design team. His solution was to accept into the weight section young men who had completed their National Service, wanted a career in aviation, were prepared to study and had a minimum qualification of School Certificate in English, Maths and a Science subject. They were to study for the Ordinary National Certificate in Engineering, being allowed a paid day off each week to attend Southampton Technical College. Their motivation proved strong and their success rate high. It was later made possible for them to obtain twelve months' practical experience in the workshops after gaining the ONC. Barrie Bryant recalls:

> At first I resented the unwelcome burdens of running the scheme in addition to keeping the Section on top of its work with a fifth of the staff absent on some days. I eventually became reconciled to it even though few stayed on weights work and not all remained long at Supermarine. This Supermarine innovation was previously unrecorded and I know of no comparable scheme elsewhere.

After the war years the pressure on the staff with regard to workload did not decrease and Barrie remembers this time well, commenting that as a nation and within the firm, collectively and individually, they were all fatigued, but this pressure continued. 'Joe Smith's response to suggestions that we were overloaded was always, "Would you prefer too little work or too much?" With memories of pre-war unemployment our answer was obvious.'

Assistant Experimental Manager at High Post and Chilbolton

During the post-war period from 1946, Denis Webb became assistant experimental manager at High Post and Chilbolton aerodromes. Webb thought that the only sad thing about the end of the war, as far as he was concerned, was the departure of Sir James Bird. Bird had taken over after the demise of H.B. Pratt but, in Webb's opinion, Supermarine did not seem the same after his departure. Wilf Elliot had been appointed manager in his place, but to Webb there was still the same flavour about the place, especially with chief designer Joe Smith, Eric Cooper, Alf Faddy, Reg Caunter, Jack Rice and Alan Clifton still on the design staff, all old colleagues from his apprenticeship days.

Spitfires Flying Today

A selection of photographs of Spitfires still flying today
taken at various locations in the United Kingdom by Alan Mansell

1 X4650 Spitfire Mk IA (KL–A) was built at Eastleigh in 1940. It collided with Al Deere's X4276 and both aircraft crashed near Catterick; both pilots bailed out safely. X4650 was recovered in 1976, restored and is flying again in March 2012.

2 P9374 Mk IA (GR–J) was built at Eastleigh in 1940. It was attacked by Bf 109s and did a forced belly landing on Calais beach on 24 May 1940. The fuselage sank and disappeared in wet sand.

3 Forty years later, P9374 reappeared, was recovered from the sand and stored in the Paris Air Museum. Acquired in 2006 and taken to the Aircraft Restoration Co. at Duxford, it flew again in 2011.

4 EP120 Spitfire LF Mk VB was built at Castle Bromwich in 1942. It joined 501 Squadron and took part in the Dieppe raid on 19 August 1942. In 1991, it was restored and first flew again on 12 September 1995.

5 BM597 Spitfire LF Mk VB (JH-C) was built at Castle Bromwich in 1942 and flew first with 315 (Polish) Squadron and then 317 (Polish) Squadron. It was restored and is now part of the Historic Aircraft Collection.

6 TA805 Spitfire LF Mk IX was built at Castle Bromwich in 1944, joining 183 and 234 Squadrons in 1945, and the South African Air Force in 1949. It was later returned to the UK for restoration. It wears 234 Squadron markings with coding FX-M.

7 TA805 with Lancing College in the background. One of the college's students, Flg Off. A.E. Hyde-Parker, killed on a reconnaissance mission on 14 September 1940, is remembered on its war memorial.

8 MH434 Spitfire Mk IX was built at Castle Bromwich in 1943. A 222 Squadron pilot flying MH434 shot down a Fw 190 and damaged another. Later, while escorting a USAAF B-17, it shot down another Fw 190.

9 In 1947, MH434 was sold to the Royal Netherlands Air Force and served in Indonesia. Later, it was acquired by UK owners and has appeared in films and on TV, including *Foyle's War*.

10 PL344 Spitfire Mk IX was built at Castle Bromwich in 1944 and served with 602 Squadron and 442 and 401 (Canadian) Squadrons. Having spent periods in the Netherlands and the USA, it is now owned by Tom Blair whose initials are in the code TL–B.

11 TD248 Spitfire Mk XVI was built at Castle Bromwich in 1945 and went to 695 Squadron. Restored more than once due to accidents, it was coded CR-S with the crest of 74 'Tiger' Squadron on the nose.

12 MV268 Spitfire FR Mk XIV was built at Eastleigh. It served with 130 Squadron, then with 401 and 411 (Canadian) Squadrons. It was Wg Cdr 'Johnnie' Johnson's last Spitfire flown in the Second World War.

13 Wg Cdr 'Johnnie' Johnson led 144 Canadian Wing flying Mk IXs and they were the first to land in France at St Croix-sur-Mer on 10 June 1944. Today it is MV293 that is displayed as MV268 (JE-J).

14 PV202 LF Mk IX was built at Castle Bromwich in 1944 and was later converted to a Tr.9 trainer for the Irish Air Corps (IAC-161). It is now painted in the Battle of Britain colours of 19 Squadron and coded QV-I.

15 PL965 PR Mk XI was assembled at Aldermaston in 1944, joining 16 Squadron and later the Dutch Air Force. After restoration it was involved in film and TV work. It is now owned and flown by Peter Teichman.

16 PS890 Spitfire PR Mk XIX (UM-E) was built at Supermarine. It went to the PRU at RAF Benson, RAF Seletar in Singapore and then to the Royal Thai Air Force. It was restored at Planes of Fame at Chino in California, and is now owned by Christophe Jacquard.

Webb was called to Smith's office and was informed that he was to become assistant experimental manager and was to take charge of High Post aerodrome. This was to be a 26-mile (41.84km) journey, as High Post was situated between Amesbury and Salisbury, but he was given a 'sweetener' of the use of a firm's car. He accepted the position and was pleased that he would get amongst some aircraft again, and also that it would 'delay my move towards South Marston', something he was not keen on! However, although Smith seemed very pleased about the appointment, Webb had the feeling that Frank Perry was not so sure. Webb was pleased with the staff he had at High Post, led by Edgar Woolridge, who ran the workshops and had a very competent, happy team of chargehands and workers. He settled down well and got acquainted with Jeffrey Quill and his team of test pilots.

Special Director of Vickers-Armstrongs Ltd

Joe Smith was appointed as a special director of Vickers-Armstrongs Ltd in 1948 and served as chairman of the board of the Society of British Aircraft Constructors from 1948 until 1951. He was also awarded the silver medal of the Royal Aeronautical Society in 1950. Although Smith had been busy with the Spitfire development, he was also responsible for a post-war Spitfire two-seat

Seagull ASR-1 PA143 first flew on 14 July 1948. There were three prototypes ordered: PA143, PA147 and PA152. Note the bombed-out Woolston factory in the background. *Solent Sky*

Seagull ASR-1 PA143 with Sea Otter JM-909 built by Saunders-Roe at Cowes on the Isle of Wight. The third prototype, PA152, was not completed. *Solent Sky*

trainer, as well as the Sea Otter replacement, the Seagull, an amphibian flying boat that incorporated a variable-incidence wing. This was developed from the Air Ministry specification S.24/37 'Dumbo', an experimental torpedo bomber with the Supermarine designation Type 322, producing an outstanding range of speed. The Sea Otter was then converted for commercial use.

The S.14/44 specification was the Supermarine Seagull ASR-1 PA143 (1948), built as a monoplane for air-sea rescue and reconnaissance, and was first test flown on 14 July 1948 by Lt-Cdr Mike Lithgow. It was intended as a replacement for the Walrus and Sea Otter. However, its use for air-sea rescue was eventually taken over by helicopters. The second prototype, PA147, first flew in September 1949 and later took part in carrier trials on HMS *Ark Royal*. In July 1950, Les Colquhoun set a 62-mile (100km) closed-circuit record of 241.9mph (389.3km/h) in PA147.

Spitfire PR XIX, Royal Swedish Air Force

After the war, a number of foreign governments wished to acquire Spitfires. Most of these were government-to-government deals, but Supermarine managed to sell fifty Spitfire PR Mk XIXs to the Royal Swedish Air Force. The deal involved Supermarine taking back fifty aircraft from the Ministry of Aircraft Production, bringing them up to full modification standard, including all removable equipment, painting them with Swedish roundels and installing Swedish labels in the cockpits.

Spitfire PR Mk XIX ordered by Sweden and waiting to be delivered. *Solent Sky*

In 1948, Smith called Murry White to his office and told him that Vickers House, which at the time did all the sales and contract work for Supermarine, had a very high profile team in Stockholm negotiating the conditions of sale of the PR Mk XIX to the Royal Swedish Air Force. The team in Sweden wanted some contract and technical help and Joe Smith asked Murry if he would accompany the commercial director, Alfred Marsh-Hunn, to Stockholm to provide the technical help:

> I jumped at it although at the time I had some misgivings. Joe said that Mr Marsh-Hunn wished to travel to Stockholm by sea and rail, but he thought I would not mind as I would be travelling first-class!
>
> I was told all arrangements would be made by his secretary and that I would have the usual £10 daily subsistence. It seemed to me too good to be true! The first surprise was our drive from Hursley Park in one of the firm's Super Snipe cars. I went to get in with the driver, but was told by Marsh-Hunn to join him and informed that as I had always called him 'Sir' from now on I was to call him by his Christian name of Peter.

Marsh-Hunn's grandson, Peter Marsh-Hunn, confirms that his grandfather's Christian names were Alfred Ernest, but for some reason he preferred to call himself Peter. Murry continues:

> We had first-class cabins on Svenska Lloyd ferry from Tilbury to Gothenburg, taking two nights and a whole day across the North Sea in glorious weather.

He told me to enjoy the journey but that he was going to remain in his cabin until we got to Gothenburg. The ferry was famous for its Smorgasbord lunch on the day at sea. I made full use of it!

The rail journey was not without interest and they arrived safely in Stockholm and joined the London office team for a briefing. There was to be a top-level meeting in a few days' time, and the agent had booked Murry into a smaller but pleasant hotel from the main party who were in the best hotel in Stockholm:

> It so happened that my parents were in Oslo, Norway, at the same time. They had been invited to sail to Oslo on the *Norge*, formerly the *Philante* which my father had built for Sir Thomas Sopwith and had converted back to a yacht after war work. She was purchased and presented to King Haakon by the grateful Norwegians.
>
> I asked Peter if he would mind if I invited my parents to stay with me for a few days. After hearing this story he thought it was a great idea, and this we did. Peter spent most of his time with me, not the London group, and we had a most enjoyable time.

The London group had very briefly explained to Murry how they intended to proceed. They wanted him to stay in the background unless they called for him; only they would negotiate, so Murry stayed in the limo while Marsh-Hunn and the group met the Swedish group:

> In due course they came out with very long faces, saying they had lost the contract, as Williamson, the vital camera manufacturer, wanted a lead time of 3 years to manufacture the cameras and the Swedes wanted 6 months delivery of the first aircraft. Whereupon I piped up and said, 'Why don't you offer them with fully serviceable and certified used cameras? We can buy them in the government surplus market. We already have an approved instrument overhaul and repair shop at Chilbolton which we can use. It is run by Roy Long, a very qualified and experimental technician.'

After further discussions, prompted by enthusiastic expressions from Murry, the London party agreed to make the offer which was accepted by the Swedes. Owing to the enthusiastic efforts and technical advice offered to the negotiators by Murry, the commercial director put in very good report, suggesting that Smith put him on the monthly staff. Murry and Roy Long were given the go-ahead and the money to make the necessary purchases. They bought up 100 per cent more than they needed at a fraction of the cost for new cameras and gear:

Roy set his chaps overhauling and certifying and the whole operation went very smoothly until we came to the dashboard clocks, a very saleable item in the domestic market. Roy and I went along to a MU [Maintenance Unit] auction sale where we had to bid against a number of dealers. The clocks were sold in 40 item lots and we needed two lots. I kept outbidding the dealers and eventually got two lots for I think about £20 a clock. This was much more proportionally than we had to pay for the other equipment but it completed our job and the aircraft were delivered on time. For all this effort I got put on the monthly staff which, apart of the extra money, was a big lift in prestige.

When the first aircraft were flown to Sweden, they asked for an instructor pilot and a technician to help them establish the squadron; Smith asked Murry to go with Guy Morgan, an experienced RAF photo reconnaissance pilot, to help them. They lived in the Officers' Mess in south Sweden for about two weeks and had a hard-working but very interesting time:

> At the 'dining in nights' the C.O. would only allow English to be spoken and Guy and I had to do the 'Skol' in turn. Guy and I returned to England feeling we had done a good job and done our bit to help the Swedes keep an eye on their neighbours to the East!

The first prototype TS409 was Supermarine's first jet design. Its inaugural flight was on 27 July 1946, but a number of modifications were needed to sort out handling problems. *Solent Sky*

Supermarine Type 392 Attacker (TS409)

Joe Smith was responsible for the design of the Supermarine Attacker (TS409) jet prototype which was designed to the Air Ministry specification E.10/44 ('E' for Experimental) for a Nene turbojet with the wing development derived from the Supermarine Spiteful, the aircraft designed as a replacement for the Spitfire. It kept the Spiteful wing (and four 20mm cannons) but had a new tail and fuselage which housed a jet engine, and was known as the 'Jet Spiteful'.

High Post Aerodrome

The Spiteful, Seafang, 'Dumbo' and Attacker (TS409) were the aircraft being tested at High Post aerodrome when Denis Webb transferred there. The prototype was worked on in the Experimental Hangar at Hursley Park and then taken to High Post for final assembly. The first flight trials took place at the A&AEE, Boscombe Down, on 27 July 1946, with Jeffrey Quill as pilot. However, one of the problems at High Post was that it was a grass aerodrome and although this did not matter in the summer, in the winter the TS409 Attacker got bogged down and tractors were required to tow it out of the mud. Furthermore, there were problems with this jet aircraft because its tail-wheel undercarriage caused damage to grass airfields with the jet tail-down exhaust creating holes or ditches in the earth. Taxiing at low thrust levels caused little damage, but full-thrust engine tests had to be at prepared sites.

When Smith became aware of the problem it was decided to open up Chilbolton aerodrome, which had concrete runways, for testing the TS409. There had been an intention to move the Experimental Department to Chilbolton when the facilities had been upgraded to accommodate the drawing office and technical staff and also provide a much-needed canteen. However, once the TS409 had been transferred to Chilbolton, it found the maintenance staff working in very cold conditions, and despite some extra stoves which burned wood to create some heat, the conditions were quite primitive for the men. Edgar Woolridge did not want to move away from his home near Salisbury, his position as foreman being taken by Bill Chandler. For Denis Webb, these were exciting times with the arrival of the jet aircraft and his involvement as assistant experimental manager in charge of the Experimental Flight Test Workshops.

Jet Aircraft Trials

After working for some time on the Sea Otter, Murry White then took on the development work, including the trials of the Attacker, Swift and Scimitar jet aircraft:

> I became manager of the team who landed the aircraft on the carrier decks. In the very early days it was Jeffrey Quill and later it was Mike Lithgow. Captain Eric 'Winkle' Brown from the RAE Farnborough was also very much involved in this, and he became a great pal of mine.

It was Brown who made the very first landing on a carrier with a tricycle-undercarriage aircraft. The aircraft was the Bell Airacobra Mk I AH574, and the landing took place on 4 April 1945 on the flight deck of HMS *Pretoria Castle*. On 3 December 1945, he became the first pilot to land a jet propelled de Havilland Sea Vampire, LZ551/G, on the light fleet carrier HMS *Ocean*.

The carrier trials with the early jets were, of course, very exciting, but one of the worst incidents occurred when the production Attacker from the first squadron, piloted by Capt. George Baldwin RN, missed the wires on HMS *Eagle* and flew into the nylon barrier. The pilot was unhurt, which was what the nylon barrier was intended to achieve, but the aircraft was a complete write-off:

> We had helped in the development of the barriers at RAE, Farnborough and had used the first prototype Attacker TS409, after its flying days were over, as a trial horse by catapulting it into the trial barrier. I had many other interesting events, some exciting, of which I feel very honoured to have witnessed, but some tragic.

Jeffrey Quill's Test Flying Career Ends

At the end of the war the jet age had arrived and Supermarine started to move towards designing and building their first jet fighter. In June 1947, Jeffrey Quill, who was then Supermarine's chief test pilot, was testing the Attacker (TS409) when he lost consciousness at approximately 40,000ft (12,192m), fortunately coming-to at 10,000ft (3048m) and landing safely. Medical checks revealed that his years as a test pilot had taken their toll and it would be the end of his test flying career. It was said at the time that the only flying Quill would do was 'flying a desk', which was not entirely correct as it was only test flying that he could not undertake. Quill then became technical sales and liaison manager for Vickers-Armstrongs in 1948 and was based at the Supermarine works in Southampton. He was assisted by Jack Rasmussen, M. Scott Mackirdy, a former RAF and later ATA pilot as anchor man, and Murry White, who recalls:

> In this capacity Jack Rasmussen and I attended every Paris and SBAC show, managing the stands and later the chalets, as well as making numerous sales tours for Spitfires and Spitfire trainers, and later the jet Attacker fighters.

Quill continued to fly Spitfires after his test flying career ended, and in *Spitfire: A Test Pilot's Story* recounts a delivery flight of a Spitfire Mk 22 to Malta in 1954. On landing at Luqa airfield, he writes:

> I remember setting the trimmers carefully, with a small amount of power on, for a gentle curving and steady landing approach, and as I chopped the throttle at the threshold of the runway the aircraft virtually landed itself. I had the same thought that I had so many years before after my first flight in the prototype – that this aeroplane was a real lady; albeit by then a much more powerful, noisy, tough and aggressive lady, but a lady just the same.

Mike Lithgow then took over as chief test pilot, and his team included Dave Morgan, Les Colquhoun, Guy Morgan, G.J. ('Chunky') Horne and J.W.C. ('Pee-Wee') Judge.

Supermarine Type 398 Naval Prototype Attackers

On 27 July 1946, the first prototype Attacker, Type 392 (TS409), flew for the first time, piloted by Jeffrey Quill. TS409 also achieved the 62-mile (100km) closed circuit record of 564.88mph (909.08km/h) on 27 February 1948, piloted by Mike Lithgow, and the record was celebrated at the Hampshire Aero Club on 11 March that same year. The second prototype was Type 398 (TS413), which was specifically built for naval use and first flown from Chilbolton on 17 June 1947, piloted by Mike Lithgow.

Lithgow landed the second prototype (TS413) on the deck of HMS *Illustrious* on 15 October 1947 for deck landing trials. However, the TS413 was lost in a crash in June 1948, killing the Royal Navy pilot, Lt T.J.A. King-Joyce. After the loss of TS413, TS409 was sent back to Hursley's Experimental Department where it was navalised to undertake trials for the Royal Navy.

There was a third prototype Attacker (TS416) which had been developed from the knowledge gained from the first two prototypes, resulting in improved

The closed-circuit record of 564.88mph on 27 February 1948; TS409 pilot and ground crew, from left to right: Dave Davenport, Rolls-Royce; George Garrett, chargehand; Mike Lithgow, pilot; Bert Mee, fitter; Bill Chandler, foreman; Jim Bowers, inspector. Behind: Eric Watts, Hubert Smith, Johnny Cruise, fitters; Harry Roberts, chargehand electrician. *Solent Sky*

Mike Lithgow piloted the first flight of the 'navalised' prototype TS413 on 17 June 1947. Carrier trials from October 1947 proved very successful, culminating in orders for the production Attacker. *Murry White*

Second prototype TS413 landing on the flight deck of HMS *Illustrious* during deck landing trials. *Murry White*

handling of the aircraft. However, the urgent need for jet aircraft and attempts at speed records left the improvements found in the TS416 behind.

The first production aircraft was the Attacker F Mk 1 (WA469) which was the first to have folding wings and flew its inaugural flight on 5 April 1950, becoming the first jet aircraft in front-line Fleet Air Arm service in August 1951, aboard HMS *Eagle*. It had a maximum speed of 590mph (949.51km/h). When facilities were added for carrying bombs, the designation was changed to the FB Mk 1, followed by the FB Mk 2 (WK319), first flown on 25 April 1952 and which replaced the FB Mk 1 Nene 101 turbojet with a Nene 102.

The FB Mks 1 and 2 were developed for the Royal Navy and carried a full load of ammunition, four 20mm Hispano cannons, two 1000lb bombs, or eight rockets under the wing, as well as a 250-gallon (1,136.52-litre) drop tank. However, due to the extended trials, the Attacker served just four years with the Royal Navy before it was replaced by the Sea Hawk.

South Marston and the Attacker

Tony Kenyon was asked to go to South Marston, Swindon, just for a fortnight because there were some problems with the Attacker. Apparently Swindon was unhappy with the drawings, but at that time there was no love lost between

An Attacker landed on HMS *Eagle* in September 1952, but it missed the wires and crashed into the barrier. *Murry White*

The wreckage of the Attacker caused by crashing into the barrier shows there was quite substantial damage to the aircraft. *Murry White*

South Marston and Southampton, South Marston being a specially built MAP 'shadow factory':

> I went up for a fortnight, but stayed up there for nine years! Barnes Wallis' son also worked in the drawing office in Swindon. The drawing office started at first with about five of us, but it started to expand because they were trying to close Hursley down. A lot of people from Hursley did not want to move there and travelled daily. Swindon was purely for production.
>
> They used to run engines outside the Experimental Hangar and when it came to jet aircraft they still used to test the engines there. As things got faster with take-offs and landings they started to use Chilbolton for most of the testing, and also used Boscombe Down. That was where the test pilot Les Colquhoun was flying the Attacker when the wing folded on it, but he managed to bring the plane down and land safely.

On 23 May 1950, Les Colquhoun was flying the Attacker F Mk 1 (WA469) with the task of testing the air brakes. It was while in a dive that the outer portion of the starboard wing folded up and the ailerons became locked. Colquhoun bravely made the decision not to eject because he wanted the cause of the wings folding to be discovered and made a high-speed landing at Chilbolton with a burst tyre. He was awarded the George Medal for his effort to save the aircraft.

WA469 was the Attacker that test pilot Les Colquhoun was flying when the starboard wing folded. *Solent Sky*

Another Attacker crash took place on Thursday, 5 February 1953, when Roy Collingwood, pilot of Attacker FB Mk 1 (WA535) took off from RNAS Stretton (HMS *Blackcap*) at 15.30 hours for a familiarisation flight. He reported to another pilot flying a Meteor jet at 13.37 hours that he was flying at 17,000ft (5,181.6m) and still climbing, but by 15.30 hours the aircraft had crashed in a field near Burtonwood. It had crashed vertically, leaving a crater 10ft (3.04m) in diameter to a depth of up to 25ft (7.62m), and within the debris spread around the crash site was one piece which had the aircraft number WA535. The Board of Inquiry eventually ruled that anoxia (a total decrease in the pilot's oxygen level) was the most likely cause of the accident.

The Attacker was the first to enter service with the Royal Navy and achieved a short but successful career in the Fleet Air Arm, as well as serving the Pakistan Air Force.

18

BREAKING THE SOUND BARRIER

Going Supersonic

With the introduction of jet aircraft there was a greater interest in high-speed flight and the challenge of breaking the sound barrier. In aviation aerodynamics the sound barrier is a term that refers to the transition of an aircraft from subsonic to supersonic speed.

The problem with the sound barrier arose during the Second World War when propeller aircraft in a dive were increasing their speed and finding that the airflow over the wings created shock waves and turbulence. The effect of this caused a number of crashes in which the pilot lost complete control of the aircraft by being unable to pull out of the dive with the control stick. In aerodynamics the term for this effect is 'compressibility' and although this is not a problem at low speeds, as the aircraft increases its speed the changes in airflow become more severe and dangerous, with the result that wartime aircraft could not safely exceed 500mph (804.67km/h).

Early claims of breaking the sound barrier came during the war when Hans Guido Mutke, the pilot of a Messerschmitt Me 262, claimed to have done just that in April 1945. However, this was discounted by experts, and a further claim by George Welch to have broken the sound barrier on 1 October 1947 was unverified. The first man officially credited with breaking the sound barrier was Chuck Yeager in the Bell X-1 on 14 October 1947 at a speed of 700mph (1,126.5km/h) or Mach 1.06. This took place at 10.42 a.m. local time over the Muroc Dry Lake in the Mojave Desert, California. The Bell X-1 was dropped from a Boeing B-29 Superfortress which was flying at 20,000ft (6,096m), and the actual flight took 14 minutes. Once Yeager had gone supersonic, those on the ground heard the first sonic boom but at first thought that the Bell X-1 had exploded. However, it was soon realised that this was not the case and that the Bell X-1 had become the first successful supersonic aircraft in the history of flight.

The first research to be undertaken in Britain into high-speed flight approaching the speed of sound was the swept-wing de Havilland DH 108 which was powered by a Goblin jet engine. It was called the Swallow and the subsequent research programme was referred to as the Swallow Project, with three prototype aircraft built. They were TG283 and TG306 in 1946, and VW120 in 1947. It was in VW120 that John Derry set the 62-mile (100km) world speed record at 605mph (973.65km/h) on 12 April 1948. TG283 was first flown on 15 May 1946 by Geoffrey de Havilland Jnr, but the aircraft were later to prove to be too dangerous to fly. All three crashed, killing the pilots.

The first pilot killed was Geoffrey de Havilland Jnr, who crashed on 27 September 1946, while flying TG306 in a high-speed dive. Capt. Eric 'Winkle' Brown was involved in the crash investigation flying VW120:

After Geoffrey de Havilland Jnr was killed I was involved in the investigation because the whole aviation industry was perturbed as to what had happened. The investigation revealed that Geoffrey de Havilland Jnr was flying in some slightly bumpy weather and this had induced a longitudinal oscillation in the aircraft which got out of control. It was a runaway oscillation which was so bad not only did it break up the aircraft, but as a tall man it was thought that his head struck the top of the cockpit and he was fatally injured.

I was much smaller than him and when I was ready to do my test I was told to put the seat right down, but I also had two big advantages. They strengthened the wings before I went up and did the test so you would be less likely to have structural failure, and they gave me an ejection seat.

I was very fortunate in the test, but it was a very near thing. I got into a very violent oscillation which got out of hand and I couldn't eject because the G's were so high. I couldn't lift my arms up, so I just had to sit it out. The doctors said that after 10 seconds I would have been unconscious, but after 7 seconds (it was just instinct) I pulled the stick and the throttle back slowly together and it stopped as suddenly as it started. It was pure unadulterated instinct! No great skill involved at all.

Swallow VW120 was later thought to have broken up in a dive at Little Brickhill on 15 February 1950, killing the pilot, Sqn Ldr Stuart Muller-Rowland, who was testing the effects of change from subsonic to transonic flight. The third crash was on 1 May 1950, when TG283 crashed killing the pilot George Genders while carrying out stalling trials at Hartley Wintney. However, John Derry was fortunate to survive an uncontrolled dive in VW120. This occurred during a test flight on 9 September 1948 when it became the first British aircraft to exceed Mach 1 going into an uncontrolled dive from 40,000ft (12,192m) to 30,000ft (9,144m). He was lucky to be able to recover the aircraft and survive.

Type 510 VV106 was the first Swift prototype, but had swept instead of straight wings. It was also the first swept-wing jet to land on a carrier. *Solent Sky*

Swift Type 510 VV106 landing on HMS *Illustrious* with the deck arrester hook ready to engage the wires. *Murry White*

The Development of the Swift

The Air Ministry issued specification E.41/46 for an experimental swept-wing version of the Attacker and this eventually became the Supermarine Swift, a single-engine jet fighter for the RAF in the 1950s. It had quite a long development period and eventually entered service as an interceptor.

The Swift prototype Type 510 (VV106), the first British jet to have swept wings and a swept tail wing, was first flown in 1948. It was also the first swept-wing jet to take off and land on an aircraft carrier, HMS *Illustrious*. To be able to land on the aircraft carrier, the Type 510 was fitted with an arrester hook and had RATOG equipment. An afterburner was added to the second Swift prototype and the designation changed from Type 510 to Type 528 (VV119), which first flew in March 1950. After further modifications to the undercarriage by changing to a tricycle arrangement, the Type 528 became the Type 535 (VV119), which first flew in August 1950. It was VV119 that starred as the 'Prometheus' in the film *The Sound Barrier*.

VV106 photographed flying over the Needles, Isle of Wight. *John Thomson*

Swift Type 535 VV119 made its first flight with the nosewheel configuration on 28 August 1950. Twin tailwheels were retained as 'bumpers' to prevent any damage to the fuselage. *Solent Sky*

The Feature Film *The Sound Barrier*

The interest in high-speed flight and breaking the sound barrier at this time led to the making of the feature film *The Sound Barrier*, which was produced and directed by David Lean and included some scenes filmed at Chilbolton airfield. The story and screenplay were by Terence Rattigan and stars who appeared in the film included Ralph Richardson, Nigel Patrick and Ann Todd, who was married to David Lean.

In the 2004 series by Alan Mansell for the Solent Sky magazine based on feature films made in the Solent area, he explains how this film was developed and the research David Lean undertook in order to obtain specific facts about breaking the sound barrier:

> During the summer of 1951 a film crew together with some well-known stars descended on the Vickers Supermarine airfield at Chilbolton, where they stayed for a hectic number of weeks. The subject of their frenetic activity was the production of a new feature film, the real star of which was the second prototype Vickers Supermarine 535 Swift [VV119] – the production version of which was destined to be the RAF's first swept-wing jet fighter. In the film the name given to the aircraft was the 'Prometheus'.
>
> For David Lean, the film's producer, the opportunity to use an aircraft that was at the forefront of technological development in combination with a story by Terence Rattigan was just too good to miss. The topicality of the film was

also right for the time – aircraft from famous names like Supermarine, whose immortal Spitfire was the nation's saviour during the dark days of 1940, instantly generated interest. Fighters – Jet Fighters particularly – and the constant quest for greater speed were of interest to the public, on both sides of the Atlantic.

The sound barrier – perhaps more properly described as the compress-ibility effect – felt by aircraft as they approached Mach 1 was at the time thought by some to be an impossible barrier to break through. That was until the American Chuck Yeager was credited as the first pilot to break through the sound barrier on 14 October 1947. This feat was put to good use by using Yeager in the promotion of *The Sound Barrier* at the US Premier.

During the making of the film David Lean spent a lot of time talking to John Derry, who was of course the first British pilot to fly through the sound barrier in a dive when flying the tailless de Havilland DH 108 Swallow. The subsequent fatal crash of this aircraft whilst being flown by Geoffrey de Havilland Jnr provided Lean with the inspiration for the film.

The film's credits list just about every British test pilot of the period, notable among whom were John Cunningham, Les Colquhoun, David Morgan and Mike Lithgow. Also listed were the aircraft used in the production, which were billed as 'The Jet Planes used in breaking the Sound Barrier'.

In 1952, *The Sound Barrier* was filmed at Chilbolton and VV119 ('Prometheus') is featured with the personnel and film crew, with signatures of David Lean and Ann Todd. *Solent Sky*

Mike Lithgow and Joe Smith visit the hangars with Dennis Dickinson, head of flight-testing at Chilbolton. *Mark Roberts*

Joe Smith and Mike Lithgow standing by the jet exhaust of VV119. *Barbara Harries*

John Derry was later killed, along with his flight-test observer Anthony Richards, on 6 September 1952, when his DH 110 broke up after just breaking the sound barrier during a flight demonstration at the Farnborough Air Show. Debris from the aircraft showered down on the spectators below, resulting in twenty-nine fatalities and over sixty injured.

The Type 541 Swift

Supermarine Type 535 (VV119) was the predecessor of the Swift Type 541 and this became the pre-production model for the Swift. The Type 541 had its Rolls-Royce Nene turbojet engine replaced with the Rolls-Royce AJ.65 (axial flow) turbojet engine, known as the Avon.

Some of the Vickers-Armstrongs design team moved from Hursley Park to South Marston, Hurn and Weybridge, and the work progressed on the fighter prototype Swift. The aircraft was tested at Chilbolton, an airfield requisitioned by the Ministry of Aircraft Production and a test landing ground bought by the Royal Navy.

There were two Type 541s: WJ960, which first flew on 1 August 1951, and WJ965, which first flew on 25 August 1952 and was later modified, breaking the sound barrier while in a dive for the first time on 26 February 1953 while flying over Chilbolton. The Air Ministry placed a production order for 100 aircraft in case the Hawker Hunter development programme was unsuccessful. The Swift was also considered as a possible replacement for the Gloster Meteor in the air defence role.

The Swift F Mk 1's first flight was in 1953 and the aircraft entered service with No 56 Squadron in February 1954, becoming the RAF's first swept-wing aircraft powered by an Avon 109 engine and with an armament consisting of two 30mm cannons. The squadron is one of the oldest and most successful squadrons of the RAF, with battle honours from many of the significant air campaigns of both World Wars.

There were some serious accidents involving both Mks 1 and 2, including one fatal crash. The Swift F Mk 1 was dogged by bad luck, one instance being when the engine of test pilot Dave Morgan's Swift failed over Chilbolton in September 1951 and he was below the safe height to eject. He glided the aircraft under power lines and aimed for a gap between a farm and a barn, but demolished a brick lavatory before belly landing in a field. After apologising to the farmer's wife, he met four farm labourers who had witnessed the crash and offered each of them a cigarette!

Owing to its poor safety record, the F Mk 1 was grounded in August 1954. From 30 August it was replaced by the second variant, the F Mk 2, sixteen of

Swift Type 541 WJ960 first flew from Boscombe Down on 1 August 1951, Mike Lithgow experiencing some handling and engine problems during test flights. *Solent Sky*

Swift F Mk 4 WK198 was the aircraft that went to North Africa for an attempt on the world air speed record. *Solent Sky*

which were built. It was simply a Mk 1 with two extra cannons. However, the airflow over the wings at high Mach numbers caused instability so this variant was also grounded. This resulted in wing shape modifications to resolve the problem.

The third Swift variant was the F Mk 3, twenty-five of which were built. Powered by an Avon 114 engine with an afterburner, this aircraft was never in service with the RAF and was used mainly for training purposes. The next variant was the F Mk 4 (Type 546) which included a variable-incidence tailplane that appeared to fix the handling problems experienced by pilots.

The FR Mk 5 (Type 549) was built for photo reconnaissance and had a longer nose to accommodate the cameras. The first example was XD903, which was flown for the first time, on 27 May 1955, by test pilot Les Colquhoun.

Despite the problems with the previous marks, the Swift FR Mk 5 was highly successful in its reconnaissance role and even won a NATO award twice in reconnaissance competitions. It was because of the strong airframe that there were no fatigue problems, and it became a popular aircraft with the pilots, much to the surprise of the crews of earlier marks.

A flight of Swift FR Mk 5s from No 2 Squadron RAF in perfect formation. *David Noyce*

Flying the Swift FR Mk 5

The Swift FR Mk 5 was a single-seat, swept-wing fighter reconnaissance aircraft powered by a single Avon turbojet engine with reheat. In its role as a recon-naissance aircraft it was fitted with three cameras, and its armaments consisted of two 30mm Aden guns. As a high-altitude combat fighter the early Swift was not very successful, and this was reflected in the comments within RAF circles, and throughout the aviation world, which focused on the accidents and dan-gers posed to pilots. However, when its role was changed to fighter low-level reconnaissance these attitudes tended to remain and in some circles tarnished its excellent reconnaissance role in the Cold War theatre. Most pilots who flew the Swift FR Mk 5 in Germany have fond memories of flying the aircraft.

Nigel Walpole was a pilot serving in RAF Germany in No 79 Squadron in the 1950s, when the aircraft became well known for its successful role as a fighter reconnaissance aircraft. In his book *Swift Justice* he defends the FR Mk 5 against the criticism levelled at it at the time. He believes that not enough credit was given to the aircraft and that despite the earlier problems experienced in its role as a high-level combat fighter, the low-level fighter reconnaissance role was very successful.

Bryan Carter was another FR Mk 5 pilot with No 79 Squadron stationed at Gütersloh in Germany, having joined the RAF in 1950:

Bryan Carter with the Swift FR Mk 5 WK281 at Tangmere Aviation Museum in April 2011. WK281 joined 79 Squadron at RAF Gütersloh in April 1959. *Richard de Jong*

I went into the recruiting office and decided to volunteer for the Royal Air Force to train to be a pilot/navigator and was very fortunate in being sent to Rhodesia for my flight training. My first jet aircraft was the Vampire and eventually I went on to convert to the Supermarine Swift.

Bryan found the training on the Swift was very much in-house, but as there was no two-seater trainer Swift they had to train a different way. The trainee pilots were handed a set of pilot notes and then went to the simulator. After lunch they would return to one of the hangars where there was a cardboard cut-out of a Swift cockpit. The trainee pilot was allocated an instructor who then ran him through the procedure of how to start the engine, including all the basics for getting airborne. Following on from this were the instructions and any important matters that the trainee needed to know about take-off, flying speed in the air and landing speed, and importantly the emergency drills, such as in the event of fire and how to eject from the aircraft. To Bryan this was crucial because at the time there had been quite a few engine failures with the Swift, so it was essential to know how to operate the Martin-Baker ejector seat. This was an early version of the ejector seat, which had a 400ft (121.92) minimum bail-out limit; anything lower and the parachute would not open:

> The Swift was a fairly long aircraft, but underpowered, and we had to put the reheat on to give sufficient thrust to get us airborne. The runway was 2,000 yards [1,828.8m] long, but we soon learned that as the temperatures go up your performance goes down.
>
> I remember standing on the Squadron Ops Room watching a Swift take off and it took almost all the runway before it left the ground, and it was good that some airmen had the sense to lower the barrier at the end of the runway because the aircraft only just cleared it.
>
> The officer on duty started to hunt around and eventually found a performance booklet that had been issued by Supermarine. On checking we found that you needed a longer runway than the 2,000 yards at particular temperatures. So we stopped flying until the temperature cooled down!
>
> The aircraft had two intakes either side of the cockpit and when taking off you used the reheat, but once the aircraft was airborne and you got to wheels up you could cancel the reheat. If you left it burning you would use a lot of fuel. The acceleration when flying at low level was quite good. However, the aircraft appeared to be a bit docile, needing a fair bit of effort on the part of the pilot, but it had nice flying controls.

The Swift had a large belly tank underneath most of the time which gave the pilots a reasonable endurance. Flying at low level they could get about 50 minutes, but by flying higher it was possible to get about 1 hour and 5 minutes. Bryan felt they were fortunate that at the time they had sixteen aircraft for twelve pilots, which meant that there were always enough aircraft available by rotation for maintenance to be undertaken, which in fact was fairly regular:

> It was a nice stable aircraft and flew quite nicely throughout the speed range, except the turning which wasn't as sharp as other aircraft, but this was a consequence of overweight. I did have a couple of hydraulic failures, but the first one I was a bit concerned with because I hadn't practised enough flying in manual control.
>
> The aircraft was armed with two 30mm cannons and also we had cameras on board because the aircraft when flying low down was a very good stable platform and had good cockpit visibility.
>
> Although you couldn't stay around very long, with a bit of careful flying you could stay around for about an hour, and by staying low level which was set officially at above 250ft [76.2m].

In Germany there were two Swift squadrons: No 2 Squadron at Jever, and No 79 Squadron at Gütersloh. Being based at Gütersloh, about 100 miles from Berlin, which was within East German territory, Bryan comments, 'If the balloon went up we would be the first up to undertake photographic reconnaissance of what was going on.'

In the training for photographic reconnaissance the pilots had to fly past various targets, normally starting them with a bridge. At that time there were no restrictions regarding the height at which the RAF could fly but, as Bryan remembers, they did tighten up because one or two people frightened themselves by meeting aircraft coming the other way:

> It was quite interesting using the cameras because what you didn't see was recorded until they were taken in for interpretation. We would train all the time and in the UK one of the training areas was Tower Bridge over the Thames. The bridge has got three spans over the water, but the middle span is a lifting one. We were proficient enough to do one fly-by at about 300 knots, and as it is not a very big bridge we would pass over it in less than half a minute, having the cameras running, looking what was going on over all three spans and the amount of traffic there was. All this had to be reported to the photo interpreter after you had landed back at base.

While in Germany, the squadron trained regularly with the Army, but at the beginning it was discovered that the Army's camouflage capability varied from regiment to regiment, although most were more successful using camouflage on level ground. However, the military forgot that the aircraft were above and when they flew over a clump of trees, the pilots could see the trucks with branches stuck in them, so to the pilots they were not camouflaged at all. The Dragoon Guards was the regiment that 79 Squadron worked most with, and on one exercise they did a number runs over and then returned to base to have the photographs checked in the photographic caravan. After they had been checked by the interpreter, he exclaimed, 'I think we got them':

> There was a whole bunch of trees with a small clearing and we could see a soldier sat on a latrine. You would have thought they had learned from that experience and it had sharpened them up, but a few days later in a similar spot and another clearing in the woods, again we saw a batman with a cup of tea in his hand marching towards some trees!

By the end of the training, the regiment proved excellent at camouflage, even thinking of reflection of light from the windscreens. At first they put their coats over the top but finally they had pieces of card cut out to put over them:

> It was a lot of fun doing the training with the regiment and sometime we had an invitation to visit them and fire some of their guns, but we preferred our own armaments. That was because we had a good stable platform for aiming accurately on to a target. You didn't bounce around a lot and had a steady aim which got you a good score. When you think about the operation, you are going out there flying along and looking for targets of opportunity, just as they do today. The role of the Swift was very interesting as it was a stopgap aircraft for the fighter/photographic reconnaissance side – I enjoyed flying it.

Bryan had a permanent commission, which meant that he could stay on until the age of 55. Having started as a sergeant pilot, he gained his officer's commission and after various training posts as an instructor he finally had a posting to 29 Squadron, flying Lightning jet aircraft until his retirement from the RAF in 1969. After leaving the service, he became a civil pilot, flying for BEA on Viscounts, Tridents and Boeing 737s, until he left to fly for Air Europe.

Swift Type 552 prototype Mk 7 XF774 first flew in April 1956 and carried Blue Sky air-to-air missiles, later renamed Fireflash. The Swift F Mk7s were the first British fighters to carry guided missiles. *David Noyce*

Swift PR Mk 6 and Swift F Mk 7

Two further variants were designed. The PR Mk 6 (Type 550) XD943 was an unarmed photo reconnaissance aircraft powered by the Avon RA.7 turbojet, but was not completed due to the programme being cancelled.

The F Mk 7 (Type 552) XF774 was the first Swift to be fitted with four Blue Sky guided missiles. Further modification was required, which involved lengthening the nose to accommodate the radar and increased the wingspan. Although fourteen aircraft were built, none ever entered service.

Type 545 'Supersonic Swift'

With the increased interest in supersonic flight, Supermarine made a proposal to the Air Ministry for a Swift (Type 545) designed specifically for supersonic flight. The Air Ministry responded by issuing the specification F.105DT and an order for two prototypes. Serial number XA181 was built at Hursley's Experimental Hangar but was never flown. The second, XA186, was cancelled before any construction of the fuselage took place, although this was after a structural test specimen had been built.

The Type 545 was referred to as the 'Supersonic Swift'. In this design, the two air intakes were moved forward to the nose of the aircraft. It was powered by a Rolls-Royce Avon RA.14R turbojet and had crescent-shaped wings.

The Type 545 'Supersonic Swift' design had the air intakes forward in the nose of the aircraft, well away from the wings, but the project was cancelled despite the prototype XA181 being almost complete. *Solent Sky*

No 79 Squadron, winners of the 1959 NATO Low Level Reconnaissance Competition code named 'Royal Flush'. No 2 Squadron came second. The C.O. has his elbow on the wing. *Solent Sky*

Although Supermarine were among the most famous of all British aircraft manufacturers, mainly because of the reputation of the wartime Spitfire, they did not fare as well in the post-war years. This was in part due to the problems of the earlier versions of the Swift jet aircraft and the withdrawal of the fighter variants from service with the RAF. Despite this setback, the Swift FR Mk 5 went on to become very effective in its low-level photo reconnaissance role and consistently beat all other makes in international competitions, including American aircraft, and remained in service with the RAF until 1961.

Harry Griffiths considered that the bad press reports about the Swift were unjustified, and remembers Joe Smith saying in his speech at the design staff dinner: 'Don't lose heart over press comments about the Swift – it's a good aircraft and the fact is that if there were a World War tomorrow we should be building it and we would bloody well win.' Smith was very proud of his achievement with the Swift, including its success in breaking speed records.

THE SWIFT WORLD
SPEED RECORD

Murry White was in charge of the organisation and management of the team for the attempt on the world speed record attempt and was very proud of the outcome. Joe Smith had called him into his office one day, where he found an Air Commodore present, and said:

We want to see if we can get the World Speed Record with a Swift Mark 4. We think the best place to do it is out in North Africa where the temperature is hot and the Air Commodore has it all lined up for us. I want you to manage the team out there. The first thing you have to do is get an Ordnance Survey Team out there to survey the course and mark it out. Mike Lithgow and Les Colquhoun will fly out with you to show you where we think the best place is.

Involving the Ordnance Survey

Murry said he was happy to take on the project and Smith told him to be firm with the Ordnance Survey and not take 'no' for an answer. He would back him up on anything he wanted, including any necessary finance.

The head of the Ordnance Survey was very negative and wanted to know who was going to pay for the four OS staff needed. Murry explained that Supermarine would finance the operation, but it took him almost the whole day to get an agreement. Murry got back at about 4 p.m. to find Smith and the Air Commodore pacing up and down, and told them that he had convinced the Ordnance Survey that they had to do it and that Supermarine would pay all their costs, including transportation and clothes, and would indemnity them. Smith was happy with the result and said he would arrange for the Ordnance Survey team to have expenses at the rate of £10 a day to do it.

Observation bases were built and manned to record the attempts on the world air speed record in Libya. *Solent Sky*

The Air Commodore arranged for Murry to have the assistance of Sqn Ldr John Harvey, an RAF liaison officer who knew the North African coast very well. The team's working base and airfield was to be RAF Castel Benito at Idris el Awal, now known as Tripoli, in Libya. They were supplied with all the clothing and resources they needed, and the team flew off to North Africa in a chartered RAF Viking.

Les Colquhoun was with them and had already selected the proposed course, which was along a straight road, approximately 10 miles (16.09km) long across the Azizia Plain, finishing at Bur el Gnem. This was to be between the 81st and 84th kilometre stones along the road. Surveying the course, setting up the concrete bases for the timing machines and laying telephone cables between them took about two weeks, then the team returned to the UK. An RAF Hastings was chartered for the main party to fly to Libya, and they left on 22 September 1953. At about the same time, Mike Lithgow, who was piloting the Swift, flew in formation with Les Colquhoun, who was piloting the Attacker. Murry talks about the flight to Libya:

In the Hastings we had the usual spares, as well as a spare Swift engine, spare windscreen, wheel tyres and brakes and a full maintenance team led by young Jeff Judd, Goldsmith from the RAF and five operators for the timing machines, and the four FAI [Fédération Aéronautique Internationale] official observers. The Hastings was manned by a full RAF crew who remained with us throughout the record attempt and eventually flew us all home.

One of the requirements set by the FAI was that Mike Lithgow should make four runs over a measured 3 kilometres [1.86 miles], two in each direction and at a constant height of 100 metres [328ft]. To prove this the two monitoring aircraft positioned at each end of the course had sealed Barographs, one in the Anson and one in the Meteor which the RAF Station supplied and flew, thus becoming part of the team. Although we had radio communication with Mike, due to the terrain and distance it was ineffective, but by having Les Colquhoun in the Attacker at 5,000ft [1,524m] he could act as a relay station and monitor all radio communications. We also had the FAI observers to see fair play and who were famous people in their own right.

The team lived in the Officers' Mess in Castel Benito, but as they were outside throughout the day in the intense heat they found no one had an appetite, so lived on iced water in thermos flasks provided by the wives and girls based at the RAF station. Murry continues:

We also had a whole fleet of journalists under Charles Gardner (of BBC fame) who were not attached to my party. Joe wished to keep our attempt as secret as possible in case we failed. We did not want any publicity which might adversely affect Swift production. I had daily briefing meetings (when we strictly kept the press out) to go over the day's work and the next day's programme at about 6 p.m. each day. Then we all showered and had our one meal of the day.

The preparation for the record attempt took some time to arrange, but Murry was very pleased with the support and assistance that the RAF station gave them:

We had numerous breakdowns and troubles. One was identifying the turning points for Mike to clearly see. In the end, after trying various markers, Les flew to Malta in the RAF Anson to collect smoke generators that John Harvey had located. Castel Benito was a fully functional RAF Station and thanks to the RAF commitment gave us full backing in all we wanted which included positioning fire engines at the course, emergency tented hospital, ambulance and RAF Regiment guards to protect it, as well as road transportation for us all. We also had the good services of a medical officer, Wing Commander Tony Barwood, who kept us, amongst a lot of other things, fully supplied with salt tablets because we were all out in the desert from 7 a.m. to 5 p.m. in intense heat and so were in constant dehydration conditions.

In his book *Mach One*, Mike Lithgow makes little of his cockpit flight conditions for the numerous record attempts: 'Unfortunately, once airborne there was at first little or no air coming through the suit and the temperature inside the cockpit was well into the 180°s.' However, Murry explains how very severe it was for Lithgow flying in such conditions:

> When one realises he was flying 100 metres [328ft] up at 750mph [1,207km/h] in a very high-performance aircraft, very sensitive to control movements, one realises how brave he was. After a run, he was on several occasions so exhausted that he had to be lifted out of the cockpit by the ground crew, who incidentally all worked under very tiring conditions happily and loyally as a great and very efficient team.

By this time Joe Smith, Ernie Mansbridge and representatives of Rolls-Royce had travelled to Libya and had witnessed the successful breaking of the world speed record by Lithgow in the Swift F Mk 4, WK198, on 26 September 1953, at 737.7mph (1,187.21km/h). (Lithgow had previously broken the London–Paris speed record, averaging 671mph [1,079.86km/h] for the 212.5 miles [342km] on 5 July 1953.) Fortunately, the team in Libya just managed to get all the equipment out before the desert wind (the *Ghibli*) and rains struck, turning the wadis into rushing streams:

On 26 September 1953, Mike Lithgow flying a Swift F Mk 4, WK198, successfully broke the world air speed record with a speed of 737.7mph (1,187.21km/h). *Solent Sky*

Everybody had worked tremendously long and hard in the exacting conditions and so I declared a 3-day holiday, with some moans from Charles Barter who looked after the money for me, before we were ready to depart for home. We all clambered into the RAF Hastings, complete with all the loot each of us had accumulated, which included things like a sack of coconuts, and arrived back at RAF Lyneham, but not without incident! Over central France the flight engineer came back to say we had developed a leak in the central fuselage fuel tank and he forbade smoking! In spite of the fuel loss, we just made RAF Lyneham without the need to refuel and landed with virtually dry tanks! And so ended what I think was a wonderful combined team effort.

The company chairman and directors, delighted with the success of the team in breaking the world speed record, arranged for a grand celebration evening and dinner in London on 10 November 1953. Murry was also delighted with Lithgow's achievement, but has one final thought:

I was very much in admiration of Mike Lithgow, both for his world speed record and his work with me on aircraft carriers. I am still very sad at his untimely death in the deep stall incident of the BAC 1-11. He was certainly a remarkable man and a great and brave pilot. I felt very proud to have worked with him.

The temperature in the aircraft was extreme during record attempts and a very exhausted Mike Lithgow can be seen climbing out of the cockpit at Idris. *Solent Sky*

On 10 November 1953, the company chairman and directors arranged a celebration dinner in London. From left to right: Murry White, Mrs Yapp, Winnie Smith, Joe Smith, Sqn Ldr John Harvey, Jean Harvey, –?–. *Murry White*

Alan Clifton (Young Alan) also remembers the tragic loss of Lithgow. Alan had been due to have an interview with the chief test pilot, but the interview date, 22 October 1963, was sadly the day on which Lithgow was killed when the prototype BAC 1-11, G-ASHG, got itself into a deep stall while stalling tests were being undertaken.

The Duke of Edinburgh Visits Supermarine

In April 1953, HRH Prince Philip, Duke of Edinburgh accompanied by the Duke of Kent visited Supermarine facilities at Chilbolton, Hursley Park and South Marston and were able to see for themselves the developments in the Supermarine jet aircraft. After the Duke had landed in a Viscount at Chilbolton, he was welcomed by Supermarine's chief designer Joe Smith, and Jeffrey Quill, chief liaison officer, and then introduced to chief test pilot Lithgow and his team. He was shown the Supermarine Type 508 (VX133) which had a V (butterfly) tail, standing near the hangar entrance. This aircraft had been modified in 1947 from the Type 505, which was without an undercarriage, into the Type 508 with a retractable nosewheel undercarriage.

Standing near the Type 508 was a Type 529 (VX136) and also the Swift F Mk 1 (WK194) and the Swift F Mk 4 (WK198). It was WK198 that had been flown in Libya for the successful attempt on the world absolute air speed record in September 1953. The Duke was also able to see a two-seat Spitfire Trainer Tr. 8 N32 (G-AIDN). G-AIDN remained at Chilbolton from 1952 until 1956 before

On a visit to the design office at Hursley Park, HRH the Duke of Edinburgh is shown examples of design plans. From left to right: Joe Smith, the Duke of Edinburgh, Gerry Gingell. *Solent Sky*

Supermarine occupied many rooms of Hursley House for various departments, with the design and technical offices on the ground floor. The Stag Room was distinctive as a result of the displays on its walls. *Solent Sky*

going to the Hampshire Aeroplane Club. Members of the technical office explained about the test equipment they used and how the test results were studied. Afterwards test pilot Dave Morgan did a short flying display using the Swift he had flown to break the London–Brussels speed record on 10 July 1952 at a speed of 665.9mph (1071.66km/h), and the Duke was able to witness him passing the control tower in excess of his record speed.

It was a busy day for the Duke. Following his visit to Chilbolton, he was taken to Hursley Park where he saw the ongoing work in the Experimental Hangar and drawing office before returning to Chilbolton from where he was flown in the Viscount to South Marston. Here he was welcomed by the superintendent, Stan Woodley, and escorted around the works to inspect the various workshop facilities. He was able to see an Attacker ordered for the Royal Navy and Swifts ordered for the RAF before returning in the Viscount to London Airport.

20

LANDING ON RUBBER MATS

The Admiralty was interested in having an aircraft without an undercarriage that would be able to land on flexible rubber decks on aircraft carriers. Flexible deck tests started on a hard installation at the RAE Farnborough in 1947, and on a flexible rubber deck on HMS *Warrior*. This was an attempt to save the weight of an undercarriage, and Eric 'Winkle' Brown proved this was possible when he landed a Sea Vampire on HMS *Warrior*.

> We did 100 landings at Farnborough and 200 landings on HMS *Warrior* at sea, and all were very successful. After landing on the flexible deck you are sitting at the end of the wire and when they pulled the aircraft fully back on the wire the aircraft was positioned over the trap door. The door would open and the aircraft slide down onto a trolley, and not having an undercarriage the carrier could store double the number of aircraft by double docking.
>
> Towards the end of the experiment we were a sort of circus act. If any visitors came to the RAE Farnborough we had to perform some flexible deck landings.

In 1945, Supermarine had designed the single-seat Type 505 undercarriage-less fighter, powered by two Rolls-Royce Avon turbojet engines positioned side by side with a V (butterfly) tail. The Type 505 had spent a long period in the project office where a wooden mock-up was built, but no actual manufacturing drawings were issued for this design. However, despite Brown flying a Sea Vampire demonstrating that a skilled pilot could land on a flexible deck, the project was cancelled. This was to be the start of a series of designs for naval jet fighters that would lead to the Scimitar jet fighter.

The Admiralty had lost interest in the undercarriage-less aircraft by 1947, and issued specification N.9/47 for a naval carrier jet fighter/research aircraft.

Type 508 VX133 ready for take-off from HMS *Illustrious*. It was a single-seat, twin-engine jet aircraft with straight wings, a butterfly tail and a retractable nosewheel undercarriage. *Murry White*

Murry White, Supermarine team manager for carrier trials, talking to chief test pilot Mike Lithgow alongside the Type 508 during the carrier trials on HMS *Illustrious* in May 1952. *Murry White*

Three aircraft were ordered from Supermarine and were built at Hursley Park Experimental Department. The first design, similar to the Type 505, became the Type 508 but with a tricycle undercarriage.

At first, the Type 508 (VX133) was a V-tailed, twin-engine, straight-winged, single-seat fighter prototype powered by two Avon engines. The aircraft first flew on 31 August 1951 from Boscombe Down airfield, and by May 1952 was tasked to carry out aircraft carrier trials on HMS *Eagle*. The second aircraft, Type 529 (VX136) also had straight wings but with its armament changed to two 20mm cannons. VX136 first flew on 29 August 1952, but the straight-wing version's flight tests showed that the maximum speed was less than required, reaching just over 600mph (965.6km/h). The third aircraft was the Type 525 (VX138), a twin-engine experimental aircraft designed with 45° swept-back wings to improve the speed.

Denis Webb took over the Type 525 project full time in 1952 under Joe Smith at Hursley Park's Experimental Hangar until it was completed. Frank Perry, manager of the Experimental Department, was to remain at Chilbolton. On 25 April 1954, Type 525 (VX138), the last Supermarine prototype built at the Hursley Park Experimental Department, left the site to be transported by road to the A&AEE at Boscombe Down. The aircraft was first flown from there by Mike Lithgow on 27 April 1954. Later in 1954, after further test flights had been carried out at Chilbolton airfield, VX138 was taken back to the Experimental Department at Hursley Park to be fitted with blown flaps.

VX133 landing on HMS *Illustrious* with arrester hook lowered ready to engage the wires. *Murry White*

Type 529 VX136 on the flight deck with its wings folded. It was the second of three aircraft ordered to specification N.9/47 and first flew on 29 August 1952. *Murry White*

The third prototype, Type 525 VX138, was built with swept wings to improve performance, and was taken by road from Hursley Park's Experimental Hangar to Boscombe Down on 25 April 1954. *John Thomson*

Mike Lithgow flew VX138 on its first flight on 27 April 1954, and in September of that year it made its first public appearance at the Farnborough Air Show. *Solent Sky*

Blown Flaps

Blown flaps was a new concept introduced in about 1950 which gave low-speed lift during take-off and also gave the pilot an improved view when coming in to land. Aerodynamicists recognised that compressed air over a deflected wing flap could increase the lift in the landing environment and allow slower and safer landing speeds.

The blown flaps were fitted on the Type 525 and worked well, but an unfortunate accident occurred on 5 July 1955 after a Royal Navy pilot, Lt-Cdr T.A. Rickell was unable to recover from a spin 20 minutes after take-off, just a short distance from Boscombe Down airfield. Although the pilot ejected from the aircraft, he was too low to the ground and died from his injuries. Joe Smith was devastated not only by the loss of the pilot but also because the loss of VX138 would cause a delay of two years before another prototype was able to take part in further trials with blown flaps. This delay seriously curtailed Supermarine's ability to gain future orders against some of their competitors.

Although Smith was special director of Vickers-Armstrongs Ltd, he was still a hands-on designer who worked with his large team developing jet aircraft, culminating in his final design which was to be the Type 544 (N113D) Scimitar.

The Type 525 was the forerunner of the Type 544 Scimitar prototype (WT854) which was first flown by Lithgow from Boscombe Down on 19 January 1956. The first production F Mk 1 Scimitar was XD212, which made its first flight on 11 January 1957 and undertook flight-test trials at Boscombe Down and deck landing trials on HMS *Ark Royal*.

Another landing by WT854, and the arrester gear can clearly be seen ready to engage the wires on the flight deck. *Murry White*

Type 544 (N113D) Scimitar WT854 was first flown by Mike Lithgow from Boscombe Down on 19 January 1956, followed by deck landing trials. Here it is landing on HMS *Ark Royal*. *Murry White*

The first flight of Scimitar XD212 on 11 January 1957. It served with 736 Naval Air Squadron at RNAS Lossiemouth. On 20 September 1961, it crashed into a hill near Huntly, Banffshire, killing the pilot. *Murry White*

The first Scimitars to enter Fleet Air Arm service were delivered to No 700X Squadron which was the Scimitar Intensive Flying Trials Unit, formed and based at RNAS Ford in August 1957. The unit was disbanded in May 1958 when the Scimitars became part of No 700 Squadron. In June 1958, eight

Scimitars joined No 803 Squadron at RNAS Lossiemouth to undertake training and then embarked on HMS *Victorious* in September 1958. In May 1962, No 803 Squadron transferred to HMS *Hermes* where they operated in the Mediterranean and the Far East until 1963. The squadron returned to RNAS Lossiemouth, where the strength was increased to sixteen Scimitars. After further service operating from HMS *Ark Royal*, HMS *Centaur* and HMS *Eagle*, the Scimitars were replaced when the Buccaneers came into service.

The Scimitar was a single-seat fighter powered by twin Avon 200 turbojet engines and was built for the Royal Navy as a low-level strike fighter. Its armament consisted of four 30mm Aden cannon, Sidewinder air-to-air missiles, Bullpup air-to-ground missiles, a Red Beard tactical nuclear bomb and a range of bombs and rockets.

Almost Vertical Take-Off

David Coombs transferred from Hursley Park to a post in design office liaison at Wisley, near Weybridge, and was able to witness the take-off of the Scimitar from the test flight aerodrome there:

> Today it is just a ploughed field, opposite the Royal Horticultural Gardens. The runway was almost a mile long and so we saw all that was happening. We worked in a small drawing office near the control tower. We were working on the Scimitar, powered by twin Avon engines, and at that time we would watch it come along the runway for take-off and go straight up, almost vertically. A television cameraman trying to capture this feature missed it, and requested a re-run!! That was the first British aircraft to be able to do that. All the aircraft we worked on at that time were for the Royal Navy, and I found it extremely interesting.
>
> The Chief of Manufacturing had decided that General Engineering should be the future of design, but this was strongly resisted by the senior design staff. I felt fortunate to have worked at the cutting edge of design in aeronautical progress of the time.

Tropical Trials on the Scimitar

Gordon Monger was one of the team that went to Libya in 1959 for tropical trials on the Scimitar. However, having broken his leg skiing earlier in the year, he had some rapid physiotherapy before going to Libya:

Scimitars were often seen taking off from the runway almost vertically. *Solent Sky*

After a troublesome week we eventually took off at dawn from Boscombe Down on a Friday in a lumbering Hastings that had long since lost its heating system, draught excluders and seat cushions. All the gear was tied down forward of the few seats. We landed at Orange in Southern France where RAF personnel there served us tea in basins and some bread for breakfast.

It was then intended to fly on to Libya, so the engines of the Hastings and escorting Canberra were started, but the starter motor for the Scimitar failed and the Hastings returned to Boscombe Down for a replacement starter. The Canberra got away, but when the Hastings had returned it was midday on Saturday and the French had closed Orange for the weekend, so the team could not leave until the Monday. The problems did not end there:

We got away on the Monday having changed into tropical clothes because it was so hot in Orange. What a mistake! As we climbed out over the Mediterranean, with the aircraft's condition and our clothing, it got very cold, only to land in Idris about 20 miles south of Tripoli in Libya, as if we were landing in an oven. We were then accommodated in a ground floor barrack room.

When the tropical trials were undertaken, the majority of flying on the Scimitar was made at 200ft (60.96m) and Mach 0.94 over the desert for 20 minutes. For an ambient temperature of 35°C this gave a total temperature of about 100°C. The exception to this low-level flying was loitering at high altitude to cool the aeroplane and then rapidly reducing altitude to very low level over the sea, where the humidity was higher, to check the demisting of the cameras and transparencies. The Scimitar was provided with cold air units to cool the equipment and the cockpit, and the pilot was provided with a ventilated suit in which cold air was blown through capillary tubes onto his body to keep him cool.

Flight-test instrumentation was fitted in the nose of the aircraft, but was changed for the different tests being carried out and was cooled by the exhaust cold air from the cockpit. Recording of the test instruments was by a 35mm camera fitted with a 200ft (60.96m) magazine:

The magazine was removed immediately after flight and was so hot that it could not be held and had to be tossed between two people. The first few feet of film was heat damaged before the start of recording and the last few feet after the conclusion of the recording. During the flight the perforated edge of the film was heat damaged, all of which protected the major part of the film. You could feel the radiant heat from the aircraft from some distance after a flight, and the pilot had to wear gloves to escape from the cockpit. Fuel leaks occurred in the wings and a drip onto one's hands was very hot after a flight. Also, flying at low altitude, the sand eroded all leading surfaces and the leading section of the cockpit windscreen had to be changed during the period. An eyelid protected the exposed camera. After the trials, Rolls-Royce had the engines back for inspection and said they were the cleanest engines internally that they had ever seen.

The test flights were carried out in the early afternoon, in the hottest part of the day, after the aircraft had been standing in the sun, followed by the debriefing. Gordon Monger analysed the results, wrote reports and attended briefings in the mornings. In the late evenings they read the film. Apart from in-flight sand blasting, a few minor wing fuel tank leaks and other minor snags, everything went very well except for the instrumentation, which gave a lot of trouble as it was not capable of withstanding such high temperatures:

> The engines performed well on take-off where on other aircraft their engines gave trouble. On one occasion where two flights were made in quick succession, a valve in the cooling airline to the lead acid battery, to protect the battery in flight should the cooling unit fail, closed between the flights. On the second flight the battery temperature slowly increased to over 100°C. On inspection of the battery the next morning, it was found to be completely dry and the plates badly distorted. The cockpit hood slid open a small amount on one flight and the hot air rushed in, but the pilot rapidly climbed to a cooler altitude.

During the tests four 1,000lb bombs painted black were left in the sunshine by the taxiway for a few days and Gordon wondered what the airline passengers must have thought when they saw them. However, when depositing the bombs in the Mediterranean, only three were seen by the pilot to have exploded:

> There was no problem with misting of the cameras or transparencies although a P.O. there for the servicing of the aircraft, at the debriefing one evening stepping out of his domain stated that the cameras misted up, but this was without foundation and was dismissed as lack of knowledge. However, this misleading remark was reiterated in the book entitled *The Scimitar File* published in 2000.

The team had very little leisure time but did manage to visit the old town of Garian, about 20 miles (32.16km) from Idris, where they saw life-size wall drawings of the Lady of Garian made during the Second World War, and also went to the Roman ruins at Sabatha. However, apart from the danger and hostile nature of places they visited, it was the stench that, Gordon comments, 'stayed in my nostrils for months'. The other discomforts were the flies, the temperature dropping only to the low 30s°C at night and the sandstorms which Gordon found uncomfortable: 'When washing with soap it was like washing with Vim!'

When the team eventually left Libya for England, they took off at dawn when the temperature was at its lowest, but suffered storms in the Mediterranean and as the Hastings could not climb above them, had to make a detour and eventually landed at Orange. However, the final flight over France was much more pleasant in the sun until arriving back in England.

The Scimitar had been designed to operate from HMS *Centaur*, as well as larger fleet carriers. All these ships had centre-line lifts with a length of 54ft (16.45m) and a width of 44ft (13.41m) and these dimensions limited the size of the Scimitar. However, the Scimitar was generally well liked by pilots, and was the first British jet fighter to carry nuclear weapons. It was also the last aircraft to carry the famous Supermarine name, and the last complete military aircraft to be designed and built in the Southampton area. Sadly, Joe Smith died before he could see the Scimitar in production.

21

Post-War Apprenticeships at Supermarine

For young people leaving school in the Southampton area there were two main opportunities for apprenticeships, either in the shipyards or in aviation, and for many it was the expectation of their family that they would become apprentices either in the docks or in aviation work.

Some of the past apprentices at Supermarine during the Second World War or in the post-war era have shared their experiences with the author. They include Gordon Monger and Tony Kenyon, who joined Supermarine during the war, and David Noyce, David Effney, Alan Clifton (Young Alan), David Coombs, Norman Crimble, John Thomson, David Faddy, Margaret Blake and her brother Christopher Legg, Garth Pearce and Leo Schefer, who were all post-war apprentices.

Although John Thomson's father and uncles encouraged him to undertake an engineering apprenticeship at the shipyards of Harland & Wolff or Thornycroft, he was not interested in marine engineering but wanted to work in aviation. His interest in aviation started at a young age when living under the flight path at Eastleigh Airport. He remembers watching DH Dragon airliners flying over his home on their way to Jersey: 'When it came to choosing a career there was only one thing I wanted to do, to work on aeroplanes.'

Not all wanted to follow in their family footsteps, as can be seen by Dr Gordon Mitchell, son of Supermarine's chief designer Reginald Mitchell, who decided on a different profession, and Martin Davis, son of Eric John (Jack) Davis, who became an historian and shares his memories of his father:

My childhood memories are from the late 1940s into the 1950s when my father used to take me to various air shows, including Farnborough and Boscombe Down, and this was especially when my father was working on military aircraft.

My father was always interested in what I was doing, always supportive, always encouraging and not over-strict. He was meticulous, very organized and very precise in everything he did.

Martin did not have as much involvement in his father's work as perhaps some others did, but he was intensely interested in history. Jack Davis was very pleased when Martin gained a place at Cambridge to read history, followed by a career in higher education:

> Interestingly, once when he visited me he met the college porter who had in fact previously worked at Supermarine and they recognised each other immediately. I remember him telling me that he had been at the maiden flight of the K5054 at Eastleigh aerodrome on March 5 1936. He continued with the development of the Spitfire throughout the war years and beyond.
>
> My father greatly respected R.J. Mitchell who he thought was very good at encouraging young people, and I remember him saying that Joe Smith was extremely important after R.J. Mitchell had died, and was the key person in the production of the Spitfire. He also thought that Alan Clifton in the area of aerodynamics was outstanding.

During his time at Supermarine, Davis worked on the Southampton, Scapa and Stranraer flying boats, prototype and production Spitfire, B.12/36 four-engine bomber and various Spitfire and Seafire developments. Other aircraft included the Seagull ASR-1 flying boat, Swift fighter, twin-engine naval fighter Type 508, and finally the Scimitar, the last of the Supermarine aircraft. He finally retired in 1971.

David Faddy shares his memories as a child of his father Alf and his later career at the Defence Operational Analysis Establishment:

> I was brought up in a very happy home. My father was a very good father. I trained as an apprentice at the Royal Aircraft Establishment, largely because my father was convinced that my brother and I ought to be apprentices. He had something of a contempt for people who hadn't served an apprenticeship, and himself had been an apprentice at Parsons at Newcastle upon Tyne. R.J. Mitchell and Joe Smith had also served engineering apprenticeships and that was one of the things they had in common. I have to say that neither I nor my brother were terribly good at engineering. I actually started again and eventually went into operational research. My brother became a violin teacher, which was what he wanted to do and should have been allowed to do at the beginning. In that respect we were, of course, influenced by our father.

David Effney was another young man who wanted to take up a career in aviation and was fortunate in getting an introduction to Supermarine because his mother had known Joe Smith just after the First World War. This was at a time when Smith and his old RNVR friends would regularly meet up and take a group of girls to Murray's Hotel at Hythe between 1918 and 1921, the year that Smith joined Supermarine as a draughtsman. David's mother said that they were 'just lads and lasses enjoying themselves'. Knowing of her son's interest in a career in aviation, she contacted Smith and told him she had a son who would like to join Supermarine as an apprentice. An appointment was made for David to meet Smith, accompanied by his father:

> I know we went up to Hursley House and when we arrived we asked to see Mr Smith. At first we sat in the entrance hallway and waited to be called into his office. He had a very nice office, fairly big overlooking the park. We sat and he discussed my options and what they could do for me, and what I ought to be trying to do. Joe Smith decided that there was a space for me as an apprentice draughtsman and called in Mr Daniels the apprentice supervisor to tell him that I would be coming on his books. There was an exchange of correspondence and I was given a date to start as an apprentice in February 1948.

Alan Clifton (Young Alan) started his apprenticeship at Supermarine in 1949 and remembers many of the apprentices he worked with, especially his association with David Effney:

> David Effney got a jazz band together. He was on saxophone, me with a phonofiddle which belonged to my uncle who was killed in the First World War. It was a one string fiddle with a sort of gramophone horn. There was somebody who played the drums, and one who played the piano. We used to go and practise our one tune 'Goodnight Irene' at David's parents' house in Southampton.

David is listed in the 1951 design office dinner programme as performing with Wally Clarke on piano; David was playing the saxophone. Young Alan joined Supermarine when the Swift was under development, but had not yet flown for the first time:

> I started off as an airframe fitter, worked in the machine shop in Woolston, then up to South Marston, also in the machine shop. I went to Itchen to work on panel beating which I found very interesting. I finished in the drawing office, where I had a year or two working for Pelham Slade. I worked in the engine sections as well. I had to defer National Service because of

my apprenticeship, and then I went to the RAF recruiting office and told them that I wanted to learn to fly. They told me they were not taking on National Service pilots, but if I wanted to fly I would have to sign on, and being a keen young man I asked for the paperwork. I signed on and became a Flying Officer, flying Hunters. When I left the RAF I went back to work for Supermarine, but later I became a commercial pilot.

He also remembers Norman Crimble when they were apprentices. Norman had left school at the age of 15 years 10 months, so before he started his apprenticeship at 16 he had to be a 'shop boy' for two months. Mention was made in Chapter 13 about the tricks played on the new boys when they joined Supermarine and of Tony Kenyon's experience with the 'struggling bar'. Norman was also tricked when he was a new boy:

At the start I was a shop boy where I was to get things for the fitters from the stores. That was known as a 'Go for'. The fitters would send you to the stores for some sort of material and would say something like, 'Go for a long wait' and you would go to the stores thinking you were asking for a 'long weight'. The storeman would then leave you standing there for about an hour, and then he would say, 'Alright, you have had your long wait so you can go now!'

Judy Monger, daughter of Ernie Mansbridge, joined Supermarine in 1951, but unbeknown to her at the time, she was to join her father's department:

The people in the office were dead worried about having the boss's daughter in the office, although I did not know that at the time. I started flight test analysis up at Chilbolton, analysing the traces and films that came out of flight tests. I progressed from there to looking after an aeroplane, and running its flight tests. There were five of us in the office and each would run an aircraft test. Aeroplanes on test all at the same time, but doing different tests, like performance tests, G-suit tests. You would have a schedule planned out and brief the pilot before the flight, then debrief the pilot afterwards.

After working on aircraft until 1959, Judy then transferred to join Vickers Hovercraft at Southampton. While still working on hovercraft she first transferred to the Isle of Wight before moving to Dover for a year. She remembers Les Colquhoun, who had previously been a well-known Supermarine test pilot: 'He was a wonderful epitome of a gentleman! He later moved to hovercraft and took over the hovercraft work in Southampton and then to Dover where he took over Hover Lloyd.'

Christopher Legg and his sister Margaret were educated at Clark's College, a private school in The Avenue, Southampton, and their father worked at Supermarine (Vickers) at Woolston. Margaret was not keen on training to be a teacher, which was the career choice her mother wanted her to make, so in 1946, at the age of 16, she joined Supermarine's technical office to undertake performance calculations. As an apprentice she was able to work around all the workshops, although this was not easy in one particular workshop:

> I was not welcomed in the sheet metal workshop, but the others were more obliging. At the time there was the Women's Engineering Society in London, but as I was so busy I was unable to attend all their meetings.

Margaret was released to attend Hartley College in Southampton to study full time before returning to Supermarine. She did work for some time at the Bristol Aeroplane Co. and undertook flight tests, but remembers that it was 'not good when you are airsick!' She remained with Supermarine until 1955, but then did train to become a teacher and taught in a grammar school, including running conferences to encourage women to take up engineering.

Her brother Christopher was at first keen to join the Royal Navy, and after leaving school he went to HMS *Collingwood* for the entrance examination and medicals. He passed everything except the eyesight test and he was very disappointed not to be able to join what he thought was his chosen career. He realised much later that not joining the Royal Navy was perhaps 'a blessing in disguise' because his father, knowing of his interest in aircraft, suggested he apply for an apprenticeship at Supermarine. He went for an interview, was successful, and joined the company on 5 January 1952 for his first day of a five-year apprenticeship as a jig- and tool-maker. At first he was working at the Itchen works in the Tooling Department where the foreman was his father!

Apprenticeship Training

As part of the apprenticeship training there was a period of approximately six months working in the shops, sometimes transferring to Eastleigh, South Marston or one or more of the other dispersed sites.

When David Noyce left Taunton's School in 1947, he heard there were some jobs going at Vickers-Armstrongs at Hursley Park, near his home at the top end of Hursley Road, Chandler's Ford. He was interviewed by the apprentice supervisor and taken on as an apprentice draughtsman, starting in September 1947:

At the time I didn't really know what a draughtsman did! However, as part of my apprenticeship I did the rounds, starting in the Experimental Hangar at Hursley Park where I spent six months before transferring to the flight shed at Eastleigh aerodrome where the final preparations of the aircraft were made. The actual old flight hangar is now part of Ford's factory and was cut off from Southampton Airport when the M27 was built through one end of the air-field. I was there for another six months, often undertaking menial tasks such as leaning over the tailplane while they revved the engines up, and getting smoke and flames from the exhausts flying back at you.

At the main factory, where the terminal buildings are today, they would complete the assembly of the aeroplane and install the engines before wheeling the aircraft across to the flight shed where they were prepared for flight.

David remembers seeing in the flight shed at Eastleigh aerodrome the new and refurbished Sea Otters, Spitfires and Seafires that were being prepared for flight-testing and final painting before being delivered to the RAF, Royal Navy and the Indian, Swedish and Pakistan air forces. After working at the Eastleigh flight hangar, he was transferred to the Shaw Works machine shop at Newbury where he spent six months learning to use lathes, capstans and grinding machines before going to the Itchen works for a further six months. He then transferred to the mould loft at Hursley Park. This department was managed by Jack Earl and Arthur Smith:

In some ways this department was a left-over from the flying boat days of Supermarine, as mould lofts were an integral part of boatbuilders' design tools. This department was responsible for the drawing of detail aluminium sheets which had been coated by carborundum dust. The aluminium sheets were prepared by placing small glass balls on the aluminium sheets, adding carborundum powder and water, then oscillating the table to roll the powder into the surface. Cellulose paint was used for 'ink' and dimensions were very precise. From these sheets prints could be made on to plywood and these were then used to produce manufacturing tools for production parts.

After this period, David moved to the drawing office to work on aircraft draw-ings on the queries section under Ron Vere. In September 1950, at the age of 21, he completed his training as a draughtsman and, as he had been deferred from National Service, left to undertake his two-year service in the RAF.

When David Effney first started work, his introduction to engineering was in the main hangar at the Itchen works. He was given a piece of ½in- (1.27cm) thick flame-cut plate and told to file the edges square:

Having completed this task I went into the detail shop, and at the time there was on old gentleman called Pop Crossland who was the detail shop foreman. I worked there for six months and then I moved to sub-assembly work. I found it very interesting work and I was able to do little jobs myself without much supervision. I joined Claude Harris who was a sheet metal worker really, but was working on sub-assembly. He was very knowledgeable, as well as Eddie Walsh and Jack Bessent. They were all very competent and Claude taught me a lot about sub-assembly and sheet metal work.

At the end of the year he won the prize for the best apprentice of the year in the Southampton area. The prize was a month at an outward bound mountain school, described by David as 'quite an interesting interlude'.

David Coombs had started as a Supermarine apprentice at Hursley Park in September 1949, working at first in the Experimental Hangar and then eventually in the drawing office. He found it to be a very pleasant place to work, and remembers that they were allowed to talk together and there was always something going on. At lunchtimes there were generally competitions at flying radio-controlled model aeroplanes, with some of the models flying over the village:

> I started in the Experimental Hangar just as they were finishing the Attacker aircraft. To a young chap the work was very interesting and initially the apprentice would be helping a fitter, and as it was an experimental hangar everything was done on a small scale, and one could go around working with the different trades, which from my point of view was very good.

From 1940, the drawing office team worked in Hursley House. The team got so large that in 1941 a purpose-built drawing office was built in the grounds, later known as X Block. *Solent Sky*

The drawing office was only one field away and I think there were a few hundred working in the drawing office in different sections. There was one building, for example, where there were about thirty people working on hydraulics. This was Bill Fear's department where they were designing undercarriages – it was that big.

There were different sections that you worked round. Initially the drawings that we started with were about A4 size. I went in there at the age of 19 after having two years in the Experimental Hangar training with all sorts of trades, gaining experience.

John Thomson's mother took him for an interview at Hursley Park where he was seen by the apprentice supervisor. The personnel manager arranged for them to be driven back home to Southampton in a company car, which, John says, 'impressed my mother!' He was successful, but as he was only 15½ years old he had to work as an office boy in the drawing office for six months. He remembers that the drawing office was huge with a large number of draughtsmen employed. At the start he was based in the queries section where mistakes on the master copies of the drawings were corrected by a small number of draughtsmen. His duties were running errands, taking messages and washing up cups. After a while, the section leader trusted him to correct some of the easier mistakes on the drawings. When things were quiet, John would go to the drawings library and book out interesting master drawings to study, showing, for example, the general arrangement of the Spitfire or even earlier aircraft.

In May 1949, John was transferred to the Itchen works at Woolston to start his apprenticeship in the detail shop of the training section, where he was shown how to make simple brackets by hand and taught how to use various tools. He was then placed with a skilled sheet metal worker to assist him making small access panels for Spitfires. From there he progressed to the Spitfire refurbishment section. At that time, Supermarine were buying back surplus Spitfires from the Air Ministry for £300 each, dismantling them and completely refurbishing them to sell to other countries, many of which appeared to want a squadron of Spitfires for their air forces:

I found myself at the age of 17, working on my own removing damaged ones as templates to make new ones, and reassembling them for riveting. I was working on real Spitfires. I thought I had died and gone to heaven!

Every now and then we put a Mark IX fuselage in the jig and our job was to take things off, but not all of the Mark IX fuselages had a rudder bar in them. The foremen told me to get my toolbox and get transport down to the Itchen works where at the back of the works was a yard which was full of

Mark IX fuselages. He gave me a shopping list of all the bits he was short of, and wanted me to dismantle and bring them back. That was another interesting interlude.

Two-Seat Trainers

Built by Supermarine in 1944, MT818 was based first with the controller of research and development at High Post and Farnborough, and then converted by Supermarine as a Type 502 two-seat Spitfire trainer in 1946 from a Mk VIII airframe. It was known as the Tr.8 N32 (G-AIDN) and was to be used for training purposes. Apart from its use as a demonstration model, it later went into private hands and was shipped to America, but then returned to the UK, was restored as MT818 and was flying again in 2011.

After the war, another attempt was made to convert old Mk IX airframes into Type 509 two-seat trainers with the second cockpit having a 'bubble canopy'. These were known as the Tr.9 two-seat trainers and there were twenty-one conversions of the aircraft, which were then sold to the Irish Air Corps, Royal Dutch Air Force, Indian Air Force and Royal Egyptian Air Force. John Thomson remembers working on these conversions at Eastleigh aerodrome, which involved removing fuselage skins and some of the structure to make way for a second cockpit.

David Effney was at first sent to the hangar at Eastleigh aerodrome to work on Wellington bombers before joining John on the two-seat trainer conversions:

We were re-engining the Wellington bombers and as the rudders weren't balanced we put horn balances on the rudders [two arms with connecting weights], and the bombers were converted into radio trainers.

At the time there were also some Seafires in the hangar. We also had some Spitfires that were being converted into two-seat trainers. We would strip the skin off the top of the fuselage and then fit in the second cockpit. I was working at that time with John Thomson who had started his apprenticeship at the same time as me. We were also given the job of sorting through a pile of parts and picking out those needed for the trainers and discarding the rest.

John also remembers working with David, and some interesting jobs came their way while in the Eastleigh main hangar working on the Spitfire trainer project. He recalls when the news came through that Supermarine we were going to build the first set of Vickers Viscount wings:

The Viscount was one of Vickers' success stories, a beautiful airliner, and turbo prop engines. We were going to be building the first set of wings. The toolmakers had come down from Weybridge, the jigs had been assembled already. All it meant then was the skilled men would fit the wing spars into the jigs, and all the ribs that made up the wings and I was drafted on to that with a skilled man. Every day was an adventure – I really loved it!

David Effney was also involved in the work on the prototype Viscount wings at Woolston where he worked with Claude Harris skinning the wings (putting the metal sheeting over them) and on some of the assembly work. He remembers the wings had de-icing systems: lots of little strips ½in (1.27cm) by ¼in (0.64cm) built around the leading edge, which let the air through. 'We had all these little bits to bend from full size mould loft plates, which was quite a job.'

Wheeling (English Wheel)

Wheeling is a highly skilled job whereby the metal skins of the Spitfire were stretched to create the shape required for the fuselage. Fred Veal, who did wheeling all of his working life and beyond, explains the skills involved:

> I worked in the wheeling squad, where you shape the skins of the aircraft. It's a skilled job, but you really can't be taught because the only way to learn is to take some metal, and go to a wheeling machine and practise the skill of stretching the metal. This obviously distorts the metal, and you have to learn how to control the distortion, until you get the shape that is required.
>
> Some people didn't want to take on wheeling because you could go in the morning and start working on a sheet of metal and it would be nowhere nearer to the shape of the job when you went home at night. That is what would put people off doing wheeling, but for me, I wanted to do it, and it served me very well.
>
> Supermarine had some hangars at Eastleigh airport and I was there wheeling, and that was where eventually Cliff Colmer started his apprenticeship and I had him working with me. That was where we first met and we have known each other right up to the present day.

Cliff Colmer was 16 when he started as an apprentice at Supermarine, working with Fred on wheeling. Their experience and skill of wheeling found both of them in later years working in the USA and helping with wheeling panels for aircraft that were being restored.

To John Thomson, wheeling was one of the most tiring jobs in sheet metal work and was not always the job that apprentices relished. He remembers his experiences when helping a sheet metal worker shaping the front panel underneath the Spitfire, and especially how 'shattered' he was when they had finished. This chin panel was about 6ft (1.82m) long, and the skill of the sheet metal worker was to form the panel to shape on the wheeling machine:

> You went to the stores and got a sheet of either 20 or 18 gauge aluminium and with somebody stood at the end of the sheet he would start wheeling the panel to shape. That meant going backwards and forwards on this wheeling machine which was two wheels, one was curved, one was flat, and gradually the panel took the shape of the underside of the Spitfire to be represented with what was called a wooden jig. This represented the underside which we were going to fit the panel to. Now even for a fit young apprentice of 16 or 17 it was quite an arduous task, but the skilled sheet metal worker had been doing it for years. You had to pay attention going backwards and forwards with him all the time, and if you started to day dream and lose attention you very quickly got shouted at to 'Wake Up!' It was a long tiring day.

Tony Kenyon also remembers working with a metal worker on the wheeling machine where he had to fair off the fuselage for the tailplane of the Attacker. It was a long day for him, having to walk backwards and forwards with the metal being shaped between the wheels. 'I thought that was the last job in the world I would want!'

When David Effney moved up to Hursley Park he worked in the mould loft where there were people such as Guy Gobel, who had experience of working on the mock-ups, with very good skills in projections and layouts on the floor and could work out any shape that was required. After a while, David began to do his own jobs but the mould loft manager had a strange system in which the drawing for the next job appeared on David's bench with his name written in the corner without there having been any previous discussion:

> We used to produce all the drawings to full size, absolutely to scale, to 10 thousandths of an inch on grained aluminium plate. Every frame and every structure was drawn on the grain plate, which could then be reproduced by inking it. Then they would run the plate through the roller and you would have a copy. Everything had to check to + or − 10 thousandths of an inch. It used to take weeks to complete these jobs.
>
> I remember I had one job that was a gun bay frame which took a long time to complete. I worked there for about a year, until I moved into the

drawing office, where at first you went to work in the 'query squad'. We used to go through all the questions raised by the workshops, check the drawings and sort out which one was right, correct them and reissue them.

I remember I had an uncle working in the project office. His name was Arthur Shirvall and he had been talking to my grandmother, who told him I had failed an exam. I was called to the project office where I got a good telling off by him for failing the exam!

Norman Crimble was at first assigned to a skilled fitter who he assisted in producing aircraft skin panels, which were curved panels made to fit wooden jigs. He also went to the machine shop where he was taught lathe work, and then later moved to the Itchen works to make drop tanks. At the age of 19, he was transferred to the mould loft where he drew full-scale lines under the supervision of Jack Earle, and from there went to the drawing office where he worked for Horace Noble on the fuel section. However, some of the jobs were quite unpleasant and on one occasion when undertaking pressure tests, one apprentice was required to climb into a leaking tank to look for bubbles in order to identify the leak. When the foreman looked around and there were no apprentices to be seen, he said, 'We've got twenty apprentices in this place and I can't find one to go in the tank and check for bubbles.' Word had got around that one of the apprentices would have to strip off and go into this tank, so they had all disappeared very quickly! However, David Coombs was not so lucky and finished up inside a fuel tank:

Joe Smith was the chief designer and we did not have any contact with him as such. I remember on one occasion because I was small I was required to climb and work inside a fuel tank. However, as Joe Smith was famous for swearing, I heard him outside while I was in the tank using some quite colourful language, possibly picked up from his time in the RNVR in the First World War.

David Faddy also remembers an incident when he heard his father using quite a colourful vocabulary, which came as quite a surprise to him. It was on a Sunday morning in 1949 when Alf Faddy received a telephone call asking him to go to Chilbolton aerodrome, and he invited David to accompany him. When they arrived they were met at the hangar door by test pilot Dave Morgan for whom Faddy had a great regard:

After a short conversation they went off to see the person in charge of the hangar, who my father subjected to a torrent of abuse, greatly to my astonishment! I knew the words, of course, but didn't think that my father ever used them. I don't remember the details but it appeared that the aircraft (I think it was the 510 prototype which much later evolved into the Swift) had not been as meticulously prepared as it should have been with the result that the pilot had had difficulty in returning safely.

Tracing Office

Norman Crimble met Ann Fear, daughter of Bill, when they travelled home on the bus together and became friendly, which eventually led to them getting married. Ann worked as a tracer from the early 1950s and explains the process:

> Copies were made of the pencil drawings from the drawing office by placing the tracing cloth, waxed linen which was a blue colour, over the drawings. It was quite transparent. Using mapping pens filled with black ink the line width was raised by adjusting a screw at the front of the pen. The ink pens were double nib so you had to manipulate the pen to make it a thicker or thinner line. The outlines were thicker and the inner lines were thin. We used to place the waxed linen over the top and trace through, like tracing paper, but with ink. It was quite a messy job and once the drawings were traced they were rolled up and sent to the print room and copies made for the various departments. If an alteration was made the draughtsman sent the drawing back with the tracing to be amended, with a note relating to the alteration made at the side of each drawing. So with tracing the pencil drawings endless copies could be made. In those days all the printing was done by hand, but in later years tracing cloth was replaced by a plastic film. Some people produced very neat work.

Having finished his apprenticeship at the age of 21, Norman had to do his National Service, after which he joined Vickers at Swindon for a while before leaving to work for a Bristol company which sent him to the Isle of Wight to work on hovercraft.

David Faddy remembers that after the war his father would take him to Hursley Park, often on Sunday, mainly to see what was going on in his office. It was one of two offices separated by a secretarial office in the middle. The other office was occupied by Eric Lovell-Cooper. David was able to see the prototypes of the Swift and other aircraft being developed at that time, and he later worked in the aerodynamics office at Hursley Park during his college holidays. The work was interesting but the calculations in those days were very primitive by today's standards. After qualifying, David went back into the RAE at Farnborough as a scientific officer.

David remembers his father telling him after the war that, at one point, he and others had to make rush visits to fighter stations to make it clear how Spitfires should be repaired:

It is well known that actually putting a stressed skin aircraft into production for the first time proved very difficult and caused delays. It is perhaps not so well known that hard-worked RAF engineers did not at first know how to maintain a stressed skin aeroplane in wartime, and Spitfires returning from dog-fights often had bullet holes in the wing or fuselage. Engineering officers, airframe fitters and airframe mechanics were familiar only with canvass-covered aircraft, and were repairing the aircraft by covering the holes with flattened biscuit tin lids, pop-riveted to the skin. They had to be persuaded that this practice undermined the structural integrity of the aircraft and institute a safe repair scheme.

Christopher Legg spent some time working at South Marston and six months in the drawing office at the Itchen works. He remembers Len Gooch, who was a very austere gentleman but a very efficient manager at the Itchen factory. It was well known that whenever he went through the shop floor, the word would go round, 'Look out, Gooch is about!'

Working in Hursley Park's Experimental Hangar

John Thomson remembers working on the Type 525 in the Experimental Hangar at Hursley Park. He considered himself fortunate to be working there because the staff were highly skilled craftsmen, the best of Supermarine.

Apprentices would often be sent on errands to the stores to get parts and sign them out. John recalls that he was working on the rear end of the Type 525 with two fitters just where the fuselage turned into the fin area. When a fuselage is built there are a number of frames at specific points all the way through the fuselage joined together with longerons, which are long pieces of sheet metal bolted to the frames to hold them together, as strength is extremely important. The bottom longerons on the Type 525 were machined aluminium lengths and they had to be accurately fitted and bolted:

Bruce, one of the fitters, looked at the drawings and asked me to go to the stores and requisition the port and starboard longerons to go at the top of the

Originally the experimental team worked in the Stable Block at Hursley, but with the urgent need for a larger area the Experimental Hangar was built to the south of Hursley House. *Solent Sky*

fuselage to join about six frames together. In Supermarine there was no left or right, it was all nautical terms – fore and aft, port and starboard.

After collecting the longerons John took them up to the planked staging where he was working and laid them out to inspect them before they were fitted in the frames. While looking at the port longerons he noticed an 18in (45.72cm) hairline crack where they formed to a right angle. This surprised him, as the longeron had already been checked because it had an inspector's stamp and number on it:

> I called Bruce's attention to it and he couldn't understand how it got through inspection and went off and got the chargehand. He had a look at it – 'Good grief' – and went and got the foreman who asked, 'Who found this?' Bruce answered, 'The nipper did.' The foreman said, 'Well done!' and that was it. I suddenly had lots of 'Brownie points'. I was Hawkeye!

The longeron was sent back to Eastleigh and scrapped. John wondered if his sharp eye helped in the next part of his training, because a few months later he was called into the foreman's office and offered a transfer to the Planning Department. He thought that was 'fantastic', and finished his apprenticeship in that department.

After completing his apprenticeship, John Thomson did his two years' National Service from 1954 to 1956 in the RAF, and then returned to

Supermarine and worked there for a few more years. It was at this time that Hursley Park was being taken over by IBM and Supermarine staff were being transferred to South Marston and other sites. However, John was shocked when, as a single man, he lost his job in the first batch of redundancies, because he thought he had a job for life at Supermarine. He was able to get an interview with Len Gooch, the production manager, who told him that the aircraft industry had become so big following the war that it needed reducing and advised him to get out and take his skills into general engineering. This was excellent advice because John did not realise just how highly the Supermarine engineers were regarded, and it was not difficult to find another job.

Working Alongside Joe Smith

When David Noyce returned to Supermarine from his National Service he was able to join the fuselage section under Pelham Slade. This was one of the largest sections in the drawing office and had about twenty-five draughtsmen working there. At the time, they were designing the Scimitar but had problems with weight. Joe Smith was determined to reduce the weight, and David was to have the experience of working alongside him for a few days. He was given the task of mustering a whole lot of machine fittings and forgings for Smith to have a look at as a way of achieving the necessary weight reduction:

> It took me about two weeks and all the production parts were assembled in boxes and Joe Smith, Eric Cooper and Pelham Slade were all gathered around my desk. I was passing these fittings one at a time to Joe, and with a marker he drew holes on each one. Joe would say, 'Right, next one' and sat at my desk day after day for at least three days marking all the fittings so that the metal could be cut out to reduce the weight of the Scimitar. I was transferring from one box to Joe and then putting the marked part into another box. My job was then to get each drawing of the part and make the changes and that then went out to be remade for production.

Joe Smith and His Team

David Noyce recalls when he was working in the Experimental Hangar and they were building the Supermarine Type 545, which was designed for supersonic flight:

They were having all sorts of problems, and I can vividly recall Joe Smith coming down with a number of others from the design team. Alf Faddy was the project manager of the Supermarine 545 and Joe was walking around the aircraft with chalk. He drew a chalk outline round the air intake and said, 'There you are Faddy, make your bloody figures fit that!'

There were three mock-ups in the Experimental Hangar in the latter years. The mock-up was a full-size aircraft and everything was wood and covered in plywood. When the Air Ministry visited the hangar, the wooden mock-ups were even painted to look like a real aircraft. The coppersmiths would use the mock-up to run a pipe to a fuel tank or hydraulics and would then bend the pipework to fit the mock-up. They would then give it to the carpenters who would make a jig that the pipe would fit in. The jig would then be sent to the Eastleigh workshop where the pipes would be bent in the jig, and then fitted in the aircraft during assembly.

There was also a Supermarine Seagull, one of the amphibians in the Experimental Hangar. Although that one did fly, it was about that time that the helicopters were beginning to challenge the work of the amphibians.

David thought very highly of Smith and his team, and of the developmental work that was achieved by them:

> Joe Smith struck me as being a gentleman, but also one of the boys in his attitude. Joe wasn't the sort of man that everybody knew; he just got on with it. Whenever you talk about the Spitfire it is always R.J. Mitchell that is mentioned, but all the development of the Spitfire was done by Joe.
>
> There was always Alan Clifton, Ernie Mansbridge, Arthur Black, Arthur Shirvall and Harry Griffiths who worked for Arthur Black. He was a really brainy guy. They were a group that worked closely with Joe Smith on design matters.

Supermarine's South Marston Factory

It was following a conversation between Garth Pearce's father and Stuart Lefever (known as 'Lefty') who was the northern area production manager for Vickers-Supermarine that Garth was invited to South Marston for an interview. When he arrived at the factory he was impressed by the sight of so many Swift fuselages lined up for assembly.

Garth started at Vickers-Supermarine on 27 September 1954, on a wage of £2 5s per week, but was shocked to find out that mathematics and physics beyond

'O' level GCE was necessary to progress, and further study would be necessary to reach the levels required. Training followed the pattern of detail fitting, hood assembly, press shop, process, template making, planning liaison, machine shop, final hydraulic installations, wind tunnel, and full-scale layout (mould loft).

Not long after he had started in 23 Shop (fitting shop) it was announced that the Swift F Mk 4 work was being dropped, but the Swift FR Mk 5 would continue but with less production. By then the Type 525 prototype of the Scimitar was flying and orders had been placed for the Type 544 Scimitar. Garth recalls:

> When the first Scimitar fuselage arrived it appeared huge compared with the Swift fuselages. This aircraft employed many unique design features to reduce weight and to minimize landing speeds for aircraft carrier operations, such items as forged fuselage frames and blown flaps being introduced.

Garth worked on the first production Scimitar XD212 hydraulics system, assisting in the installation of the high-pressure hydraulic lines in the aft end of the fuselage, while other teams installed systems in the wings and centre fuselage:

> The hydraulic lines operated the tailplane, rudder, snubber, A frame hook, A frame doors (not fitted) and dive brakes. Our hydraulics ran through the Radio Bay at the tail of the fuselage, and accessed through two tiny doors on the underside of the fuselage.

This was a very cramped area to work in and Garth remembers spending one Bank Holiday doubled up in the tiny space for up to eight hours. He describes how the hydraulic pipes were prepared to a 'master sample' made up by the coppersmiths and then handed to the carpenters who then made the jig.

Owing to the decline in the aircraft industry, Supermarine began to close the dispersal factories at Trowbridge, Eastleigh and Shaw near Newbury, as well as the design and experimental facilities at Hursley Park and Chilbolton. South Marston then became the centre for apprenticeship training, with apprentices from the Hursley Park design office and some apprentices from Follands, which was also lacking in orders, moving there.

Later, while working in the wind tunnel, Garth spent some time working on 'secret' military aircraft, later finding out that this was Supermarine's version of what was to become the TSR2. After having worked in the Hydrodynamics (Hovercraft) section until 1966, Garth decided that with an impending relocation to Southampton it was time to move on. He left to work for Lockheed on the C-5A Galaxy.

Jeffrey Quill in the cockpit with Gordon Monger before flying Spitfire AB910 to the RAF Historic Flight at Coltishall in 1965. *Gordon Monger*

Spitfire AB910 arrives at the RAF Historic Flight at RAF Coltishall. It is now with the Battle of Britain Memorial Flight and is based at RAF Coningsby. *Gordon Monger*

AB910 was presented to Air Marshal Sir Douglas Morris, AOC Fighter Command. Others present at the ceremony are, from left to right: Dave Morgan, Ernie Mansbridge, Les Colquhoun, Sam Hughes, Jack Rasmussen, Les Ashby, Air Commodore Al Deere, Jeffrey Quill. *Gordon Monger*

Spitfire Mk VB AB910

Garth had completed his five-year apprenticeship back in 1959, but he remembers the week preceding Battle of Britain Day when he and the other apprentices sneaked outside to watch a 'dogfight' between Jeffrey Quill flying Spitfire AB910 and Bill Bedford flying a Hawker Hurricane. 'This was the first time any of us young people could see what marvellous manoeuvrability and speed these piston engines had.'

During the war AB910 had an interesting career, flying 143 operational missions between August 1941 and July 1944. On one mission it joined 133 (Eagle) Squadron at Biggin Hill in 1942 and was involved in air-combat support on the Dieppe raid. However, on 14 February 1945, the aircraft became famous for having taken off from Hibaldstow airfield with LACW Margaret Horton, a WAAF ground-crew fitter, on its tail. Fortunately, after one circuit the pilot, Flt Lt Neil Cox DFC, realised there was a problem and landed the aircraft and his 'passenger' safely back on the airfield.

After the war the aircraft took part in air racing until it was purchased by Vickers-Armstrongs and refurbished in 1953. Quill then flew AB910 regularly in air displays until the decision was made by the British Aircraft Corporation in 1965 to present the Spitfire to the RAF Historic Flight at Coltishall as a Battle of Britain gesture. Quill's penultimate flight in a Spitfire was in September 1965, when he took off from Wisley in AB910 to fly to RAF Coltishall, accompanied by a Hawker Hunter, to hand the aircraft over to the RAF Historic Flight. On arrival, both aircraft gave an impressive flying display. His final flight in AB910 was on 16 June 1966 (thirty years after his first flight in the prototype) for the purposes of a documentary film made by a French television company.

22

GOODBYE HURSLEY PARK

Not a Popular Move!

The move from Hursley Park to South Marston was not popular with many of the staff, who considered it a journey too far, as Murry White recalls:

> Stan Woodley who was running the company along with the board of directors decided to move the company to South Marston; a former shadow factory near Swindon, and take on commercial work like office furniture, television back projection and accelerated freeze dried food equipment.
>
> Joe was very ill at this time and the writing was on the wall and we were all going to be taken to South Marston, and that was the last thing I wanted to do was to work under Stan Woodley, although he was always very good to me.

At that time, Murry was interested in working overseas in the aviation industry and by chance he had a telephone call from Lt-Cdr Norman Wadsworth, who he knew quite well, inviting him to lunch. Wadsworth explained that he had had a call from Alan Greenwood asking him to go to Canada to set up an office for him there. He asked Murry what he thought and how he should handle it. Murry told him that he knew Greenwood very well but advised that the first thing to do was ask for double the salary they were offering and to make sure that he got a good contract covering all the things that he wanted, especially in terms of his wife and family:

> I was furious about this and at the time was sharing an office with Jeffrey Quill and told him about the drawing people from the services, and how I would like a job like that, especially overseas. Jeffrey said, 'Oh, would you? Well, we will have to see what we can do.'

The opportunity to work overseas came about a year or so later when Greenwood invited Murry, accompanied by Jeffrey Quill, to a meeting at the RAC Country Club. It was suggested at the meeting that because Wadsworth was being inundated with work, he thought that Murry could be sent out to be his assistant:

> I told him I would be happy to do it, but took my own advice to Norman Wadsworth and told him what I wanted in the way of contract and things. I went back and discussed it with my wife who was overjoyed about it. I was told it was to be in Montreal, but Alan Greenwood telephoned me a few days later to apologise and tell me that the job would be based in Winnipeg, which was another 2,000 miles inland. Little did I know what Winnipeg was like in the winter! He asked who would tell Joe Smith, and I said that I was the only one who could do that, to which Alan Greenwood replied, 'I'd hoped you would say that.'
>
> I telephoned Winny, Joe's wife, and although I knew them well I still called Joe 'Sir', and by this time he called me Murry. When I went to his home he was in his dressing gown, but his wife said that he was very ill and got tired very quickly and asked me not to take long. I told him I had been offered a job in Canada and he looked at me and said, 'Is that what you want to do?' I told him I didn't want to go to South Marston and that I would love to travel, and would love to go to Canada. Joe said, 'Well, you go with my blessing.' That was the last time I saw poor old Joe. He died about six months later.
>
> I later took a course on the Viscount aircraft because one of the things I said was that I would not go out to Canada unless I really understood the aircraft in complete detail. Alan Greenwood said that they could fix that up for me.

Stan Woodley's Letter to Design Staff

The year 1956 was one in which significant changes were to take place for the Supermarine Design Department. Joe Smith was totally against the department being moved to South Marston, and resisted any attempt to do so, but he was ill and passed away on 20 February 1956. It was just one month later, on 22 March, that the Design Department received a letter from Stan Woodley informing them of the decision to relocate the department from Hursley Park to South Marston:

> In view of the impending termination of the lease at Hursley Park consideration has been given by the management to the future location of the

Supermarine design organisation, and the decision has been taken to transfer existing department to South Marston over the next two years.

As a matter of policy Mr G.R. Edwards, the firm's managing director, has decided that Weybridge and Supermarine divisions will retain their separate identities. In implementing this policy it is considered essential that the Supermarine works should now function in the main design, development and manufacturing, which will be South Marston. Steps are, therefore, being taken to set up a design unit there, and when this is complete it is anticipated that the establishment will constitute one of the most modern and well-equipped units for integrated aircraft design and manufacture in the country with full provision for continued expansion.

In making this decision it was fully appreciated that transferring involved dislocation of domestic arrangements of the individual, and every effort will be made to minimise this in arranging details.

The letter informed staff that there would be an enquiry office set up in Hursley House which would open daily from 10 a.m. for staff to discuss their personal concerns about transferring to South Marston, but that appointments should be made beforehand. It concluded:

> You will shortly receive a questionnaire relating to requirements for housing, education, etc., and arrangements about facilities in these matters will be announced.
>
> S.P. Woodley, Superintendent

Life After Supermarine

Barrie Bryant in his paper 'How Super – Supermarine Reflections' of October 1998 concludes with his thoughts on the demise of the design team from 1958:

> I believe that the nation lost an irreplaceable capability when the team scattered in 1958. For that wanton event those who drafted the Sandys White Paper of 1957 bear much of the burden, but not all. The firm's own culture altered insidiously throughout its two final decades, responding as then deemed best to the nation's evolving interests. We ought not however to forget the numerous people whose skills were founded or extended while working at Supermarine but who left for other employers, sometimes in other countries. Having trained some who departed, I deplored the 'brain drain' of the post-war decade but I was later pleased to learn something of ex-Supermariners' contributions elsewhere, notably in North America and Australasia.

Harry Griffiths in his book *Testing Times: Memoirs of a Spitfire Boffin* concludes, 'What I do regret is the fact that the Supermarine team is no more. There is no doubt it was the finest collection of aircraft designers, technicians and builders of its day.'

In 1958, there were some long-service staff members who were nearing retirement and had no wish to live near Swindon. Vickers showed some consideration to these staff by setting up a small Itchen office where they could work until their retirement. Among them were Reginald Caunter, Eric Lovell-Cooper, Miss Leach, Arthur Shirvall and George Kettlewell.

With the imminent transfer of Supermarine staff to South Marston, Jeffrey Quill transferred to Vickers at Weybridge in 1957, as head of the military aircraft office of Vickers-Armstrongs. Following the formation of the British Aircraft Corporation he was deeply involved in the development of the TSR2 supersonic bomber until the project was cancelled in 1965 by the Labour Government. The following year, Quill was appointed sales director of the Anglo-French company developing the Jaguar supersonic fighter; later he became marketing director of Panavia, the Anglo-German-Italian consortium engaged in developing the Tornado swing-wing fighter. After retiring in 1978, he was elected Fellow of the Royal Aeronautical Society in 1980, and also served as president of the Spitfire Society. He died, aged 83, at his home on the Isle of Man on 20 February 1996.

The VA-2 was one of three hovercraft versions designed and built as part of the Vickers Hovercraft venture. *David Coombs*

Vickers Hovercraft

By 1958, Sir Christopher Cockerell, inventor of the hovercraft, had managed to convince the National Research Development Corporation to issue a contract to Saunders-Roe, the flying boat firm at Cowes on the Isle of Wight, to build the SR.N1 (Saunders-Roe Nautical 1). The first prototype SR.N1 was completed in May 1959, and on 25 July it crossed the English Channel from Calais to Dover on the 50th anniversary of the first aeroplane crossing of the Channel. French aviator Louis Blériot had set off at dawn on 25 July 1909 to pilot his Blériot XI from Sangatte to Dover.

In 1960, Vickers-Supermarine started to develop hovercraft, initially at South Marston, before the whole team working on the hovercraft was moved to Woolston, on the bank of the River Itchen. David Coombs worked on the Vickers hovercraft at the Itchen works, and describes the speed the hovercraft was achieving at the time:

> I worked for a short time for Supermarine when they moved to South Marston before I got sidetracked on to working on Vickers Hovercraft in the early 1960s at the Vickers Itchen works, just above where the old floating bridge was. We did trials on Southampton Water and by 1961 we were then doing 60mph [96.56km/h] down Southampton Water. I worked on the VA-2 right through to the finish.

The Vickers Hovercraft designs started with the VA-1 (Vickers-Armstrongs 1) which was a full-sized wooden prototype. This was followed by a five-seat light alloy craft, VA-2, that could be transported in an Argosy aircraft for demonstration around the world. These hovercrafts were trialled over ice in Sweden on the sea crossing between Malmö and Copenhagen, and also in Africa. The VA-3 was developed as a passenger ferry, crossing from Rhyl in North Wales to Wallasey on Merseyside. Later, in 1966, Vickers Hovercraft amalgamated with Saunders-Roe on the Isle of Wight to form the British Hovercraft Corporation.

Hovercraft services are run around the world in various roles. The hovercraft has special attributes, being able to cross mud banks, shallow water, snow and ice, where conventional shipping cannot go, and also has the ability to transfer from water to land at full speed. Today, regular hovercraft services ply between Southsea and Ryde, and the sound of hovercraft propellers in the Solent is reminiscent of the sound of the Spitfire in earlier years.

The Attraction of North America

For many Supermarine ex-apprentices the training they received and the quality of their experiences while working with the company were a passport to success, often leading to offers of work with aviation companies around the world. This was true of Leo Schefer, who spent his early teenage years in Melbourne, Australia, where his family were on a government posting from 1950. Having been brought up with rationing in post-war Britain, he comments: 'I was a well-disciplined little Brit, but the Australians taught me not to stand in line, and I've been grateful to them ever since.' Leo returned to England in 1953, a completely different person. In 1957, Leo learned to fly a glider in the RAF Cadet Force at school and had gained his 'A' levels. He wanted to join the RAF as a pilot, but his eyesight let him down:

> I considered immigrating to Australia, but their aircraft industry was rather modest, so I looked for an apprenticeship in the UK. I had been enthralled by the stories surrounding the Schneider Trophy and the Spitfire, so Supermarine was my first choice. I was accepted at South Marston and began my 5-year training in September 1957.

With the conversion of the South Marston works by Vickers to a food processing division, the apprentices were given the option to join that division or move to Vickers-Armstrongs (Aircraft) Limited at Weybridge. Most, if not all, went to Weybridge:

> By 1961, it had become apparent to the Weybridge apprentice school that I was unlikely to be an engineering success, and I was removed from the design office in the interest of public safety. The apprentice school transferred me to the sales publicity office, where I proved more useful. Shortly after my apprenticeship ended, I was moved to be in the Sales Publicity Office at the Hurn factory where the BAC 1-11 was moving towards first flight. The BAC 1-11 gained orders from Braniff, Mohawk, Aloha and American Airlines in the United States. Vickers-Armstrongs (Aircraft) had by now merged with English Electric and Hunting Percival and Bristols to form British Aircraft Corporation. BAC's subsidiary in the United States was Vickers-Armstrongs (Aircraft) USA Inc. based in Arlington, Virginia.

This was the beginning of the 'brain drain' as Fleet Street called it, in which the US and Canadian aerospace industries recruited talent from the British industry. However, Leo was fortunate to have links with the US subsidiary and when the American executive responsible for press relations and customer promotional support was taken ill, he was given the opportunity in August 1964 to replace him for four months. After returning to the UK in December 1964, Leo was invited to return permanently to the US subsidiary in March 1965 as the American executive had to retire due to ill health:

Murry White was the President of the US subsidiary and I was most fortunate to work under him until he retired in about 1982. Murry didn't really understand my job, but he trusted me, left me to it, and provided support as needed. No one could have had a better situation. In fact, I have good memories of the tolerance and understanding shown to me at Supermarine and Weybridge by the apprentice school managers, by the chargehands and managers I was assigned to. At Weybridge and Hurn following my apprenticeship, I again found myself working for real professionals who looked for results, put the project first, and looked after their team. By then I was two years out of my apprenticeship, and was, I believe, the only member of the 1957 intake who had not emigrated to the aerospace industry in the United States or Canada.

The American subsidiary had now become BAC (USA) Inc., and I remained with it in its successive guises until July 31, 1988, when I resigned to take up my current employment as President of the Washington Airports Task Force.

From 1965, Leo worked with their US customers, helping them introduce the BAC 1-11, and was also involved with Concorde. As part of the BAC team, he handled public relations and press relations for the aircraft in the USA, including the successful fight to gain it landing rights. In the late 1960s, the USA wanted to involve Europe in the Space Transportation System, which besides the shuttle would involve a space lab – now evolved into the International Space Station:

BAC teamed with Rockwell contributed technically and designed 15 per cent of Rockwell's winning bid. Unfortunately, the British Government wasn't willing to fund 15 per cent of the space shuttle, so we lost out. But for five years or so, I had an interesting part-time involvement as the link between the company's space division in the UK, the BAC team at Rockwell in Downey, California, and the U.S. Government.

With the merger of BAC and Hawker Siddeley into British Aerospace, our product interests in the United States expanded to include the HS-125 business jet, the Harrier, the Hawk – known as the T-45 in U.S. Navy service – the

BAe-146, the Jetstream, and for a while the Avro-748. British Aerospace USA Inc. was totally responsible for marketing the HS-125 and the Jetstream 31, and we soon had those aircraft as the sales leaders in their class. We ended up selling 70 per cent of British Aerospace's civil aircraft output. Unfortunately, we didn't have the same autonomy to sell the 146 or the Avro-748, which weren't as successful. We did put the three regional aircraft together as a family of aircraft with common engineering integrity and support; this probably helped their sales.

At the Washington Airports Task Force, Leo found himself advising American officials on international aviation policy, and local officials on noise and land use policies around airports, among many other issues:

All my BAe experience proved invaluable, and 20 years later, I'm still using many of those Vickers/BAC/BAe lessons.

At the Task Force, I increasingly found myself representing US interests on occasions, leading a US consortium to work with the Canadians for a new air service agreement between the two countries. Ironically, the Canadian team was led by a US citizen – a juxtaposition which created great amusement to the two teams: the Americans being led by a Brit, and the Canadian cities by a Yankee, who incidentally had been a senior executive with Capital Airlines when they introduced the Vickers Viscount.

My wife and I became American citizens like our three children in 1995, and found ourselves being sworn under the nose of the first Boeing 777 to enter commercial service during the inaugural ceremonies for the flight to London from Washington Dulles.

My current job has continued to give me huge satisfaction, as it involved aviation's role in modern society. At this Task Force, our goal is to ensure that people and goods can be shipped from any part of our region to any part of the world within 24 hours. That involves the multi-modal aspects of aviation. Good air service, for example, doesn't do the region much good if you cannot easily get to the airport, so we find ourselves heavily involved in surface connections to the airports, as well as in the creation of new air services, effective air traffic control, and user-friendly facilities at the airport.

Restoring Warbirds in the USA

Cliff Colmer was very pleased that he had the opportunity to learn the skills of wheeling from working with Fred Veal during his apprenticeship at

The 'Three Wheelers'; from left to right: Cliff Colmer, Bob Cunningham, Fred Veal. *Cliff Colmer*

Bob Cunningham wheeling and shaping a fuselage part for an aircraft. *Richard de Jong*

Supermarine, and elsewhere with him over the years. After completing his apprenticeship in 1950, Cliff did his National Service in the RAF, in the workshops. He then joined Moorgreen Metal Industries where Fred Veal was a foreman, and so they met up again. Together with Bob Cunningham, another skilled sheet metal worker, Cliff was offered employment with Northrop in California, working on the F-18 fighter. Although Bob decided not to go, Cliff and his wife Pam spent three interesting years in California while he worked for Northrop. When he returned to England, he joined Fred and Bob to work at C.F. Taylor's in Christchurch. The firm is known today as Beagle Aircraft.

After retirement, Bob started his business, Cunningham Aero, making parts for Spitfires, and has become well known worldwide for the supply of aircraft parts. While doing a job for Ray Middleton of QG Aviation in Colorado, who was restoring a Hurricane, he found that Ray had nobody to do the wheeling so introduced Cliff to him. For the last decade, Cliff has regularly travelled to Colorado to work on the restoration of the Hurricane and other aircraft. He also became involved in some work being done for Eddie Kurdziel in the workshop, and Cliff and his wife would go out and attach the restoration work to a holiday which sometimes was as long as seven weeks!

Eddie Kurdziel

Capt. Eddie Kurdziel had learned to fly while attending undergraduate and graduate school in engineering. He became a US Navy pilot flying A-4s, F-8s, A-7s and the Lockheed S-3. On leaving the US Navy he was hired by Northwest Airlines and moved first to Minnesota and later to San Diego. He became interested in aircraft restoration and shipped a partly restored Fairey Firefly from Australia to the USA. Eddie asked Ray Middleton of QG Aviation if he was interested in taking on the restoration of the aircraft, and so the project began. Eddie talks about when he first met Cliff and Pam Colmer:

> I first met Cliff and his wife Pam Colmer through Ray Middleton, my chief engineer at QG Aviation of America in Fort Collins, Colorado. Ray is the owner of the business that was tasked with the restoration of Firefly WB518. There had been a lot of wear and tear on the airframe accumulated during its time in service with the Royal Australian Navy, along with the many moves, and of course its tenure as a 'birdhouse' in Griffith NSW.
>
> Cliff was contracted to help with the sheet metal repairs. A dapper Englishman, Cliff first appeared to me in an apron that looked like he was a chef of sorts. He worked tirelessly to reproduce or repair many of the dam-

Capt. Eddie Kurdziel and his restored Firefly. *Eddie Kurdziel*

aged parts. His other half, Pam, who is really the unsung hero in all of this, catered to Cliff's whims and kept him supplied with sandwiches, tea and cakes in the pursuit of his profession.

Cliff Colmer is certainly an anachronism when it comes to the current process of aircraft construction. Educated through an apprentice program at Supermarine in the United Kingdom before the advent of computers and CAD machines, he comes from another world of slide rules and rooms of design engineers. The skill set that he possesses is no longer taught and barely even exists in our current aircraft and automotive industries. With the aid of two metal wheels and his innate skills he can quickly make objects of fine art that would take weeks to program and produce via our current computers and CAD machines. These things of beauty are all one of a kinds tailored to their particular application. In this case the repairs were made to metal cowls, drop tanks and propeller spinners. New wing fairings (complex curves) were all produced by Cliff with a keen eye, his hands, and the English wheel. He can quickly ascertain size and shape and make it all happen to a raw piece of sheet aluminum. I suppose to a casual observer it's a bit like a 'dog watching television', we're not sure of what we're seeing ... all magic. I used to watch him carefully eye a damaged fairing, take a piece of aluminum to the wheels, roll it between them, return to the aircraft and eye it again before repeating the process. The results are extraordinary. A flying kinetic sculpture as it were.

Cliff Colmer is on the far left discussing the Seafire restoration work he is undertaking in Minneapolis, USA. *Cliff Colmer*

Cliff Colmer and Fred Veal using the English wheel to shape a long panel for an F-82 Twin Mustang in Minneapolis. *Cliff Colmer*

I may be a bit prejudiced but others have shared my same views and enthusiasm for this objet d'art. The Firefly has garnered the following awards: Grand Champion at Oshkosh, the Smithsonian/Rolls-Royce Aviation Heritage Trophy that resides at the Udvar-Hazy Center in Washington DC, and the People's Choice Award at the Reno Air Races. Not too bad considering Cliff learned these skills so many years ago. The fact they are still so relevant today, albeit on an aircraft from those same times, is pretty amazing when you really think about it.

One of the other projects Cliff did for Ray was the restoration of a Supermarine Seafire in Minneapolis. He would fly to Minneapolis to work on the Seafire, and then fly down to Colorado to work on the other jobs. On one occasion, Cliff was in the USA for two weeks to work on the Seafire:

> We would hire a camper and go sight-seeing, looking at the Presidents' heads at Rushmore. Fred Veal came along with us, but in the three days before we picked up the camper a guy from Cargill asked me to work on a panel. It was too long a panel for one person to do and Fred came and we did the job together.

Cliff still visits Fort Collins to work on Bill Greenwood's Spitfire N308WK. His most recent visit was in October 2012. The Spitfire was damaged when it ran into the rear of a recently restored Hawker Hurricane while taxiing during the Galveston Spirit of Flight Air Show on 26 April 2008. There were no injuries.

This Spitfire was built at Castle Bromwich in 1944 as a single-seat fighter, and stored until 1950, when it was converted at Eastleigh to a Tr.9 trainer before being sold to the Irish Air Corps as IAC163. In 1968 the aircraft was sold and took part in the filming of *Battle of Britain*, before being owned by a Canadian businessman. Bill Greenwood acquired it in 1983, using QG Aviation to regularly maintain and service it at Fort Collins.

Cliff had originally been asked by Ray Middleton to work on the Hurricane involved in the above accident. Both Cliff and his wife Pam remember seeing the damaged Hurricane after the accident, but it is currently being stored in the hangar until a decision is made on repairs. During his recent visit, Cliff also worked on Capt Eddie's Firefly which had a damaged undercarriage.

Good Fortune to be Living in Southampton

For young lads living in Southampton in the early twentieth century there was the choice of a career at sea working on the ocean liners, working in the docks or working in the expanding aviation world. Charles Labette comments:

Living in Southampton was one of the keys to our good fortune in our professional lives. The whole basis of our training was obtained from Supermarine and its excellent design team and staff. Nobody can have had better. It stood us in good stead for our executive roles in the aviation world in the following years.

Supermarine to me was something personal and very important in my life's scheme of things. I did not see it as something to be compared with any other achievements elsewhere. It stood out with absolute clarity for the British nation to see and a very big plus for the Woolston chaps and Southamptonians.

Charles left Supermarine at the end of 1946 to join Aer Lingus as their chief project engineer. In August 1949, he joined the National Airways Corporation in Wellington, New Zealand, as chief engineer until his retirement in November 1977 at the age of 65.

Ted Faggetter left for Melbourne, Australia, in 1938 to be project engineer for the Commonwealth Aircraft Corporation, designing aircraft for the RAAF. In 1948, he was invited by the general manager of the Dunlop Rubber Co. in Australia to set up the Australian Dunlop Aviation industry, manufacturing aircraft for the RAAF. After a very successful aviation career, Ted retired in 1971.

Jack Rasmussen MBE transferred to the British Aircraft Division when Supermarine moved to South Marston in 1956. He worked in the Caribbean islands, based in Trinidad, before returning to the Sales Department at Weybridge on the Viscount.

In 1956, Murry White was based with Trans-Canada Air Lines in Winnipeg as Viscount technical representative for Vickers-Armstrongs, and then in 1958 took up a similar position in Denver, Colorado, with Continental Airlines. From 1959, he transferred to Washington DC as CEO and director of the US subsidiary company of Vickers-Armstrongs, later renamed British Aircraft Corporation and finally to become British Aerospace. Murry White CBE retired on 31 December 1980, but remained a director of BAe Inc. until 1982, and still lives in the USA.

Leo Schefer joined Murry at BAC (USA) Inc. and in 1988 took up his present position as president of the Washington Airports Task Force.

Christopher Legg found that his apprenticeship with Supermarine and National Service in the RAF were an excellent start to his future career in engineering, and in 1969 he joined the Melroe Manufacturing Co. in North Dakota. Now retired, he still lives in the USA.

23

MEMORIES OF JOE SMITH

B arbara Harries remembers her 21st birthday celebrations, when her father was very ill and in bed:

My father was a wonderful father and I had a very happy childhood because of him. I wanted to be with daddy, all little girls want to be with daddy. I admire what he achieved, what with the Spitfire and the aircraft afterwards. My father died of cancer, and was very ill [during the time leading to his death]. I remember when it was my 21st birthday party in September I was having a cocktail party. Supermarine works had made my cake and dad was up in bed. By the end of the evening half the party was up in dad's bedroom. It was lucky the doctor was a family friend because the next morning when mum took him up to see dad, he was horrified because there was a row of glasses on the window sill!

My mother wanted him to retire because of the strain of the war years and also he didn't look well in the early 1950s. My father planned to take early retirement when he was 58, but sadly he passed away. It was all the end of an era and I have never seen so many people at a funeral, and it was all recorded down to South Marston and people were lining the streets in Hursley.

My father more or less worked himself to death as he was travelling up and down to London and other places on the train in wartime, and after taking over from R.J. Mitchell he had to fight to get the Spitfire into production. It was a battle to get everything out on time.

The British Gold Medal for Aeronautics

Joe Smith died at Chandler's Ford on 20 February 1956 and was posthumously awarded the British Gold Medal for Aeronautics. The award was received by his son David as part of the 44th Wilbur Wright Memorial Lecture and Presentation of Awards by the Royal Aeronautical Society in 1956.

The British Gold Medal for Aeronautics was awarded for outstanding practical achievement leading to advancement in Aeronautics. The British Gold and Silver Awards were founded by the Society in 1933 following a request from Lord Amulree, Secretary of State for Air, that some award be given for outstanding feats in aviation.

The gold medal commemorates Sir George Cayley and his first model aeroplane of 1804. The first award was presented to Capt. Geoffrey de Havilland in 1934, and other recipients included E.W. Hives in 1948 and G.R. Edwards in 1952, both of whom Smith had known and worked closely with.

Joe Smith's Character

Smith had been responsible for the development of so many marks and variants of the Spitfire, including the naval version of the Seafire, the Spiteful and the Seafang, and of jet aircraft culminating in the Scimitar. He was a very loyal man, especially to his mentor R.J. Mitchell, and to all his team, yet always shied away from personal publicity. Basically, he was a shy man who had come into aviation from an engineering background, and was not always comfortable when he had to appear in public in his role as chief designer.

Jeffrey Quill wrote that Smith was 'a very human man who liked the company of young people and all the fun and excitement of aeroplanes and airfields and flying in general and thus he remained young in heart'. Smith was essentially a fighter and would not give in to the immense challenges of aircraft design, and his engineering background and experience gave him a good basis on which to ensure that the designs were expertly detailed and precise when entering the workshops for production purposes. He expected much from his staff, but took overall responsibility for their well-being and especially for the safety of the test pilots who flew the aircraft.

His good humour, combined with his fun attitude, especially when drumming on 'McNamara's Band' at the annual drawing office dinners, showed him to be 'the life and soul of the party'. Cyril Russell referred to this, commenting that Smith was a dedicated, clever and polite man with a sense of humour that bubbled out as an after-dinner speaker.

Tony Kenyon remembers being thanked by Smith for escorting his daughter Barbara for the evening at a dance and afterwards looking after her. Tony thought that it was Eric Lovell-Cooper who recommended him to Smith because he had proved that he did not drink too much at the apprentice dinners at the Polygon Hotel. However, he remembers years later attending a Swift dinner-dance at Tangmere at which Barbara Smith was present. Tony went to introduce himself, but Barbara did not remember him as the young man who escorted her to the dance:

> I know that Joe was very much respected, and he used to give his speech at the Design Office dinners and everybody used to listen intently as he could be amusing, crack a joke and everything else. He was a man's man really!

One of Smith's tricks involved a papier-mâché Spitfire drop tank he had in his office which looked identical to the real thing. It weighed only a few ounces, whereas the real thing would have been very heavy. When a visitor came into his office he would make a great effort pretending to lift the tank and would then throw it to the visitor, shouting 'Catch!'

Dr Gordon Mitchell, R.J.'s son, got to know Smith very well, both before and after his father's death, and felt that he did not get the credit he deserved. After reading some reminiscences of ex-Supermarine staff in a newsletter, he was prompted to write some of his memories:

> One person I got to know very well both before the war in the years following my father's death, and then after the war, was Joe Smith. We had long chats about the B.12/36 Bomber in the 1930s which Joe had great hopes for and desperately hoped it could be built. It was, of course, Joe who, as Chief Designer following R.J.'s death, masterminded the development of the Spitfire throughout the war and kept it continuously in the front line and superior to the German fighters. A vital contribution for which, I am afraid, Joe does not always receive the credit he deserves. My father would have been delighted, I am sure, with the way his Chief Draughtsman [Joe] developed his original work on the design of the Spitfire.

Alan Clifton (Cliffy) took over as chief designer after Smith died, and when Supermarine ceased to function he transferred to Weybridge and led the military project team. He then ran the Tornado variable-geometry wing programme after Barnes Wallis retired. Alan Clifton (Young Alan) remembers that his father retired in 1966, and thought that what held his father back from greatness was that he was not a political animal:

> I think my father and Ernie Mansbridge were very alike in some ways, and would stand back, but if they thought something important needed saying then they would say it. Joe Smith's great strength was that he understood the politics of big companies. He was really a front man, but my father was a backroom man. They were called backroom boys anyway! They were all very loyal to Joe and thought tremendously of him.

After Smith had died, Cliffy gave this tribute to his colleague:

> The close association between Supermarine and Rolls-Royce which existed in Mitchell's time continued under Joe Smith, who greatly admired the drive and energy of Ernest Hives (now Lord Hives) and his team. The Merlin engine development, and later the Griffon, made possible the continued improvement in Spitfire performance and propeller development, first by de Havillands and afterwards by Rotols, which was available to match the increased powers.
>
> Frequent meetings were held between the firms at managerial and technical level and the team spirit characteristic of the war period was nowhere more evident. Joe was never satisfied with the rate of progress, although the joint effort of Ernest Hives of Rolls-Royce, Len Fairhurst of Rotols, and Joe Smith was indeed something to remember, and resulted in new marks of Spitfire or Seafire at an average rate of one every three months.
>
> The meetings were attended on the Supermarine side by James Bird, who had returned as general manager for the later war period. He and Joe hatched many a plot to surmount any difficulties in the way of getting the new marks to the production stage. James Bird and Joe Smith were both fighters, and any opponents to their plans were in for an uncomfortable time. Nevertheless Joe had a remarkable capacity for making friends even of his opponents, and he was quite incapable of bearing a grudge.

In the foreword to the 40th anniversary booklet of the first flight of the prototype Spitfire, Alan Clifton (Cliffy), president of the Southampton branch of the Royal Aeronautical Society, wrote:

> It was my good fortune to be associated with R.J. Mitchell when the Spitfire prototype was designed and built and with Joe Smith during the development of its many production marks. I feel sure they would have welcomed this symposium. They lived and carried out all their work as aeroplane designers in the Southampton area. Both were Fellows of the Royal Aeronautical Society.

The main aim of the symposium was to commemorate the first flight of the prototype Spitfire, but also importantly to gather and record first-hand evidence and recollections from the surviving members of the Supermarine design team while it was still possible.

It is fitting to conclude with the contribution that Mrs Winifred Smith gave in the foreword of the 40th anniversary booklet:

I feel very honoured and deeply moved to have been asked to write this short foreword for the Mitchell Memorial Lecture. My husband was, of course, very deeply involved with the war-time development of the Spitfire and I believe that the unshakeable faith he had in its qualities as a flying machine is borne out by the many years it was in production. From the early days until his untimely death, Joe was devoted to finding ways of improving not only performance but also the safety of the men flying the Spitfire and this determination to better an existing mark characterised his whole approach to aircraft development. Linked with his single-mindedness of purpose was a strong awareness that he was very much one of a team and it was as such that he always tried to portray himself. I know that if he was still with us he would be delighted there is still such interest and enthusiasm about the Spitfire and very proud that his work has not been forgotten.

EPILOGUE

The Spitfire Legend Lives On

Aircraft of all types fascinate both young and old, especially when watching the skills of the Red Arrows or seeing the historic Battle of Britain Memorial Flight when visiting the many and varied air shows, including Farnborough, Duxford, RAF Cosford, Shuttleworth and RNAS Yeovilton and Culdrose, where a range of historic aircraft, warbirds and jet aircraft are displayed. There are opportunities to visit aviation museums such as the RAF museums at Hendon and Cosford, Solent Sky in Hampshire and the Imperial War Museum at Duxford. Many like making and flying model aircraft, and of course many aviation books and magazines are on sale or can be loaned from libraries. However, a highlight must be the sight of a Spitfire in flight, and it is often its beautiful profile and the unmistakable sound of the engine that draw the attention to the sky.

It is still possible to have a flight in a Spitfire. There are some two-seat trainers flying today, but it can be quite expensive. However, there are companies that advertise home-build kits for the enthusiast to make and fly themselves. Some even have easily recognisable names, such as The Spitfire Co. in California, and Supermarine Aircraft in Texas, which sells Spitfire flatpack kits.

Supermarine as a company disappeared in the late 1950s, but Mike O'Sullivan, CEO of Supermarine Aircraft in Texas, has been granted the rights to use the legendary name by descendants of the British family members.

The final Supermarine Spitfire Mk 24 was developed by Joe Smith and his team in 1946, and forty-five years later, in 1991, Mike O'Sullivan designed his 75 per cent scale Mk 25 single-seat Spitfire replica in Brisbane, Australia, followed by the Mk 26, 80 per cent scale two-seat version. The Supermarine Aircraft factory has since moved to Cisco, Texas, and now produces the all-aluminium Mk 26B 90 per cent scale, two-seat flatpack version of the company's home-build kits, and many of these aircraft have been sold around the world. The cost of a kit, plus engine, is less than £135,000, but compared to a Spitfire that came up for auction at £1.25 million that is quite cheap. However, once the kit arrives you will need another 1,200 hours to build the aircraft.

The Enstone Flying Club, based at Enstone airfield near Chipping Norton in Oxfordshire, have their own Spitfire project, whereby they plan to build their own 'City of Oxford' Squadron. The squadron will consist of twelve of the Supermarine Aircraft Mk 26B 90 per cent scale Spitfires kits that they hope will be flying by the end of 2013.

Finally, ex-Supermarine apprentice Leo Schefer shares his thoughts on the legendary Spitfire and the impact it still has today:

Today the Spitfire is a thing of beauty first, a historic weapon second. What made the Spitfire an effective weapon is what young, dedicated airmen could do with it. Its shape and movement stirred the visceral juices of the imagination, bringing out the Walter Mitty latent in all of us; 76 years after the first Spitfire flew, it still does.

But, an airplane is just a collection of largely metal parts until given life by the user. It's the people, women as well as men, who created, made, maintained, directed, and above all, used the assembled whole that make the collection of parts we call a Spitfire into a legend.

Nearly 70 years after formal production ceased in 1945, demand for flyable Spitfires has led some wealthy cognoscenti to buy already built Spitfires – no guns, just the beauty of flight and the emotional pull of flying a beautifully balanced machine that in the hands of an earlier generation played a key role in the defence of democracy. Some spend millions on a Rembrandt or Picasso; others on a Spitfire!

BIBLIOGRAPHY

Andrews, C.F. & Morgan, E.B., *Supermarine Aircraft Since 1914* (Putnam, 1981)

Arthur, Max, *Lost Voices of the Royal Air Force* (Hodder & Stoughton, 1993)

Barfield, Norman, *Supermarine* (Chalford Publishing Co., 1996)

Birtles, P., *Supermarine: Attacker, Swift and Scimitar* (Ian Allan, 1992)

Bishop, Patrick, *Battle of Britain* (Quercus, 2009)

Bishop, Patrick, *Fighter Boys* (Harper Perennial, 2004)

Cawthorne, Nigel, *Britain's Finest Hour: Spitfire* (Abbeydale Press, 2011)

Charles, David, *The Story of Aircraft: Seven Decades of Powered Flight* (Octopus Books, 1974)

Clostermann, Pierre, *The Big Show* (Cassell, 2004)

Deighton, Len, *Battle of Britain* (Book Club Associates, 1980)

Dickson, Bonner W.A., *Aircraft: From Airship to Jet Propulsion 1908–1948* (Published for Vickers-Armstrongs Ltd by The Naldrett Press, 1948)

Franks, Norman, *Battle of Britain* (Bison Books, 1981)

Griffiths, H.G. *Testing Times: Memoirs of a Spitfire Boffin* (United Writers Publications, 1992)

Haining, P., *Spitfire Summer* (W.H. Allen, 1990)

Henshaw, Alex, *Sigh for a Merlin: Testing the Spitfire* (Crécy Publishing Ltd, 1996)

Isaacs, J.O., *Aeroplane Affair* (Air Research Publications, 1988)

Jablonski, Edward, *Seawings* (Robert Hale & Co., 1972)

Jackson, Robert, *History of the Spitfire* (Marks & Spencer, 2003)

Jackson, Robert, *Spitfire: Life of The Legend* (Metro Books, 2010)

Johnson, 'Johnnie', *Wing Leader* (Chatto & Windus, 1956)

Kershaw, Alex, *The Few* (Da Capo Press, 2006)

Korda, Michael, *With Wings like Eagles* (Harper Perennial, 2010)

Lithgow, Mike, *Mach One* (Allan Wingate Ltd, 1954)

McKinstry, Leo, *Spitfire: Portrait of a Legend* (John Murray, 2007)

Mitchell G., *R.J. Mitchell: Schooldays to Spitfire* (Clifford Frost Ltd, 1997)

Morgan, Eric B., and Shacklady, Edward, *Spitfire: The History* (Key Publishing Ltd, 1987)

Munson, Kenneth, *Aircraft of World War II* (Ian Allan, 1962)

Oxford Dictionary of National Biography (OUP, 2004)

Price, Alfred, *Spitfire at War* (Ian Allan, 1974)

Price, Alfred, *Spitfire: A Documentary History* (Macdonald & Jane's Publishers Ltd, 1977)

Price, Alfred, *Spitfire at War 2* (Ian Allan, 1983)

Price, Alfred, *The Spitfire Story* (Arms & Armour Press, 1986)

Price, Alfred, *The Spitfire Story* (Haynes Publishing, 2010)

Prior, Rupert, *Flying: The Golden Years* (Tiger Books International, 1994)

Quill, Jeffrey, *Spitfire: A Test Pilot's Story* (John Murray, 1983)

Quill, Jeffrey. *Birth of a Legend: The Spitfire* (Quiller Press, 1986)

Robertson, B., *Spitfire – The Story of a Famous Fighter* (Garden City Press, 1960)

Russell, C.R., *Spitfire Odyssey* (Kingfisher Railway Publications, 1985)

Russell, C.R., *Spitfire Postscript* (Published by the author, 1994)

Scott J.D., *Vickers: A History* (Weidenfeld & Nicolson, 1962)

Shelton, John, *Schneider Trophy to Spitfire: The Design Career of R.J. Mitchell* (Haynes Publishing, 2008)

Sherborne J., *When the Clouds Roll By* (Rockbourne Publications, 2010)

Smith, Peter C., *Stuka at War* (Ian Allan, 1980)

Smithies, Edward, *Aces, Erks & Backroom Boys* (Cassell, 1990)

Taylor, J.W.R. & Allward, M.F., *Spitfire* (Harborough Publishing, 1946)

Van Ishoven, Armand, *The Luftwaffe in the Battle of Britain* (Ian Allan, 1980)

Webb, Denis Le P., *Never a Dull Moment* (J&KH Publishing, 2001)

Wellum, Geoffrey, *First Light* (Penguin, 2002)

Williams, Ray, *Royal Navy Aircraft Since 1945* (US Naval Institute Press, 1989)

Wragg, David, *Boats of the Air* (Robert Hale & Co., 1984)

Bibliography Sources

East, R.A. & Cheeseman, I.C.F., '37/34 Fighter K5054: Forty Years of the Spitfire', RAeS Southampton branch, 1981

Faddy, David, 'The Forgotten Spitfire Designer', *Aeroplane*, July 2006

Frimston, Ian, 'Birth of a Spitfire: Spitfire 70th Anniversary', *Aeroplane*, April 2006

Gingell, G.N.M., 'Supermarine Spitfire 40th Anniversary', RAeS Southampton branch, 1976

Henshaw, A., 'Tribute to Jeffrey Quill', *Aerospace*, 1996

Mansbridge, Ernest, Obituary, *Aerospace*, November 1996

Quill, J.K., 'Notes on service in the RAF Meteorological Flight, 1933–35'

Smith, Joe, Obituary, *Journal of the Royal Aeronautical Society*, June 1956

Smith, Joe, Obituary, *Vickers News*, March/April 1956

Courtesy of flightglobal.com:

Flight, 11.9.31, 'Schneider Trophy Contest, Schneider Team at Calshot, History of the Schneider Trophy Contest'

Flight, 7.2.35, 'The 200mph bomber American Northrop 2E Purchased by the Air Ministry K5053'

Flight, 18.4.40, '1912–1940: A History of Marine Aircraft Development. Supermarine's Twenty-eight Years of uninterrupted Work: A Great Racing Record'

Flight, 7.9.44, 'Sea Otter and Seafire'

Flight, 26.12.46, 'Spitfire and Seafire: Their development described by Supermarine Chief Designer', Lecture delivered by Joe Smith at the RAeS

Flight, January 1953, 'The Supermarine Swallow-Aircraft described Number 53', G.A. Gull

Flight, 2.10.53, 'Sires of the Swift' by H.F. King MBE, with contribution from Jeffrey Quill OBE, AFC

Flight, 29.1.54, 'In Memory of R.J. Mitchell', First Mitchell Memorial Lecture – given by Joe Smith at the RAeS

Flight, April 1956, 'A Colleague's Memory of Joe Smith', Alan Clifton

INDEX

Aircraft Index